Blaise Pascal

The Provincial Letters of Blaise Pascal

A new translation, with life of the author

Blaise Pascal

The Provincial Letters of Blaise Pascal
A new translation, with life of the author

ISBN/EAN: 9783337017361

Printed in Europe, USA, Canada, Australia, Japan

Cover: Foto ©Thomas Meinert / pixelio.de

More available books at **www.hansebooks.com**

THE PROVINCIAL LETTERS

OF

BLAISE PASCAL.

A NEW TRANSLATION, WITH LIFE OF THE AUTHOR.

GLASGOW:
AM COLLINS, PUBLISHER & QUEEN'S PRINTER.
1863.

PROVINCIAL LETTERS.

CONTENTS.

	Page
LIFE OF THE AUTHOR,	9

LETTER FIRST.

Discussions in Sorbonne. Invention of Proximate Power: how used by the Jesuits to secure the censure of M. Arnauld, ... 33

LETTER SECOND.

Sufficient Grace, ... 42

ANSWER OF THE PROVINCIAL to his Friend's first two Letters. . 52

LETTER THIRD.

Injustice, Absurdity, and Nullity of the Censure of M. Arnauld, 54

LETTER FOURTH.

Of Actual Grace always present, and Sins of Ignorance. 62

LETTER FIFTH.

Design of the Jesuits in establishing a new Morality. Two sets of Casuists among them Many of them Lax, some Strict. Ground of this Diversity. Doctrine of Probability explained. Herd of Modern and Unknown Authors substituted for the Holy Fathers . . 74

LETTER SIXTH.

Artifices of the Jesuits to evade the authority of Scripture. Councils, and Popes. Consequences of the Doctrine of Probability. Their corruptions in favour of Beneficiaries, Priests, Monks, and Domestics. History of John of Alba. 87

CONTENTS.

LETTER SEVENTH.

The Method of directing the Intention according to the Casuists. Of their permission to Kill in defence of Honour and Property. This extended to Priests and Monks. Curious question proposed by Caramuel: May the Jesuits lawfully kill the Jansenists? . . . 100

LETTER EIGHTH.

Corrupt Maxims of the Casuists concerning Judges, Usurers, the Contract Mohatra, Bankrupts, Restitution, etc. Various extravagances of the Casuists, . . . 114

LETTER NINTH.

Of Spurious Devotion to the Blessed Virgin introduced by the Jesuits. Different expedients which they have devised to Save themselves without pain, and while enjoying the Pleasures and Comforts of Life. Their Maxims on Ambition, Envy, Gluttony, Equivocation, Mental Reservation, Freedom allowable in Girls, Female Dress, Gaming, hearing Mass, ... 128

LETTER TENTH.

How the Jesuits have softened down the Sacrament of Penitence, by their Maxims touching Confession, Satisfaction, Absolution, Proximate Occasions of Sin, Contrition, and the Love of God, ... 142

LETTER ELEVENTH.

Ridiculous Errors may be refuted by Raillery. Precautions to be used. These observed by Montalte: not so by the Jesuits. Impious Buffoonery of Father le Moine and Father Gerasse, ... 157

LETTER TWELFTH.

Refutation of the Jesuit quibbles on Alms and Simony, . 171

LETTER THIRTEENTH.

The Doctrine of Lessius on Homicide the same as that of Victoria: How easy it is to pass from Speculation to Practice: Why the Jesuits have made use of this vain distinction; and how little it serves to justify them, . 185

LETTER FOURTEENTH.

The Maxims of the Jesuits on Homicide refuted from the Fathers. Answer in passing to some of their Calumnies: Their Doctrine contrasted with the forms observed in Criminal Trials, ... 200

LETTER FIFTEENTH.

The Jesuits erase Calumny from the list of sins, and make no scruple of using it to cry down their Enemies, . . 215

LETTER SIXTEENTH.

Horrible Calumnies of the Jesuits against pious Ecclesiastics and holy Nuns, ... 230

LETTER SEVENTEENTH.

Proof on removing an Ambiguity in the meaning of Jansenius, that there is no Heresy in the Church. By the unanimous consent of all Theologians, and especially of the Jesuits, the authority of Popes and Œcumenical Councils not Infallible in questions of Fact. . . . 251

LETTER EIGHTEENTH

Proved still more invincibly by Father Annat's reply, that there is no heresy in the Church: every body condemns the doctrine which the Jesuits ascribe to Jansenius, and thus the views of all the faithful on the Five Propositions are the same: difference between Disputes as to Doctrine, and as to Fact: in Questions of Fact, more weight due to what is seen than to any human authority, ... 270

LIFE OF THE AUTHOR.

BLAISE PASCAL was born at Clermont, in Auvergne, June 19, 1623. His father, Stephen Pascal, president in the Court of Aids, in that city, married Antoinette Begon, by whom he had four children: a son born in 1619, who died in infancy; Blaise, the subject of the present memoir; and two daughters, Gilberte, born in 1620, who was married to M. Perier, and Jacqueline, born in 1625, who took the veil in the Convent of Port Royal.

The family of Pascal had received a patent of nobility from Louis XI. about the year 1478, and from that period had held official situations of importance in Auvergne. Besides these hereditary advantages, Stephen Pascal was distinguished, not only for his legal knowledge, but for superior attainments in literature and science, combined with great simplicity of manners, and an exquisite relish for the calm and pure delights to be met with in the bosom of his family. The death of his amiable and excellent wife, Antoinette Begon, in 1626, a stroke most deeply felt, increased his interest in the education of his children, an object for which he had always been solicitous, but which, from that time, became paramount to every other. In order to pursue it without distraction, he resigned his official situation in favour of his brother, and removed, in 1631, to Paris. Here he had free access to persons whose taste was congenial with his own, and enjoyed the amplest means of information from books and other sources. His principal attention was directed to his only son, who gave indications, almost from his cradle, of his future eminence; at the same time he instructed his daughters in the Latin language and general literature, studies which he looked upon as well adapted to produce a spirit of reflection, and to secure them from that frivolity which is the bane and reproach of either sex.

The famous Thirty Years' War at that time raged through Europe; but, amidst all its disasters, Eloquence and Poetry, which had flourished in Italy for more than a century, began to unfold their lustre in France and England; the severer sciences issued from the shades in which they had been enveloped; a sound philosophy, or rather a sound method of philosophising, made its way into the schools, and the revolution, which had been commenced by Galileo and Des Cartes, rapidly advanced. Stephen Pascal partook of the general impulse, and united himself with men of similar talents and pursuits, such as Mersenne, Roberval, Carcavi, Le Pailleur, and others, for the purpose of discussing philosophical subjects, and of opening a correspondence with the promoters of Science in France and other countries. To this association may be traced the origin of the Academy of Sciences, established under royal authority in 1666.

Young Pascal sometimes joined in the scientific conversations held at his father's house. He listened to every thing with extreme attention, and eagerly investigated the causes of whatever fell under his observation. It is said that at the age of eleven years, he composed a small treatise on Sounds, in which he endeavoured to explain why the sound made by striking a plate with a knife ceases on applying one's hand to it. His father, fearful that too keen a relish for the sciences would impede his progress in the languages, which were then considered the most important part of education, decided, in concert with his friends, to abstain from conversing on philosophical subjects in his presence. To pacify his son under this painful interdiction, his father promised that when he had acquired a complete knowledge of Greek and Latin, and was in other respects qualified, he should learn Geometry; only observing that it is the science of extension, or of the three dimensions of the body, length, breadth, and thickness; that it teaches how to form figures with accuracy, and to compare their relations, one with another. Slight as these hints were, they served as a ray of light to develop his genius for mathematics. From that moment his mind had no rest; he was eager to explore the mysteries of a science withheld from him with so much care. In his hours of recreation he shut himself up in a chamber, and with a piece of charcoal drew on the floor triangles, parallelograms, and circles, without even knowing the names of these figures; he examined the different positions of convergent lines, and their mutual relations. By degrees he arrived at the conclusion that the sum of the three angles of a triangle must be measured by a semi-circumference; or, in other words, are equal to two right angles, which is the thirty-second proposition of the First Book of Euclid. While meditating this theorem, he was surprised by his father, who, having learnt the object, progress, and result of his researches, stood for some time dumb with astonishment and delight, and then hastened, almost beside himself, to tell what he had witnessed to his intimate friend M. Le Pailleur.

The young Pascal was now left at full liberty to study Geometry. The first book on the subject put into his hands, at twelve years old, was Euclid's Elements, which he understood at once, without the slightest assistance. He was soon able to take a distinguished station among men of science, and at sixteen composed a small tract on Conic Sections, which evinced extraordinary sagacity.

The happiness which Stephen Pascal enjoyed in witnessing the rapid progress of his son was for a short time interrupted by an unexpected event. In December, 1638, when the Government, whose resources had been impoverished by a succession of wars, made some reduction on the interest of the public debt, a measure which, though very easily adopted, excited great dissatisfaction among the proprietors, and occasioned meetings which were denounced as seditious. Stephen Pascal was accused as one of the most active on this occasion, which his having laid out the greatest part of his property in the purchase of shares rendered somewhat plausible. An order was issued for his arrest, but having received timely notice from a friend, he secreted himself, and withdrew into Auvergne. His recall was owing to the good offices of the Duchess d'Aiguillon, who prevailed on his daughter Jacqueline to perform a part in a comedy before Cardinal Richelieu. On the Cardinal expressing his satisfaction with the performance, she presented him with a copy of verses applicable to her father's situation, on which Richelieu immediately procured his recall, and within two years made him Intendant of Rouen.

During Pascal's residence at Rouen, when scarcely nineteen years old, he invented the famous arithmetical machine which bears his name. It was two years before he brought it to a state of perfection, owing not merely to the difficulty he found in arranging and combining the several parts of the machinery, but to the unskilfulness of the workmen. Many attempts have since been made to simplify it, particularly by Leibnitz, but, on the whole, its advantages have not compensated for the inconvenience arising from its complexity and bulk.

Soon after this, he entered on a course of inquiry relative to the weight of the atmosphere, a subject which engaged the attention of all the philosophers of Europe. The venerable Galileo had opened the way to correct views of it, but left to his disciple Torricelli and others to establish the true explanation of the phenomena connected with this branch of physics. Pascal published an account of his experiments, in a work entitled "New Experiments Relating to a Vacuum," in 1647. He wrote also two treatises on the equilibrium of fluids, and the weight of the atmosphere, which were first printed in 1663, the year after the Author's death. These tracts were succeeded by some others on geometrical subjects, none of which appear to have been preserved. We deeply regret that they were not published at the same time as his other philosophical treatises, as they would have contributed to give us more accurate conceptions of the extent to which their author pushed his researches.

Besides this, the productions of a man of genius, though, owing to the advance of science, they may present nothing new, are always instructive from the exhibition they make of his mode of arranging his thoughts and reasonings. They are not to be valued so much, perhaps, for the actual knowledge they communicate, because in scientific researches there is a constant progression, and works of the highest order in one age are succeeded in the next by others more profound and complete. It is not so in matters of taste and imagination; and a tragedy which gives a vivid and correct representation of the passions common to mankind, will never become obsolete. The poet and the orator have also another advantage; they address, though a less select yet a far more numerous auditory, and their names speedily attain celebrity. Yet the glory of scientific discoveries appears more solid and impressive; the truths they develop circulate from age to age, a common good, not subject to the vicissitudes of language; and if their works no longer contribute to the instruction of posterity, they remain as monuments to mark the height to which the human mind had reached at the time of their appearance. Of Pascal's genius there remain memorials sufficient to place him in the first rank of mathematicians; such are the Arithmetical Triangle, his papers on the Doctrine of Chances, and his treatise on the Cycloid.

Intense application gradually undermined his health. Towards the end of the year 1647 he was attacked for three months by a paralytic affection, which almost deprived him of the use of his limbs. Some time after he removed to Paris with his father and his sister Jacqueline. Whilst surrounded by his relations, he somewhat relaxed his studies, and made several excursions into Auvergne and other parts. But he had the misfortune to lose his father in 1651, and two years after his sister Jacqueline entered the Convent of Port Royal. His other sister and her husband, M. Perier, resided at a distance at Clermont. Thus left alone, he gave himself up to such excessive mental labour as would have soon brought him to the tomb. The failure of his bodily powers forced him to relax his studies, which his physicians had in vain advised. He therefore entered into society, and though his disposition was tinged with melancholy, always gave pleasure from his superior understanding, which accommodated itself to the various capacities of those he conversed with. He gradually acquired a relish for society, and even indulged thoughts of marriage, hoping that the attentions of an amiable and sensible companion would alleviate his sufferings and enliven his solitude; but an unexpected event changed all his projects. In the month of October, 1654, as he was one day taking his usual drive in a coach and four, and was passing over the bridge of Neuilly, the two leaders became ungovernable on a part of the bridge where there was no parapet, and plunged into the Seine. Happily the first shock of their descent broke the traces which connected them with the hindmost horses, so that the coach stopped on the edge of the precipice. The concussion given to the feeble frame of Pascal may be easily conceived; he fainted away, and a considerable time elapsed before he came to himself again. His nerves were so violently agitated, that in many of the sleepless nights which succeeded during the subsequent period of his life, he imagined that he saw a precipice by his bedside, into which he was in danger of falling. He regarded this event as an admonition from heaven to break off all worldly engagements, and to live henceforward to God alone. His sister Jacqueline had already prepared him by her example and her conversation for adopting this resolution. He renounced the world entirely, and retained no connection but with friends who held similar principles. The regular life he led in his retirement gave some relief to his bodily sufferings, and at intervals a portion of tolerable health; and during this period he composed many works of a kind very different to those on scientific subjects, but which were new proofs of his genius, and of the wonderful facility with which his mind grasped every object presented to it.

The convent of Port Royal, after a long interval of languor and relaxation, had risen to high reputation under the direction of Angelica Arnauld. This celebrated woman, desirous of augmenting the reputation of the establishment by all lawful means, had drawn around her a number of persons distinguished for learning and piety, who, disgusted with the world, sought to enjoy in retirement the pleasures of reflection and Christian tranquillity. Such were the two brothers, Arnauld d' Andilli, and Antoine Arnauld, Le Maitre, and Saci, the translator of the Bible, Nicole, Lancelot, Hermant, and others. The principal occupation of these illustrious men was the education of youth; it was in their school that Racine acquired a knowledge of the classics, a taste for the great models of antiquity, and the principles of that harmonious and enchanting style, which places him on the summit of the French Parnassus. Pascal cultivated their acquaintance, and was soon on terms of the most familiar intimacy. Without making his fixed residence with them, he paid them, at intervals, visits of three or four months, and found in their society everything that could instruct him, reason, eloquence, and devotion. On their part, they were not slow to apprehend the extent and profundity of his genius. Nothing appeared strange to him. The variety of his knowledge, and that fertility of invention which animated him, gave him the ability to express himself with intelligence, and to scatter new ideas over every subject he touched upon. He gained the admiration and the love of all these eminent recluses, but especially of Saci. This laborious student, who spent his life in the study of the Scriptures and the Fathers, was devoted to the writings of St. Augustin, and never heard any striking sentiment on theology to which he did not imagine he could find a parallel in his favourite author. No sooner had Pascal uttered some of those elevated thoughts which were familiar to him, than Saci remembered having read the same thing in Augustin; but without diminishing his admiration of Pascal; for it excited his astonishment that a young man who had never read the Fathers, should, by his native acuteness, coincide in his thoughts with so celebrated a theologian; and he looked upon him as destined to be a firm supporter and defender of Port Royal, which was at this period exposed to the virulent assaults of the Jesuits.

Cornelius Jansen, bishop of Ypres, a man esteemed for his talents and character, and who was very far from foreseeing that his name would one day become the signal of discord and hatred, had occupied himself in meditating and in reducing to a system the principles which he believed were contained in the writings of St. Augustin. He wrote his work in Latin, with the title of Augustinus. It was scarcely finished when its author was taken off by the plague, which he caught while examining some manuscripts belonging to one of his clergy, who had died of that malady. The Augustinus made its appearance in 1640, a huge folio, written without order or method, and not more obscure from the nature of the subject, than from the diffuseness and inelegance of the style. It owed its unfortunate celebrity to the illustrious men who forced it into notice, and to the implacable animosity of their enemies.

The Abbe de St. Cyran, a friend of Jansen, entered with the same sentiments, and abhorring the Jesuits and their tenets, extolled the Augustinus even before it appeared, and spread its doctrine by means of an extensive correspondence. The recluses of Port Royal soon after publicly professed their approbation of it. The Jesuits, irritated to the extreme when they beheld their own theology falling into contempt before it, and jealous of the Port Royalists, who eclipsed them in every department of literature, set themselves with all their might to oppose the work of Jansen. The nature of the subject laid it open to ambiguities of language; and by garbling the words of the author, they formed five propositions which presented a sense evidently false and erroneous, and thereupon procured a censure from Pope Innocent X., issued May, 31, 1653, though without its being determined whether they were exactly contained in the work of Jansen or not. The clergy of France, in their convocation of 1655, demanded a fresh sentence, and represented the Jansenists as rebels and heretics. Alexander VII., on October 16, 1656, issued a bull which again condemned the five propositions, with a clause declaring that they were faithfully extracted from Jansen's work, and heretical in the sense of their author.

This bull served as the basis of a formulary which the clergy prepared in 1657, and of which, four years after, the Court undertook to exact the signature rigorously. Alexander VII. issued, in 1657, a second bull, with a formulary on the same subject.

It is probable that the Jesuits would have failed in their persecution of the Jansenists, if the first statesmen in Europe had not felt it their interest to support them. Cardinal Richelieu, who had a personal hatred to the Abbé St. Cyran, had tried, at first, to procure the condemnation of his writings by the Papal See; but as he was not a man to endure the ordinary delays of the Romish court for an object so frivolous in his eyes as the censure of four or five theological propositions, put forth by a single ecclesiastic, he found it more easy and convenient to lodge St. Cyran in confinement at Vincennes.

Mazarin, less violent, but more skilful in concealing his hatred, and in effecting his vindictive purposes, aimed in secret the most deadly blows at the Jansenists. In his heart he was indifferent to all theological opinions; he had little affection for the Jesuits, but knew that the Port Royal party kept up a connection with his most formidable enemy, the Cardinal de Retz. Without enquiring into the nature of this connection, he decided on its criminality, and to avenge himself, he excited the clergy to demand the Bull of 1656. Thus the State was disturbed for a century, because the defenders of a book, which, had it depended on its own merits, would have sunk into oblivion, were the friends of an archbishop of Paris, who was the enemy of the prime minister of France. Mazarin, doubtless, did not foresee the melancholy consequences of his error in introducing the secular power into a theological warfare, of the very existence of which he ought to have been ignorant. Let princes and prime ministers take a lesson from his example.

The recluses of Port Royal, and many other theologians, without defending the literal sense of the five condemned propositions, professed that they were not in the Augustinus; or that if they were, that their meaning as therein expressed was agreeable to the Catholic faith. They were answered by contrary assertions; the controversy became every day more violent, and a multitude of works appeared, which, from the indulgence of human passions, and the violations of Christian charity they exhibited, gave the enemies of religion a sad occasion of triumph.

Of all the abettors of Jansenism, none showed greater zeal than Arnauld, a man of elevated mind and austere manners. When he entered on the clerical function, he gave almost all his property to the institution of Port Royal, declaring that poverty became a minister of Jesus Christ. His attachment to what he believed to be truth was as inflexible as truth itself. He detested the corrupt morality of the Jesuits; and was equally the object of their hatred, not only on his own account, but because he was the son of the advocate who had pleaded with vehemence on behalf of the university that they should be interdicted from engaging in the instruction of youth, and even be banished from the kingdom. The following anecdote will show the intense interest with which he espoused the cause of Jansenism. One day, his friend and fellow-soldier in the same cause, but naturally of a mild and yielding disposition, complained that he was weary of the conflict and longed for repose. "*Repose!*" replied Arnauld, "*will you not have all eternity to repose in?*"

With this disposition, Arnauld published in 1655 a letter, in which he said that he had not found in Jansen the five condemned propositions; and in relation to the question at issue respecting special grace, added, that St. Peter in his denial of Christ was an example of a true believer to whom that grace, without which we can do nothing, was wanting. The first of these assertions appeared contemptuous to the Papal chair; the second made him suspected of heresy; and both excited great ferment in the Sorbonne, of which Arnauld was a member. His enemies used every means to bring upon him a humiliating censure. His friends urged on him the necessity of self-defence. He was possessed of great native eloquence, but his style was harsh and negligent. Aware of its defects, he was the first to point out Pascal as the only man capable of doing justice to the subject. Pascal willingly consented to use his pen in a cause so dear to his heart.

On January 23, 1656, he published, under the name of Louis de Montalte, his first letter to a Provincial, in which he ridiculed the meetings of the Sorbonne on the affair of Arnauld with a delicate and refined humour, of which there then existed no model in the French language. This letter met with prodigious success; but the party whose object was to destroy Arnauld, had so well taken their measures, and had brought to the assembly so many doctors and monks devoted to their authority, that not only the two propositions above named were condemned by a majority of votes, but their author was excluded for ever from the faculty of theology, by a decree dated Jan. 31, 1656. The triumph of his enemies was somewhat checked by the 2nd, 3rd, and 4th letters to a Provincial, which followed close upon the decree of the Sorbonne. The Dominicans, who, to maintain their credit and to gratify their paltry resentments, appeared on this occasion to have abandoned the doctrine of Aquinas, were overwhelmed with ridicule; but the Jesuits in particular, who had contributed most to Arnauld's condemnation, paid dearly for the joy their success gave them. From their own writings Pascal drew the materials for rendering them odious and ridiculous; and he was the remote instrument of their destruction. The absurd and scandalous decisions of their casuists furnished him with pleasantries and sarcasms in abundance. But it required a genius such as his to combine his materials into a work which might interest not merely theologians, but men of the world and of all ranks. So much has been said of the Provincial Letters that it is needless to eulogize them. They are universally acknowledged to be unequalled in their kind, and from their publication the fixation of the French language may be dated. Voltaire declares that they combine the wit of Moliere with the sublimity of Bossuet. I will only remark that one great merit of these compositions appears to be the admirable skill with which the transitions are made from one topic to another. The destruction of the Jesuits may have diminished the attractions of the work to certain classes of readers, but it will always be esteemed by men of letters and taste as a master-piece of style, wit, and eloquence. Unfortunately for the Jesuits, they had not a single good writer among them to reply to it; and the answers they attempted were as defective in style as they were objectionable in sentiment. In short, they met with a total failure, while all France was eager to read the Provincial Letters, which the Jansenists, to increase their circulation, translated into Latin and the principal modern languages.

Among other works put forth by the Jesuits on behalf of their casuists, there was one which gave general dissatisfaction, entitled, *An Apology for the New Casuists against the Calumnies of the Jansenists.* The clergy of Paris and some other places attacked this book with a powerful and vehement eloquence, worthy of Demosthenes. These productions proceeded chiefly from Arnauld, Nicole, and Pascal. The two former furnished the materials, which were elaborated by the latter. They produced a powerful sensation against the Jesuits, and in spite of all the credit the Fathers possessed with the clergy, many eminent bishops published express mandates against *The Apology for the Casuists.*

The controversy carried on by Pascal against the Jesuits lasted three years; and it prevented his labouring as soon as he had wished, at a great work he had long meditated, on the truth of religion. At different times he set down on paper reflections connected with it, and fully intended to execute the work in 1658; but at that period his infirmities increased so rapidly as to prevent its completion, and nothing but the fragments are left to us. He was first attacked with an excruciating pain in the teeth, which deprived him almost entirely of sleep. During one of his wakeful nights the recollection of some problems relative to the Cycloid roused his mathematical genius. He had long renounced the study of the sciences: but the beauty of the problems and the necessity of diverting his mind by some powerful effort from his bodily sufferings, led him into researches of which the results are, even at the present day, reckoned among the finest efforts of the human mind.

The curve well known to mathematicians by the name of Trochoid or Cycloid, is the line described by the motion of any one point in the circumference of a wheel running on the ground. It is not certain by whom this curve was first distinctly noticed, though an allusion to it occurs in Aristotle. Roberval first demonstrated in 1637, that its area is triple that of its generating circle. He also determined, soon after, the solid described by the revolution of the Cycloid on its base, and, what was more difficult for the geometry of that day, the solid described by its revolution on the diameter of its generating circle. Torricelli published most of these problems, as discovered by himself, in a work printed 1644; but it was asserted in France that Torricelli had found the solutions of Roberval among Galileo's papers; and Pascal, in his history of the Cycloid, hesitates not to treat Toricelli as a plagiarist; but after examining the papers on this subject, I must confess that Pascal's opinion seems to have been too hastily formed, and there is reason to believe that Torricelli resolved these problems independently of Roberval.

It still remained to find the length and the centre of gravity of the Cycloid, and of the solids, both those around the base and round the axis. But these researches required a new geometry, or at least a novel application of the principles already known. Pascal, within a week, and amidst extreme suffering, found a method which included all the problems just mentioned, founded on the summation of certain series of which he has given the elements in some papers which accompany his tract on the Arithmetical Triangle. From this to the differential and integral calculus there was only a step, and there is good reason for believing that had Pascal been able to devote more time to his scientific inquiries, he would have deprived Leibnitz and Newton of the glory of their inventions. Having communicated his meditations to some friends, and particularly to the Duke de Roannez, the latter conceived the design of making them contribute to the triumph of religion.

Pascal furnished an incontestable proof that it was possible for the same person to be a consummate mathematician and an humble believer. His friends therefore thought, that even if other mathematicians should succeed in resolving those questions which were to be propounded, and a reward offered for the solution of them, they would at least perceive their difficulty; and thus, while science would be promoted, the honour of accelerating its progress would always belong to the first inventor; if, on the contrary, they could not solve these problems, unbelievers would, thence forward, have no pretext for being more difficult in regard to the proofs of religion than Pascal was, who had shown himself so profoundly skilled in a science founded altogether on demonstration. Accordingly, in June, 1658, a program was published, in which it was proposed to find the measure and centre of gravity of any segment of a cycloid, the dimensions and centres of gravity of solids, demisolids, etc. which such a segment would produce by turning round the absciss or the ordinate; and as the calculations for the complete solution of all these problems would require much trouble and labour, in default of such a solution, the competitors for the prizes were required to furnish the application of these methods to some remarkable cases, such, for example, as when the absciss is equal to the radius, or to the diameter of the generating circle. Two prizes were offered, one of 40, the other of 20 pistoles. The most celebrated mathematicians in Paris were selected to examine the papers of the competitors, which were to be transmitted, before the 31st of October following, to M. de Carcavi, one of the judges, with whom also the premiums were deposited. In the whole affair, Pascal concealed himself under the name of Amos Dettonville, an anagram of Louis Montalte, the name he had assumed as writer of the Provincial Letters.

The program excited afresh the attention of mathematicians to the properties of the Cycloid, which had been for some time neglected. Hughens squared the segment contained between the summit and the ordinate which answers to a fourth part of the diameter of the generating circle. Sluze, canon of the Cathedral of Liege, measured the area of the curve by a new and ingenious method: Sir Christopher Wren showed that any arc of a cycloid, measured from its summit, is double the corresponding chord of the generating circle; he also determined the centre of gravity of the Cycloidal arc, and the surfaces of its solids of revolution. Fermat and Roberval, on the simple announcement of Wren's theorems, each gave demonstrations. But all these investigations, though very ingenious, did not fully answer the requisitions of the program. Only two persons laid claim to the prize: Lallouère, the Jesuit, and Wallis, who is so justly celebrated for his Arithmetic of Infinites, published in 1655. After a strict scrutiny, however, by the appointed judges, it appeared that their methods were too defective to satisfy the conditions. On the 1st of January, 1659, Pascal published his own treatise on the Cycloid, which Wallis himself described in a letter to Hughens as a 'work of great genius.'

Meanwhile Pascal was descending rapidly to the grave. The last three years of his life were little else than a perpetual agony, and he was almost totally incapacitated for study. During the short intervals of comparative ease, he occupied himself with his work on religion; his thoughts were set down on the first piece of paper that came to hand, and when he was no longer able to hold a pen, they were dictated to an intelligent domestic who constantly attended him. These fragments were collected after his death by the members of Port Royal, who published a selection in 1670, under the title of *Pensées de M. Pascal sur la Religion, et sur quelques autres sujets.* The first edition of the Thoughts omitted many very interesting fragments, and even some complete Essays, such as those on Authority in matters of Philosophy, the Reflections on Geometry, and on the Art of Persuasion, which are invaluable for their justness and originality.

In private life, Pascal was continually engaged in mortifying his senses and elevating his soul to God. It was a maxim with him to renounce all indulgences and superfluities. He removed from his apartment all articles of ornament; he ate only to satisfy the necessary calls of hunger, and not to gratify his palate. When he first retired from general society, he ascertained what quantity of food was necessary for his support, which he never exceeded, and whatever disgust he felt, never failed taking it; a method of which the motive may be respected, but which is very ill adapted to the variable state of the human frame.

His charity was very great; he regarded the poor as his brethren, and never refused giving alms, though often at the cost of personal privation, for his means were very limited, and his infirmities at times called for expenses which exceeded his income. Some time before his death, he received under his roof a poor man and his son, moved only by Christian pity. The child was seized with the small pox, and could scarcely be removed without danger. Pascal himself was very ill, and needed the constant assistance of Madame Perier. But as her children had never had the small pox, Pascal would not expose them to the danger of infection. He therefore decided against himself in favour of the poor man, and occupied a small incommodious apartment at his sister's. We may here mention another remarkable instance of his benevolence. One morning, returning from church, a beautiful girl, about sixteen years of age, came to him to beg alms, pleading that her father was dead, and that her mother had that morning been taken ill and carried to the Hotel-Dieu. Impressed with the danger to which the poor girl was exposed, he placed her immediately in a seminary under the care of a venerable ecclesiastic, to whom he gave a sum of money for the expenses of food and clothes, and continued his aid till she was placed in a respectable family. The purity of his manners was most exemplary. He carried his scrupulosity so far as sometimes to reprove Madame Perier for the caresses she bestowed on her children. To repress feelings of self-complacency, he wore a girdle of iron armed with points, which he used to strike with violence whenever he felt any undue elation of mind. Persuaded that the law of God forbids the surrender of the heart to created objects, he carefully controlled his affection, even for his nearest relations. Madame Perier sometimes complained of the coldness of his manners; but when an occasion presented itself for his services, he evinced so deep an interest in her welfare, that she could no longer doubt of his sincere affection. She then attributed his former insensibility of behaviour to the influence of bodily disorders, not aware that it had a purer and more elevated source.

While the disputes between the Jesuits and the Jansenists were at their height, an event happened which was looked upon by the latter as a testimony from heaven in their favour. A daughter of Madame Perier, between ten and eleven years old, had been afflicted for three years and a half with a lacrymal fistula of the worst kind; purulent and extremely offensive matter was discharged from the eye, nose, and mouth. On Friday, March 24, 1656, she was touched with what was deemed a relic of the Holy Thorn, which had been lent to the convent of Port Royal by M. de la Poterie, an ecclesiastic of eminent piety; the consequence is asserted to have been an instant cure. Racine, in his History of Port Royal, says that such was the silence habitually maintained in the convent, that for more than six days after the miracle, some of the sisters had not heard of it. It is not usual for persons of ardent faith to behold a miracle wrought under their eyes, without being struck with astonishment and impelled to glorify God by communicating it to others. The reserve of the members of Port Royal, on this occasion, may appear to some persons to cast doubts upon the fact itself; by minds favourably disposed, it will be considered an argument that the cure was not one of those pious frauds which are adopted by the leaders of a party in order to gain over a credulous multitude. The directors of Port Royal, believing it was their duty not to conceal so signal a favour of Providence, wished to confer on the fact the highest marks of credibility. Four celebrated physicians, and several eminent surgeons, who had examined the disease, certified that a cure was impossible by human means. The miracle was published with the solemn attestation of the vicars-general who governed the diocese of Paris in the absence of Cardinal de Retz. The manner in which it was received by the world completed the confusion of the Jesuits. They endeavoured to deny it, and, to support their incredulity, employed this ridiculous argument: Port Royal is heretical, and God never works miracles for heretics. To this it was replied, The miracle at Port Royal is certain; you cannot bring into doubt an ascertained fact; the cause of the Jansenists is good, and you are calumniators. A particular circumstance gave weight to this reasoning; the relic wrought no miracles except at Port Royal; transferred to the Ursulines or Carmelites, no effects were produced; it cured none: it was said because these latter establishments had no enemy, and needed not a miracle to prove that God was with them. Whatever judgment may be formed of this event, whether the cure (for that seems indisputable) is to be imputed to the operation of natural causes, not ascertained by the medical science of the times; to the influence of a credulous imagination in the patient, or to what some persons will perhaps admit, the divine power supernaturally excited in condescension to a sincere and genuine piety, though mixed with many errors, (and such the leading members of Port Royal, will be allowed by candid Protestants to have possessed,) one thing is certain, Pascal, of whose integrity and love of truth there can be no doubt, remained satisfied that the cure was the work of God, and his niece retained the same conviction during the whole course of a long life.

During the last two years of Pascal's life, his sufferings both of mind and body were extreme. In 1661 he endured the pain of witnessing the rise of that long persecution under which the institution of Port Royal at last sunk. The favour in which the Jansenists were held by the public only exasperated the Jesuits. To ensure their destruction, the Jesuits obtained an order for all the members of the Convent to sign the formulary of 1657, being certain that the advice of their directors would be either not to sign it, or to sign it with limitations equally favourable to their projects of vengeance. The Vicar-general of Paris, in consequence, received orders to execute this mandate with the utmost rigour. It is needless to describe the sad dilemma in which the Port Royalists found themselves placed: forced to pass a judgment on the work of Jansen, of which they understood neither the language nor the matter; on the one hand, honouring the authority which oppressed them, on the other, dreading to betray the truth: rebels in the eyes of the government if they refused to sign, and culpable in the eyes of their directors if they signed a document which they considered as drawn from the clergy and the Pope by the intrigues of the Jesuits. These cruel perplexities shortened the life of Jacqueline Pascal. At the time of the visit of the Vicar-general, she was sub-prioress of Port Royal; the violent conflict she endured, arising from her anxiety to submit, and the fear of violating her conscience, brought on an illness of which she died, Oct. 4, 1661, *the first victim* (as she expressed it) *of the Formulary*. Pascal loved her tenderly, and when informed of her death, said, " God grant us grace that our death may be like hers."

The members of Port Royal addressed some temperate complaints to the Court, which were construed by the Jesuits as a criminal resistance, and they insinuated that the directors of the monastery were fomenting a dangerous heresy. Yet they had never hesitated to condemn the five propositions abstractly; they had only distinguished in the *Constitution* of Alexander VII. two questions, the one of right, the other of fact; they received as a rule of faith the question of right, that is the censure of the five propositions in the sense they offered at first sight, and abstracted from all the circumstances which could restrict or modify them; but they did not consider themselves obliged to adhere to the assertion of the Pope when he said that the five propositions were formally contained in Jansen, and were heretical in the sense of that author, because it was possible, according to them, that the Pope, and even the Church, might be deceived on questions of fact. Pascal adopted this distinction very fully, and makes it the basis of his reasoning in the last two Provincial Letters, which appeared in 1657. Four years after, when it was again attempted to procure signatures to the Formulary, the Jansenists made a fresh concession; they consented that the nuns should sign it, declaring simply that they could not judge whether the propositions condemned by the Pope, and which they also condemned sincerely, were taken or not from Jansen. But this slight and reasonable limitation would not content the Jesuits, whose object was to destroy the Port Royalists, or to force them to a dishonourable recantation. This result Pascal had foreseen; and, far from approving of the concessions of the Jansenists, he always told them, 'You aim to save Port Royal; you will not save it, and you will betray the truth.' He even changed his opinion as to the distinction between the question of right and of fact. The doctrine of Jansen on the five propositions appeared to him to be exactly the same as that of St. Paul, St. Augustin, and St. Prosper, Whence he inferred that the Pope, in condemning the sense of Jansen, was mistaken, not only on a point of fact, but of right, and that no one could conscientiously sign the Formulary. He charged the Port Royalists with weakness; he told them plainly, that in their different writings they had had too much regard to present advantage, and had changed with the times. The elevation and rectitude of his mind saw in these temporising measures, nothing but subterfuges, invented to serve an occasion, and perfectly unworthy of the true defenders of the Church. They replied to these reproaches by explaining, in a long and ingenious manner, a method of subscribing to the Formulary without wounding their consciences or offending the government. But all these explanations produced no change of sentiment in Pascal; they had an opposite effect to what was desired: they occasioned a degree of coolness in his intercourse with the recluses of Port Royal. This little misunderstanding, which was not concealed on either side, was the occasion of a singular misrepresentation, of which the Jesuits were very ready to take advantage. M. Beurier, minister of St. Stephens-on-the-Hill, a pious but not well informed man, who attended Pascal in his last illness, having

heard it vaguely said by this celebrated man that he did
not think with the Port Royalists on the question of grace,
believed that these words implied that he thought with their
adversaries. He never imagined that it was possible for
any one to be more a Jansenist than Nicole and Arnauld.
About three years after Pascal's death, M. Beurier, on the
confused evidence of his memory, attested in writing to the
Archbishop of Paris, Hardouin de Perefixe, a zealous
Molinist, that Pascal had told him that he had withdrawn
himself from the Port Royalists on the question of the
Formulary, and that he did not consider them sufficiently
submissive to the Holy See. Precisely the contrary was the
fact. But the Jesuits made a pompous exhibition of this
declaration: unable to reply to the Provincial Letters, they
endeavoured to persuade the world that their author had
retracted them, especially the last two; and finally, had
adopted their theology. But the Jansenists easily confuted
these ridiculous assertions. They opposed to the evidence
of M. Beurier, contrary testimonies infinitely more circum-
stantial and positive; and, to remove every doubt, produced
the writings in which Pascal explained his sentiments.
Overpowered by these proofs, M. Beurier acknowledged
that he had misunderstood Pascal's words, and formally
retracted his declaration. Henceforward the Jesuits were
forced to acknowledge that Pascal died in the principles of
the most rigorous Jansenism. To return to his last illness.
In June, 1662, he was attacked by a severe and almost
constant colic, which nearly deprived him of sleep. The
physicians who attended him, though they perceived that
his strength was much reduced, did not apprehend immediate danger, as there were no febrile symptoms. He was
far from having the same security; from the first moment
of the attack, he said that they were deceived, and that the
malady would be fatal. He confessed himself severa
times, and would have taken the viaticum, but not to alarm
his friends, consented to a delay, being assured by the
physicians, that in a day or two, he would be able to receive
the communion at Church. Meanwhile his pains continued
to increase, violent headaches succeeded, and frequent

numbness, so that his sufferings were almost insupportable. Yet so resigned was he to the will of God, that not the least expression of complaint or impatience escaped him. His mind was occupied with plans of beneficence and charity. He made his will, in which the greater part of his property was left to the poor; he would have left them all, if such an arrangement had not been to the injury of the children of M. and Madame Perier, who were by no means rich. Since he could do no more for the poor, he wished to die among them, and urgently desired to be carried to the Hospital of the Incurables, and he was induced to abandon this wish only by a promise, that if he recovered, he should be at liberty to consecrate his life and property entirely to the service of the poor. On the 17th of August, however, he was seized with violent convulsions. His attendants reproached themselves for having opposed the ardent desire he had so often expressed of receiving the Eucharist. But they had the consolation of seeing him fully recover his recollection. The minister of St Stephen's then entered with the Sacrament and said, 'Behold Him whom you have so long desired!' Pascal raised himself, and received the viaticum with a devotion and resignation that drew tears from all around him. Immediately after, the convulsions returned, and never left him till he expired on the 19th August, 1662, aged thirty-nine years and two months.

On examining his body, the stomach and liver were found much diseased, and the intestines mortified; it was remarked with astonishment that the quantity of brain was enormous, and of a very solid and dense consistence.

Such was this extraordinary man, who was endowed with the choicest gifts of mind, a geometrician of the first order, a profound dialectician, an eloquent and sublime writer. If we recollect that in the course of a short life, oppressed with almost continual suffering, he invented the arithmetical machine, the principles of the calculation of probabilities, the method for resolving the problems of the Cycloid; that he reduced to certainty the opinions of philosophers relative to the weight of the atmosphere; that he was the first to establish on geometrical demonstration, the general laws of the equilibrium of fluids; that he was the author of one of the most perfect specimens of composition in the French language; that in his *Thoughts*, (unfinished and detached as they are for the most part,) there are fragments of incomparable profundity and eloquence, we shall be disposed to believe that there never existed in any nation a greater genius, or, we may add, a more devout believer.

THE PROVINCIAL LETTERS.

LETTER FIRST.

DISCUSSIONS IN SORBONNE. INVENTION OF PROXIMATE POWER: HOW USED BY THE JESUITS TO SECURE THE CENSURE OF M. ARNAULD.

PARIS, 23rd *January*, 1656.

SIR,—We were greatly mistaken. I was not undeceived till yesterday. Till then I thought that the subject debated in Sorbonne was very important, and of the utmost consequence to religion. So many meetings of such a celebrated body as the Theological Faculty of Paris, and at which things so strange and unexampled have taken place, give so high an idea of the subject that one cannot but believe it to be very extraordinary. And yet you will be surprised when you learn from this letter what it is that has caused all the noise. This I will tell you in a few words, after having thoroughly acquainted myself with it.

Two questions are considered; the one of fact, the other of doctrine. That of fact is, whether M. Arnauld is chargeable with presumption, for having said in his second Letter that he has carefully read the work of Jansenius, without finding the propositions condemned by the late Pope; and nevertheless, as he condemns these propositions wherever they are met with, he condemns them in Jansenius, if they are in Jansenius.

The question here is, whether he could, without presumption, thus declare that he doubts whether the propositions are in Jansenius, after the bishops have declared that they are.

The affair is brought forward in Sorbonne. Seventy-one

doctors undertake his defence, and maintain that he could not give any other answer to those who, in so many publications, asked him if he held that these propositions are in that book, than that he has not seen them in it, and that he nevertheless condemns them in it if they are in it.

Some even going further, have declared that after all the search which they could make, they have never found them, and have even found others of quite an opposite nature. They have then urgently requested that any doctor who has seen them, would have the goodness to show them; that a thing so easy could not be refused, since it was a sure means of silencing all of them, and M. Arnauld himself; but the request has always been refused. So much for what has taken place on that side.

On the other side are eighty secular doctors, and some forty mendicant monks, who have condemned M. Arnauld's propositions without choosing to examine whether what he has said is true or false; and have even declared that they had to do not with the truth, but only with the rashness of the proposition.

Besides these, there are fifteen who were not for the censure, and are called neutrals.

Thus has it fared with the question of fact, as to which I give myself very little trouble. For be M. Arnauld rash or not, my conscience is not concerned; and if I felt curious to know whether these propositions are in Jansenius, his book is neither so rare nor so large that I could not read it through to inform myself, without consulting the Sorbonne.

But if I did not fear likewise to be rash, I believe I would follow the opinion of most people I see, who having believed hitherto on public report that these propositions are in Jansenius, begin to suspect the contrary from the odd refusal to show them; indeed I have not yet met with any person who says he has seen them. So that I fear this censure will do more harm than good, and give those who learn its history an impression directly the reverse of the conclusion. For in truth the world is becoming suspicious, and believes things only when it sees them. But, as I have already said, the point is unimportant, faith not being concerned.

The question of doctrine seems much more weighty, inasmuch as it touches faith. Accordingly, I have taken particular care to inform myself upon it. But you will be pleased to see that it is of as little importance as the other.

The subject examined is a passage in the same letter in which M. Arnauld says, that "the grace without which we cannot do any thing was wanting to St. Peter in his fall." Here you and I thought that the greatest principles of grace were in question, such as whether it is not given to all men, or whether it is efficacious; but we were much mistaken. I am become a great theologian in a short time, and you are going to see proofs of it.

To learn the real state of matters, I paid a visit to Mr. ——, a doctor of Navarre who lives near me, and is, as you know, a most zealous opponent of the Jansenists: and as my curiosity made me almost as keen as himself, I asked him if they would not formally decide *that grace is given to all*, and so set the question at rest. But he bluntly rebuffed me, and told me that that was not the point; that there were persons on his side who held that grace is not given to all; that even the examinators had said in full Sorbonne, that this opinion is *problematical;* and that it was his own sentiment, which he confirmed by this passage from Augustine, which he says is famous: "We believe that grace is not given to all men."

I apologized for having mistaken his sentiments, and prayed him to tell me then if they would not at least condemn that other opinion of the Jansenists which is making so much noise, namely, that "grace is effectual, and determines our will to do good." But I was no happier in this second question. 'You don't understand it at all,' said he; 'that is not a heresy, it is an orthodox opinion: all the Thomists hold it; and I myself maintained it in my Thesis.'

I durst not propose my doubts to him, and I did not even know where the difficulty was, when, to get light upon it, I begged him to tell me in what the heresy of M. Arnauld's opinion consists. 'It is,' said he, 'in his not acknowledging that believers have the power of fulfilling the commandments of God, in the manner in which we understand it.'

I left him after this information; and, quite proud of having the kernel of the affair, I called for Mr. ———, who is getting better and better, and was in sufficient health to go with me to his brother-in-law, who is a Jansenist if ever there was one, and a very worthy man notwithstanding. To be better received, I feigned to be strongly of his party, and said to him, 'Can it be possible that the Sorbonne will introduce into the Church this error, "that all believers have always the power of fulfilling the Commandments?"' 'What are you saying?' asked my doctor; 'do you give the name of error to a sentiment which is strictly orthodox, and which the Lutherans and Calvinists alone call in question?' 'What,' said I to him, 'is that not your opinion?' 'No;' said he, 'we anathematize it as heretical and impious.' Surprised at this answer, I saw well that I had over-acted the Jansenist, as I had before over-acted the Molinist. But not being able to give full credit to his answer, I begged him to tell me in confidence if he held *that believers have always a real power of observing the commandments*. My friend warmed at this; but with devout zeal, he said, that he would never disguise his sentiments for any man; that this was his belief, and that he and all his party would defend it to the death, and as being the pure doctrine of St. Thomas, and Augustine their master.

He spoke so seriously that I could not doubt him. With this assurance I returned to my first doctor, and told him with much complacency, that I was sure there would soon be peace in Sorbonne; that the Jansenists admitted the power which believers have to fulfil the commandments; that I would be their security, and make them sign it with their blood. 'All very fine,' said he; 'it is necessary to be a theologian to see the bearing of it. The difference between us is so subtle, that we can scarcely define it ourselves; it would be too difficult for you to understand it; be contented therefore to know that the Jansenists will indeed tell you, that believers have always the power to fulfil the commandments; as to this we have no dispute: but they will not tell you that this power is *proximate*. That is the point.'

The word was new and unknown to me. Hitherto I had

understood matters, but this term threw me into the dark; and I believe it has only been invented for strife. I asked for explanation, but he made a mystery of it; and without further satisfaction sent me back to ask the Jansenists, if they admitted this *proximate* power. I charged my memory with the term, for my understanding had no part in it. For fear of forgetting it, I hastened back to my Jansenist, to whom, after the first exchange of civilities, I forthwith said, 'Tell me, I pray, if you admit *proximate power.*' He fell a laughing, and said to me coolly, 'Tell me yourself in what sense you understand it, and then I will tell you what I think of it.' As my knowledge did not go so far, I felt at my wits' end for an answer; and nevertheless, not to make my visit useless, I said to him on chance, I understand it in the sense of the Molinists. My friend, without changing a feature, asked, 'To which of the Molinists do you refer me?' I offered him the whole of them, as forming only one body, and actuated by one spirit.

But he said to me, 'Your information is very imperfect. They are so far from being of the same, that they are of the most opposite sentiments. Being all leagued in the project of ruining M. Arnauld, they have fallen upon the device of agreeing to this term *proximate*, which they might all equally use, though understanding it differently, in order to speak the same language, and by this apparent conformity form a considerable body, and swell their numbers so as to make sure of crushing him.'

This answer astonished me. But without being persuaded of the wicked designs of the Molinists, which I am unwilling to take on his word, and with which I have no concern, I endeavoured merely to ascertain the different meanings which they attach to this mysterious word *proximate*. He said; 'I would readily explain them, but you would see such a repugnance and gross contradiction, that you would scarcely believe me. I would be suspected by you. Your safer plan will be to learn it from themselves, and I will give you their addresses. You have only to see separately M. Le Moine, and Father Nicolai.' 'I don't know either of them,' said I. 'See then,' said he, 'if you are not acquainted with some of those whom I am going to mention, for they hold the views of M. Le Moine. I did know some of them: he then said, 'See if you have not some acquaintances among the Dominicans, for they are all with Father Nicolai.' I likewise knew some of those he mentioned; and being resolved to take his advice and have done with the affair, I left him and called first on one of the disciples of M. Le Moine.

I begged him to tell me what was meant by having *proximate power to do any thing*. 'That is easy,' said he: it is to have whatever is necessary to do it, so that nothing is wanting, in order to act.' 'And so,' said I, ' to have *proximate power* to cross a river, is to have a barge, bargemen, and oars, etc. with nothing wanting.' 'Very well,' said he. 'And to have the proximate power of seeing,' said I, 'is to have good eye-sight, and be in open day. For a person with good eye-sight, but in darkness, would not have the proximate power of seeing according to you.' 'Like a Doctor!' said he. 'Consequently,' I continued, 'when you say that believers always have the proximate power of observing the commandments, you mean that they always have all the grace necessary to perform them; nothing being wanting on the part of God.' 'Stay,' said he, 'they always have all that is necessary to observe them, or to ask God for it.' 'I see perfectly,' I said; ' they have all that is necessary to pray to God to assist them, without needing any new grace from God to pray.' 'You understand it,' said he. 'It is not necessary, then, to have an effectual grace to pray to God?' 'No,' said he, 'according to M. Le Moine.'

To lose no time, I went to the Jacobins, and asked for those whom I knew to be New Thomists. I begged them to tell me the meaning of *proximate power*. ' Is it not,' I asked, a power to which nothing is wanting in order to act?' ' No,' said they.' 'What, father! if this power wants something, do you call it *proximate?* and will you say that a man in the night time, and without any light, has the *proximate power of seeing?*' 'Yes,' indeed he has,' according to us, if he is not blind.' 'So be it,' said I, ' but M. Le Moine understands the contrary.' 'True,' said they, ' but we understand it thus.'

'I have no objections,' said I, 'for I never dispute about a word, provided I am made aware of the meaning which is given to it; but I see that when you say, believers have always a *proximate power* to pray to God, you understand, that they have need of other assistance, without which they will never pray.' 'Very well explained,' replied the fathers, embracing me, 'very well explained: they require moreover an effectual grace, which is not given to all, and which determines their will to pray; and it is heresy to deny the necessity of this effectual grace, in order to pray.'

'Very well explained,' said I to them in my turn; 'but according to you, the Jansenists are orthodox, and M. Le Moine heretical: for the Jansenists hold that believers have power to pray, but that notwithstanding an effectual grace is necessary, and this you approve; M. Le Moine says, that believers pray without effectual grace, and this you condemn.' 'Yes,' said they, 'but M. Le Moine calls this power, *proximate power.*'

'What, fathers!' said I, 'it is a play upon words, to say that you are agreed because of the common terms you use, while you give them contrary meanings.' The fathers made no answer: and on this my disciple of M. Le Moine arrived by good chance, which I thought extraordinary; but I have learned since that their intercourse is not rare, and that they are constantly in each other's company.

I then said to my disciple of M. Le Moine, 'I know a a man who says that believers have always power to pray to God; but that, nevertheless, they will never pray without an effectual grace which determines them, and which God does not always give to all believers. Is he heretical?' 'Stay,' said my Doctor, ' you might take me by surprise; softly, if you please! *distinguo*: if he calls this power, *proximate power*, he will be a Thomist, and of course catholic: if not, he will be a Jansenist, and of course heretical.' 'He does not,' said I, 'call it either proximate, or not proximate.' 'He is heretical,' then said he: 'ask these worthy fathers.' I did not take them as judges, for they were already nodding assent, but I said to them, 'He refuses to admit this word *proximate*, because it is not explained.' On this, one of the fathers was going to give his definition, but he was interrupted by the disciple of M. Le Moine, who said, Do you wish, then, to renew our squabblings? Have we not come under an agreement, not to explain this word *proximate*, but to use it on either side, without saying what is meant?' The Jacobin assented.

By this I penetrated their design, and on rising to go said to them: 'Verily, fathers, I much fear that all this is mere chicanery; and whatever comes of your meetings, I venture to predict, that, though the censure were passed, peace would not be established. For though it were declared necessary to pronounce the syllables *proximate*, who does not see that, not having been explained, each of you will claim the victory. The Jacobins will say that the word is understood in their sense; M. Le Moine will say that it is in his; and thus there will be far more disputes in explaining than in introducing it. After all, there would be no great danger in receiving it without any meaning, since it is only by the meaning that it can do harm. But it would be unworthy of the Sorbonne and of theology, to use equivocal captious terms, without explaining them. In fine, fathers, tell me once for all, what I must believe in order to be orthodox.' 'You must,' exclaimed all in a body, 'say that all believers have *proximate power*, wholly abstracting from any meaning; *abstrahendo a sensu Thomistarum, et a sensu aliorum Theologorum.*'

'In other words,' said I, on quitting them, 'it is necessary to pronounce this word, for fear of being heretical in name. Is it a Scripture term?' 'No,' said they. 'Is it from the Fathers, or Councils, or Popes?' 'No.' Is it from St. Thomas?' 'No.' 'What necessity then, is there for saying it, since it has neither authority nor meaning in itself?' 'You are obstinate,' said they: 'you shall say it, or you shall be heretical, and M. Arnauld also; for we are the majority, and if need be, we will bring Cordeliers enough to carry it!'

I have just left them on this last reason, in order to send you this narrative, from which you will see that none of the following points are agitated or condemned by either party. 1. *Grace is not given to all men.* 2. *All believers have power to perform the commandments of God.* 3. *Nevertheless, in order to perform them, and even to pray, they require an effectual grace, which determines their will.* 4. *This effectual grace is not always given to all believers, and depends on the mere mercy of God.* So that nothing but the word *proximate*, without meaning, runs any risk.

Happy the people who know it not! Happy those who lived before its birth! For I see no remedy, unless the members of the Academy banish from Sorbonne this barbarous term, which causes so much division. Without this, the censure appears certain; but I see, that the only harm of the proceeding will be, to give less weight to Sorbonne, and deprive it of the authority which it needs so much, on other occasions.

Meanwhile, I leave you free to espouse the word *proximate* or not: for I love you too much to make it a pretext for persecuting you. If this narrative is not disagreeable, I will continue to acquaint you with all that takes place.

I am, etc.

LETTER SECOND.

SUFFICIENT GRACE.

29th January, 1655.

Sir,—As I was closing my letter to you, I had a call from our old friend, Mr. ——. Nothing could be more fortunate for my curiosity, for he is well informed on the questions of the day, and perfectly acquainted with the policy of the Jesuits, with whom, and with the leading men among them, he has hourly intercourse. After speaking of the occasion of his visit, I begged him to tell me, in one word, the points debated between the two parties.

He immediately complied, and told me that there were two principal points; the first respecting *proximate power,* and the second respecting *sufficient grace.* My former letter explained the first; I will now speak of the second.

In one word, then, I learned, that their difference respecting grace lies here. The Jesuits hold that there is a grace given generally to all men, but so far subject to free will, which, as it chooses, renders it effectual or ineffectual, without any new assistance from God, and without any thing wanting on his part, to enable it to act effectually. Hence they call it *sufficient,* because by itself it suffices for acting. The Jansenists, on the contrary, hold that there is no grace actually sufficient, without being effectual; in other words, that all grace which does not determine the will to act effectually, is insufficient for acting, because they maintain that we never act without *effectual grace.* Such is the difference between them.

On inquiring as to the doctrine of the New Thomists, 'There is an oddness about it,' said he; 'they agree with the Jesuits in admitting *a sufficient grace* given to all men; but they insist, notwithstanding, that men never act with this grace alone; and that in order to make them act, God must give an effectual grace, which really determines their will to action, but which God does not give to all.' 'So that according to this doctrine,' said I, 'this grace is *sufficient* without being so.' 'Precisely,' said he, 'for if it suffices, no more is necessary for action; and if it does not suffice, it is not sufficient.'

'What then,' I asked, 'is the difference between them and the Jansenists?' 'They differ,' said he, 'in the Dominicans having at least this much good in them, that they refuse not to say that all men have sufficient grace.' 'I understand, replied I, 'but they say it without thinking it, since they add that in order to act, it is necessary to have *an effectual grace, which is not given to all;* thus if they are conformable to the Jesuits in a word which has no meaning, they are contrary to them, and conformable to the Jansenists in substance.' 'That is true, said he.' 'How then,' said I, are the Jesuits united with them? and why do they not combat them, as well as the Jansenists, since they will always find in them powerful opponents, who, maintaining the necessity of an effectual determining grace, will prevent them from establishing that which they hold to be of itself sufficient?'

'The Dominicans are too powerful,' said he, 'and the Company of the Jesuits too politic to make open war upon them. They are satisfied with having gained from them an admission, at least, of the name of *sufficient grace*, although they understand it differently. Their advantage in this is, that whenever they judge it expedient, they will be able, without difficulty, to discredit the opinion of the Dominicans, as not maintainable. For assuming that all men have sufficient grace, nothing is more natural than to infer that effectual grace is not necessary in order to act, since the sufficiency of this grace excludes the necessity of any other. *Sufficient,* includes all that is necessary in order to act, and it would little avail the Dominicans to cry out that they give a different meaning to the word *sufficient*. The people, accustomed to the common acceptation, would not so much as listen to their explanation. Thus the Company have a sufficient advantage in the reception of the term by the Dominicans, without pushing them farther; and if you were acquainted with what took place under Popes Clement VIII. and Paul V. and knew how much the Company were thwarted by the Dominicans in establishing sufficient grace, you would not be surprised at their not quarrelling with them, and consenting to let them hold their opinion, the Company also being free to hold theirs, and more especially the Dominicans favouring it by the term *sufficient grace*, which they have agreed to use publicly.

The Company are very well satisfied with this concession. They do not insist on a denial of the necessity of effectual grace; this were to press them too hard: one must not tyrannise over one's friends: the Jesuits have gained enough. For people deal in words, without giving heed to the meaning of them; and thus the term *sufficient grace* being received by both parties, although with different meanings, none but the nicest theologians will imagine that the thing meant by it is not held as well by the Jacobins as by the Jesuits.'

I admitted to him that they were a clever race; and to turn his information to account, went straight to the Jacobins, when at the gate I found one of my intimate friends, a great Jansenist, (for I have friends among all parties,) who was inquiring for some other father than the one I was in quest of. By force of entreaty, I got him to accompany me, and asked for one of my New Thomists. He was delighted to see me again. 'Well, father,' said I to him, 'it is not enough that all men have a *proximate power*, by which, however, they in fact never act. They must have moreover a *sufficient grace*, with which they act as little. Is not this the opinion of your school?' 'Yes,' said the worthy father, 'I mentioned it this morning in Sorbonne; I spent my whole half hour upon it, and but for the sand-glass, I would have changed the sad proverb now current in Paris, *He thinks by the bonnet like a monk in Sorbonne.*

'What do you mean by your half hour and your sand-glass?' I asked. 'Do they cut your opinions to a certain measure?' 'Yes,' said he, 'for some days past.' 'Are you obliged to speak half an hour?' 'No, we speak as little as we please.' 'But not so much as you please,' said I; 'an excellent rule for the ignorant, a fine pretext for those who have nothing good to say! But in short, father, is the grace given to all men *sufficient?*' 'Yes.' 'And yet it has no effect without effectual grace?' 'True.' 'And all men,' I continued, 'have the *sufficient,* but not all the *effectual?*' 'True.' 'In other words,' said I, 'all have enough of grace, and yet all have not enough; in other words, this grace suffices though it suffices not; in other words, it is sufficient in name, and insufficient in fact. In good sooth, father, this doctrine is very subtle. Have you, on retiring from the world, forgotten what the word *sufficient* signifies? Do you not remember that it includes whatever is necessary to act? But you have not lost the recollection of it; for, to use an illustration to which you will be more sensible, Were you served at table with only two ounces of bread and a glass of water a day, would you be satisfied with your Prior when he told you it was sufficient for your nourishment, on the pretext that with something else which he did not give you, you would have all that was necessary for your nourishment? How then can you allow yourself to say that all men have *sufficient grace* to act, while you confess that in order to act there is another absolutely necessary grace which all men have not? Is it because this belief is unimportant, and you leave men at liberty to believe or not believe that effectual grace is necessary? Is it a matter of indifference to hold that with sufficient grace we do in effect act?' 'How indifferent!' said the worthy man. 'It is a *heresy,* a formal *heresy.* The necessity of *effectual grace* to act effectually is a point of *faith:* it is *heresy* to deny it!'

'Where are we then,' exclaimed I, 'and which side must I take? If I deny sufficient grace, I am *Jansenist*; if I admit it in the sense of the Jesuits, as if effectual grace were not necessary, I will be *heretical;* so you say; and if I admit it in your acceptation, as if effectual grace were necessary, I sin against common sense, and am *preposterous;* so say the Jesuits. What, then, must I do in this inevitable necessity of being either preposterous, or heretical, or Jansenist? And to what straits are we reduced, if the Jansenists are the only persons who have no quarrel either with faith or with reason, and who escape alike from folly and error!'

My Jansenist friend took what I said as a good omen, and thought me already gained to his party. He said nothing to me, however, but, addressing the father, 'Tell me, I pray, father, in what you are conformable to the Jesuits.' 'In this,' said he, 'that the Jesuits acknowledge *sufficient grace* given to all.' 'But,' replied he, 'there are two things in the expression *sufficient grace;* there is the sound, which is only wind, and the thing signified by it, which is real and effective; and thus while you are at one with the Jesuits touching the words *sufficient grace,* and contrary to them in the meaning, it is plain that you are contrary to them as to the substance, and at one only as to the sound. Is this to act sincerely and from the heart?' 'But why,' said the worthy man, 'of what do you complain, since we do not mislead any one by this mode of speaking? For in our schools we say openly that we understand it in a contrary sense to that of the Jesuits.' 'I complain,' said my friend to him, 'of your not publishing, in all quarters, that you mean by sufficient grace, a grace which is not sufficient. While thus changing the meaning of the ordinary terms of religion, you are obliged in conscience to say, that when you admit a *sufficient grace* in all men, you understand that they have not a grace which is sufficient in fact. All the persons in the world understand the word *sufficient* in one same sense; the New Thomists alone understand it in another. All women, who form the half of mankind, all persons at court, all military men, all magistrates, all connected with courts of justice, merchants, artizans, the whole people in short, all classes except the Dominicans, understand that the word *sufficient* comprehends every thing that is necessary. Scarcely any person is made aware of this single exception. The only thing said every where, is, that the Jacobins hold that all men have *sufficient grace.* What conclusion can be drawn, but just that they hold that all men have all the grace which is necessary to act, more especially when they are seen leagued and intriguing with the Jesuits, who so understand it? Is not your agreement in expression, taken along with your party union, a manifest interpretation and a confirmation of uniformity of sentiment?

'All the faithful put the question to theologians, What is the true state of human nature since the fall? St. Augustin and his disciples answer that it has no longer sufficient grace, except in so far as God is pleased to impart it. The Jesuits afterwards come and say, that all have the grace which is actually sufficient. The Dominicans are consulted as to this contrariety; and what do they? They unite with the Jesuits, by this union forming the majority; they separate from those who deny sufficient grace, and declare that all men have it. What can be thought of this, but just that they give their sanction to the Jesuits? After all this, they add that *sufficient* is useless without *effectual grace,* which is not given to all.

'Would you see a picture of the Church in regard to these different views? I consider it like a man who, having set out on a journey, is attacked by robbers, who wound him in several places, and leave him half dead. He sends to the neighbouring towns for three physicians. The first having probed his wounds, thinks them mortal, and declares that God only can recover him. The second, coming after, and wishing to flatter him, tells him that he has still sufficient strength to reach his home, and, insulting the first for opposing this view, seeks to ruin his credit. The wounded man, in this dubious state, seeing the third at a distance, stretches out his hand to him as the person who must give the decision. He, after examining his wounds, and hearing the opinions of the other two, embraces the second, and unites with him. Both combine against the first, and, being the stronger party, drive him away with insult. The wounded man judges by this procedure that the third agrees in opinion with the second; and, in fact, on putting the question to him, is distinctly informed that he has sufficient strength to complete his journey. Feeling his weakness, however, he asks him why he thinks his strength sufficient. The answer is, 'Because you have still your limbs, and the limbs are the organs which naturally suffice for walking.' 'But,' rejoins the patient, 'have I all the strength necessary to use them, for to me they seem useless, I feel so feeble?' 'Certainly you have not so much strength,' says the physician, 'and, in fact, you will never walk unless God send you extraordinary assistance to sustain and conduct you.' 'What!' says the patient, 'I have not then in myself a strength which is sufficient, and wants nothing to enable me actually to walk!' 'Far from it,' says he. 'Your opinion, then, in regard to my real condition,' rejoins the wounded man, 'is contrary to that of your comrade.' 'I confess it,' he replies.

'What do you think the patient said? He complained of the strange behaviour and ambiguous language of this third physician. He blamed him for having leagued with the second, to whom he was opposite in sentiment, and with whom he had only an apparent conformity, and for having driven away the first with whom he in fact agreed. Having made trial of his strength, and ascertained by experience the real extent of his weakness, he dismisses both of them, and, calling back the first, places himself in his hands. Taking his advice, he asked of God the strength which he confessed he had not, was heard, and obtained assistance which enabled him to reach his home.'

The worthy father, confounded at this parable, made no answer. To bring him to himself, I said to him mildly, 'After all, Father, what made you think of giving the name of *sufficient*, to grace which you say it is a point of faith to regard as insufficient in fact?' 'You speak very much at your ease,' said he. 'You are free and single. I am a monk, the member of a community. Can you not allow for the difference? We depend on superiors, who themselves also depend elsewhere. They have promised our votes; what would you have me to become?' We understood what he would say. It brought to our minds the case of one of his brethren who has been banished to Abbeville for a similar cause.

'But what,' said I, 'led your community to admit this grace?' 'That is a different affair,' said he. 'All that I can say to you, in one word, is, that our order has, as long as it could, maintained the doctrine of St. Thomas in regard to effectual grace. How eagerly did it oppose the growth of Molina's doctrine! How much has it laboured to establish the necessity of the effectual grace of Jesus Christ! Are you ignorant of what took place under Clement VIII. and Paul V., and that death overtaking the one, and some Italian affairs preventing the other from publishing his Bull, our arms have remained in the Vatican? But the Jesuits, who, from the commencement of the heresy of Luther and Calvin, had taken advantage of the little ability which the people have to discriminate between error and the truth of St. Thomas's doctrine, had in a short time made such progress in spreading their views, that we soon saw them masters of the popular belief, and ourselves in danger of being cried down as Calvinists, and treated like the Jansenists in the present day, if we did not modify the doctrine of effectual grace, by an admission at least apparent of *sufficient grace.* In this extremity, what better could we do in order to save the truth without losing our credit, than just admit sufficient grace in name, while denying it to be so in fact? In this way the thing has happened.'

He said this so dolorously that I felt pity; but not so my companion, who said to him: 'Do not flatter yourself with having saved the truth; had it not had other protectors it had perished in such feeble hands. You have admitted into the Church the name of her enemy; this is to have received the enemy himself. Names are inseparable from things. If the word *sufficient* grace once gets a firm footing, it will be in vain for you to understand by it a grace which is insufficient; you will not be listened to. Your explanation will disgust the world, where less important things are spoken of more seriously: the Jesuits will triumph; their grace, sufficient in fact, and not yours, sufficient only in name, is the grace which will be held to be established, and the opposite of your belief will become an article of faith.'

'We will all suffer martyrdom,' said the father, 'sooner than consent to the establishment of *sufficient grace* in the sense of the Jesuits: St. Thomas, whom we vow to follow till death, being directly opposed to it.' On this my friend, who was more earnest than I, said: 'Pooh! father, your order has received an honour of which it proves unworthy. It abandons that grace which had been entrusted to it, and which has never been abandoned since the creation of the world. This victorious grace, which was longed for by the Patriarchs, foretold by the Prophets, brought by Jesus Christ, preached by St. Paul, explained by St. Augustine, the greatest of the Fathers, embraced by his followers, confirmed by St. Bernard, the last of the Fathers, sustained by St. Thomas, the angel of the schools, transmitted from him to your order, maintained by so many of your fathers, and so gloriously defended by your body under Popes Clement and Paul; this efficacious grace, which had been placed as a deposit in your hands, that it might have, in a holy order always subsisting, preachers who would publish it until the end of time, now finds itself as it were forsaken for paltry interests. It is time for other hands to arm in its cause. It is time that God raise up intrepid disciples of the doctrine of grace; men who, knowing nothing of worldly engagements, will serve God for God. Grace may indeed no longer have the Dominicans for defenders; but it will never want defenders, for it trains them for itself by its almighty power. It demands hearts pure and disengaged; it purifies them itself, and disengages them from worldly interests incompatible with the truths of the Gospel. Think well of this, father, and beware lest God remove your candlestick out of its place, and leave you in darkness and without a crown, to punish your lukewarmness in a cause which is so important to his Church.'

He would have said much more, for he waxed warmer and warmer. But I interrupted him, and said, on rising, 'In truth, Father, if I had credit in France, I would proclaim by sound of trumpet: NOTICE IS HEREBY GIVEN, *that when the Jacobins say sufficient grace is given to all, they mean that all have not the grace which effectually suffices.* Were this done, you might use the term as often as you please, but not otherwise.' Thus ended our visit.

You see then that we have here a politic *sufficiency* similar to *proximate power*. I may however say to you that the denial of *proximate power* and *sufficient* grace seems dangerous to none but a Jacobin.

While closing my letter, I learn that the censure is passed; but as I do not yet know in what terms, and it will not be published till the 15th February, I will not write about it till the first post thereafter.—I am, etc.

ANSWER OF THE PROVINCIAL

TO HIS FRIEND'S TWO FIRST LETTERS.

2nd February, 1656.

Sir,—Your two first Letters have not been for me only. Every body sees, every body hears, every body believes them. They are not only esteemed by theologians; they are moreover interesting to men of the world, and even intelligible to females.

A member of the Academy, (one of the most distinguished of a body whose members are all distinguished,) who had only seen the first Letter, writes me as follows:

"I wish that the Sorbonne, which owes so much to the memory of the late Cardinal, would recognise the jurisdiction of his French Academy. The author of the Letter would be satisfied; for in my capacity of Academician, I would authoritatively condemn, banish, proscribe, little keeps me from saying *exterminate* to the extent of my power, this proximate power which makes so much noise for nothing, and without knowing what it would be at. The evil is, that our Academical power is very remote and limited: I am sorry for it, and much more sorry that my little power does not enable me to discharge all my obligations to yourself, etc."

A personage, whom I will not designate in any way, writes to a lady who had sent her your first Letter:

"I am more obliged than you can imagine by the letter which you have sent me; it is most ingenious and admirably composed. It narrates without narrating, it clears up the most puzzling of all matters, and has a fine vein of irony in it; it instructs even those who do not know much of the case, and redoubles the pleasure of those who understand it. It is moreover an excellent apology, and, if you will, a delicate and innocent censure. There is, in fine, so much ability, wit, and judgment in this Letter, that I should like to know who has composed it," etc.

You would also like to know who it is that writes in these terms; but be contented to honour her without knowing her, and when you know her you will honour her much more.

Continue your Letters then on my word, and let the censure come when it will, we are very well prepared to receive it. The words *proximate power* and *sufficient grace*, which they use as bugbears, will not frighten us. We have learned too much of the Jesuits, the Jacobins, and M. Le Moine—how many shapes they take, and how little substance there is in those new terms—to feel any concern about them. Meanwhile, I am ever, etc.

LETTER THIRD.

INJUSTICE, ABSURDITY, AND NULLITY OF THE CENSURE OF M. ARNAULD.

Paris, *9th February*, 1656.

Sir,—I have just received your letter, and at the same time been handed a copy of the censure in manuscript. I find myself as well treated in the one as M. Arnauld maltreated in the other. I fear there is excess in both cases, and that we are not sufficiently known to our judges. I am sure if we were more so, M. Arnauld would deserve the approbation of Sorbonne, and I the censure of the Academy. Thus our interests are directly opposite. He should make himself known to defend his innocence, whereas I should remain in obscurity not to lose my reputation. Hence not being able to appear, I commit to you the office of returning thanks to my distinguished patrons, and undertake that of giving you news of the censure.

I confess, Sir, that it has surprised me exceedingly. I expected to find the most dreadful heresies condemned, but you will wonder, like me, how all this noise, and all these preparations, have become abortive at the moment of producing the grand result.

To understand it satisfactorily, recollect, I pray, the strange impressions which have for so long a time been given us of the Jansenists. Call to mind the cabals, the factions, the errors, the schisms, the crimes with which they have so long been charged; how they have been cried down and blackened in the pulpit and by the press; and how much this torrent, so violent and so lasting, has grown during the last year or two, in which they have been accused openly and publicly of being not only heretics and schismatics, but apostates and infidels; *of denying the mystery of transubstantiation, and abjuring Jesus Christ and his Gospel.*

In consequence of these many startling accusations, it was resolved to examine their books in order to give judgment upon them. Choice was made of the second Letter of M. Arnauld, which was said to be full of the grossest errors. The examinators assigned him are his most avowed enemies. They employ their utmost diligence to discover something reprehensible, and they bring forward a proposition of a doctrinal nature, which they submit to censure.

What could one think from the whole procedure, but that this proposition, selected in such remarkable circumstances, contained the essence of the blackest heresies imaginable? And yet such is its nature, that there is nothing in it but what is so clearly and formally expressed in the passages which M. Arnauld has quoted from the Fathers, at the place where the proposition occurs, that I have not seen any person who is able to comprehend the difference. People nevertheless presumed it must be great; since the passages from the Fathers being undoubtedly orthodox, the proposition of M. Arnauld behoved to be extremely opposite to them to be heretical.

The Sorbonne was expected to give the explanation. All Christendom was looking intent to see in the censure of these Doctors a point which, to ordinary men, was imperceptible. Meanwhile M. Arnauld frames his 'Apologies,' in which he gives his proposition, and the passages of the Fathers from whom he took it, in separate columns, in order to make their conformity apparent to the most undiscerning.

He shows that Augustine says in a passage which he quotes that, "Jesus Christ exhibits in the person of St. Peter a believer, who teaches us by his fall to guard against presumption." In another passage which he quotes, the same Father says, "God, to show that without grace we can do nothing, left St. Peter without grace." He gives a passage from St. Chrysostom, who says, "The fall of St. Peter was not occasioned by lukewarmness to Christ, but by want of grace; was occasioned not so much by negligence as by abandonment by God, to teach the whole Church that without God we can do nothing." After this he gives his accused proposition, which is as follows: "The Fathers show us, in the person of St. Peter, a believer to whom the grace without which we cannot do any thing, was wanting."

Hereupon people try in vain to discover how it possibly can be, that the proposition of M. Arnauld is as different from that of the Fathers as truth from error, and faith from heresy. For wherein lies the difference? Can it be in his saying that "the Fathers show us a believer in the person of St. Peter"? St. Augustine has used the very words. Is it in saying that "grace was wanting to him"? Augustine, who says that " St. Peter was a believer," also says that "he had not grace on this occasion." Is it because he says that "without grace we can do nothing"? But is not this what St. Augustine says in the same place, and what St. Chrysostom also had said before him, with this single difference, that Chrysostom expresses it in a much stronger manner, as when he says that "his fall was not owing either to his lukewarmness or his negligence, but to want of grace and abandonment by God"?

All these considerations were holding the world in breathless suspense to learn wherein the difference consisted, when the censure, so famous and so eagerly looked for, at length, after numerous meetings, appears. But alas! it has indeed disappointed our expectations. Whether the Molinist Doctors have not deigned to lower themselves so far as to instruct us, or for some other secret reason, they have done nothing more than pronounce these words: *This proposition is rash, impious, blasphemous, anathematised, and heretical.*

Can you wonder, Sir, that most people, seeing their hopes deceived, have lost temper, and turned against the censors themselves? They draw very strong inferences from their conduct, in favour of M. Arnauld. What! they say, after all this time, have all these Doctors, with all their inveteracy against a single individual, been able to do no more than find three lines to censure in all his works, and these expressed in the very words of the greatest Doctors of the Greek and Latin Churches? Is there an author whom it was wished to ruin, whose writings would not afford a more plausible pretext? Could a stronger proof be given of the soundness of the faith of this illustrious accused?

How comes it, they ask, that this censure is so filled with imprecations? that the terms *poison, pestilence, horror, temerity, impiety, blasphemy, abomination, execration, anathema, heresy,* the very worst that could be found for Arius, or Antichrist himself, are raked together to denounce an imperceptible heresy, and that even without discovering it? If quotations from the Fathers are to be treated in this manner, what becomes of faith and tradition? If the only object of attack is the proposition of M. Arnauld, let them show us where the difference lies, since we see only perfect conformity? When we perceive the heresy in it, we will hold it in detestation; but so long as we see it not, and only find the sentiments of the Fathers conceived and expressed in their own words, how can we do otherwise than hold it in holy veneration?

Such is the way in which many feel; but they belong to the class of those who are too sharp-sighted. Let us who do not go so deep into things, keep ourselves at ease on the whole matter. Would we be more knowing than our masters? Let us not undertake more than they. We should lose ourselves in the search. The least thing in the world would make the censure heretical. The truth is so delicate, that any deviation from it, however small, plunges us into error; while the error is so minute that a single step away from it brings us to truth. There is only one imperceptible point between this proposition and sound faith. The distance is so insensible, that my fear, while not seeing it, has been, that I might become contrary to the Doctors of the Church in my anxiety to be conformable to the Doctors of Sorbonne. In this fear I judged it necessary to consult one of those who from policy were neutral on the first question, that I might learn how the case truly stands. Accordingly I waited on one of them, a very clever person, and begged him to have the goodness to specify the particular points of difference, frankly confessing to him that I saw none.

Laughing, as if amused at my simplicity, he replied: 'How silly you are to believe there is any difference! Where could it be? Do you imagine that if any could have been found, it would not have been distinctly specified, and that they would not have been delighted to expose it to the view of all the people in whose minds they desire to lower M. Arnauld?' I saw plainly by these few words, that all who were neutral on the first question would not have been so on the second. Still, however, I wished to hear his reasons, and said, 'Why then did they attack this proposition?' He replied, 'Are you ignorant of two things, which the least informed on these matters know? the one, that M. Arnauld has always avoided saying any thing that was not strongly founded in the tradition of the Church: the other, that his enemies were determined to exclude him from it, cost what it might; and that these his writings, giving no handle to their designs, they, to gratify their passions, have been compelled to take up a proposition at hazard, and without saying why or wherefore? For do you not know how the Jansenists keep them at bay, and press them so very closely, that whenever a word escapes them in the least degree contrary to the Fathers, they are forthwith borne down by whole volumes, and forced to succumb? After the many proofs of their weakness, they have judged it more expedient and less laborious to censure than to rejoin, because it is far easier for them to find monks than arguments.'

'But the matter so standing,' said I, 'their censure is useless; for what credit will it have when it is seen to be without foundation, and is overthrown by the answers which will be made to it?' 'If you knew the spirit of the people, said my Doctor, 'you would speak in a different manner. The censure, most censurable though it be, will have almost full effect for a time; and though by dint of demonstrating its invalidity, it certainly will come to be understood, just as certainly will the first impression of the great majority be that it is perfectly just. Provided the hawkers in the streets cry: *Here you have the censure of M. Arnauld! Here you have the condemnation of the Jansenists!* the Jesuits will have gained their object. How few will read it? How few who read will understand? How few perceive that it does not meet the objections? Who do you think will take the matter to heart, and probe it to the bottom? See, then, what advantage the enemies of the Jansenists have here. In this way they are sure of a triumph, (though according to their wont, a vain triumph,) for several months at least. This is a great deal for them: they will afterwards look out for some new means of subsistence. They are living from hand to mouth. It is in this way they have maintained themselves hitherto; at one time by a catechism, in which a child condemns their opponents; at another by a procession, in which sufficient grace leads effectual grace in triumph; at another by a comedy, in which the devils carry off Jansenius; once by an almanac, and now by the censure.'

'In truth,' said I, 'the proceedings of the Molinists seemed to me objectionable in every point of view; but after what you have told me, I admire their prudence and their policy. I see well that there was nothing they could do either more judicious or more sure.' 'You understand it, said he. 'Their safest course has always been to be silent, and hence the saying of a learned theologian, that *the ablest among them are those who intrigue much, speak little, and write none.*'

' In this spirit they had, from the commencement of their meetings, prudently ordered that if M. Arnauld made appearance in Sorbonne, it should only be to give a simple exposition of his belief, and not to enter the lists with any one. The examinators having chosen to deviate somewhat from this rule, did not get well out of it. They saw themselves very roughly handled by his second Apology.

'In this same spirit they have fallen upon the rare and very novel device of the half-hour and the sand-glass. They have thereby rid themselves of the importunity of those Doctors who undertook to refute all their arguments, to produce books convicting them of falsehood, and challenge them to reply, while putting it out of their power to reply with effect. Not that they were unaware that this want of liberty, which caused so many Doctors to withdraw their attendance, would do no good to their censure; and that the protest of nullity which M. Arnauld took before it was concluded, would be a bad preamble for securing its favourable reception. They know well that all who are not prejudiced, attach at least as much weight to the judgment of seventy Doctors who had nothing to gain by defending M. Arnauld, as to that of the hundred who had nothing to lose by condemning him.

'But still, after all, they thought it always a great matter to have a censure, although it were only by a part of Sorbonne, and not by the whole body; though it were passed with little or no freedom, and secured by many paltry, and some not very regular methods; although it explains nothing as to the point in dispute, does not specify wherein the heresy consists, and says little from fear of mistake. This very silence gives the thing an air of mystery to the simple, and gains this singular advantage to the censure, that the most critical and subtle theologians will not be able to find any false argument in it.

'Set your mind at rest then, and fear not to be heretical in using the condemned proposition. It is bad only in the second Letter of M. Arnauld. Are you unwilling to take this on my word? Believe M. Le Moine, the keenest of the examinators, who, speaking this very morning with a friend of mine, a Doctor, who asked him wherein the difference in question lies, and whether it would no longer be lawful to say what the Fathers have said, gave this admirable reply: "*This proposition would be orthodox in any other mouth: it is only in M. Arnauld that the Sorbonne has condemned it.*" And now admire the engines of Molinism, which effect such prodigious revolutions in the Church, making that which is orthodox in the Fathers become heretical in M. Arnauld, that which was heretical in the Semi-Pelagians become orthodox in the writings of the Jesuits; making the ancient doctrine of St. Augustine become an intolerable novelty, while the new inventions which are daily fabricated under our eyes pass for the ancient faith of the Church.' On this he left me.

This lesson was enough. It taught me that the heresy here was of a new species. It is not the sentiments of M. Arnauld, but his person that is heretical. It is a personal heresy! He is not heretical because of any thing he has said or written, but only because he is M. Arnauld. This is all that is objectionable in him. Let him do what he may, unless he cease to live, he will never be a good Catholic. The grace of St. Augustine will never be true so long as he shall defend it. It would become so if he were to combat it. This were a sure stroke, and almost the only means of establishing it and destroying Molinism; such misfortune does he bring on the principles which he supports.

Here, then, let us have done with these disputes. They are the quarrels of theologians, not questions of theology. We who are not Doctors have nothing to do with their squabbles. Give the news of the censure to all our friends, and love me as much as—I am, Sir, your very humble and obedient servant,

E. A. A. B. P. A F. D. E. P.

LETTER FOURTH.

OF ACTUAL GRACE ALWAYS PRESENT, AND OF SINS OF IGNORANCE.

Paris, *25th February,* 1856.

Sir,—There are none like the Jesuits. I have seen many Jacobins, Doctors, and all sorts of people, but a visit like this was wanting to complete my instruction. Others only copy them. Things are always best at the source. I have accordingly visited one of the cleverest of them, accompanied by my faithful Jansenist, who went with me to the Jacobins. And as I wished particularly to be enlightened on the subject of a difference which they have with the Jansenists touching *actual grace,* I told the worthy father how much I should be obliged to him if he would have the goodness to instruct me, as I did not even know what the term meant; I therefore begged him to explain it to me. 'Very willingly,' said he, 'for I like inquisitive people. Here is the definition of it. *Actual grace is an inspiration from God, by which he makes us know his will, and excites in us a desire to perform it.*' 'And wherein,' I asked, 'are you at variance with the Jansenists on this subject?' 'It is,' said he, 'in our holding that God gives actual grace to all men on every temptation, because we maintain that if on every temptation actual grace not to sin were not given, no sin whatever that might be committed could be imputed. The Jansenists say, on the contrary, that sins committed without actual grace are imputed notwithstanding: but they are dreamers.' I had some idea of what he meant, but, to make him explain himself more clearly, I said, 'Father, the term *actual grace* confuses me; I am not accustomed to it: if you will have the goodness to tell me the same thing without using that term, I will be infinitely obliged.' 'Yes;' said the Father, 'in other words, you wish me to substitute the definition in place of the thing defined; that never makes any change on the meaning: I am very willing to do it. We maintain, then, as an indubitable principle, that *an action cannot be imputed as sinful, unless God gives us, before we commit it, a knowledge of the evil which is in it, and an inspiration prompting us to avoid it.* Do you understand me now?'

Astonished at this language, according to which all sins of surprise, and those done in complete forgetfulness of God, cannot be imputed, I turned towards my Jansenist, and saw plainly by his manner that he did not believe a word of it. But as he made no answer, I said to the father, 'Father, I wish much that what you tell me were true, and that you could furnish good proof of it.' 'Do you wish it?' said he immediately, 'I will furnish you, and with the very best: leave that to me.' On this he went to fetch his books. I said meanwhile to my friend, 'Does any other of them speak like him?' 'Is that so new to you?' he replied; 'rest assured that no Father, Pope, or Council, neither Scripture, nor any book of piety even in these last times, ever spoke in that manner; but as to casuists and new schoolmen, he will bring you them in abundance.' 'What!' said I, 'I care not a straw for those authors if they are opposed to tradition.' 'You are right,' said he. As he spoke, the worthy Father arrived loaded with books, and, offering me the first in his hand, 'Read,' said he, the Sum of Sins, by Father Bauni. Here it is; the fifth edition, moreover, to show you that it is a good book.' 'It is a pity,' whispered my Jansenist, 'that this book was condemned at Rome, and by the bishops of France.' 'Look,' said the Father, 'at page 906.' I looked and found as follows: *To sin and incur guilt before God, it is necessary to know that the thing which we wish to do is worthless, or at least to suspect this; to fear, or rather judge, that God takes no pleasure in the action we are contemplating, that he forbids it, and notwithstanding to do it, to take the leap and go beyond.*

'This makes a good beginning,' said I. 'And yet,' said he, 'see what a thing envy is.' It was for this that M. Hallier, before he was a friend of ours, jeered at Father

Bauni, applying to him the words, *Ecce qui tollit peccata mundi! Behold him who taketh away the sins of the world!*' 'It is true,' said I, 'that this is a new redemption, à la Father Bauni.'

'Are you desirous,' he added, 'to have a graver authority? Look at this work of Father Annat. It is the last which he has written against M. Arnauld. Look at page 34, where it is folded down, and read the lines which I have marked with a pencil: they are all letters of gold.' I read accordingly: *He who has no thought of God, nor of his sins, nor any apprehension*, that is, as he explained to me, *any knowledge of the obligation to do acts of love to God, or of contrition, has no actual grace to do those acts; but it is also true that he does not sin in omitting them, and that if he is damned, it will not be in punishment of this omission.* Some lines farther down: *And we may say the same thing of a culpable commission.*

'Do you see how he speaks of sins of omission and sins of commission? For he forgets nothing. What say you?' 'O how I am delighted,' replied I. 'What beautiful consequences I see! The whole series is already in my eye; what mysteries rise into view! I see incomparably more people justified by this ignorance and forgetfulness of God, than by grace and the sacraments. But, father, are you not giving me a false joy! Is there nothing here akin to the *sufficiency* which suffices not? I am dreadfully afraid of the *Distinguo*; I was caught by it before. Are you in earnest?' 'How,' said the Father, warming; it is no jesting matter; there is no equivocation here.' 'I am not jesting,' said I, 'but I fear it is too good to be true.'

'To make you more sure, then,' said he, 'turn to the writings of M. Le Moine, who has taught it in full Sorbonne. He learned it from us, it is true, but he has well expounded it. O how firmly he has established it! He teaches, that before an act *can be sinful, all these things must take place in the soul.* Read and weigh every word.' I read in Latin what you will here see in French: 1. *On the one hand, God infuses into the soul some feeling of love, inclining it towards the thing commanded, while, on the other hand, rebellious concupiscence urges it to the contrary.* 2. *God inspires it with a knowledge of its weakness.* 3. *God inspires it with a knowledge of the Physician who is to cure it.* 4. *God inspires it with a desire of cure.* 5. *God inspires it with a desire to pray to him, and implore his assistance.*

'Unless all these things take place in the soul,' said the Jesuit, 'the action is not properly sin, and cannot be imputed, as M. Le Moine says in the same place, and in the sequel throughout.

'Would you have more authorities? Here they are.' 'But all modern,' quietly observed my Jansenist. 'I see,' I replied; and, addressing the father, said, 'O father, what a blessing to some persons of my acquaintance! I must bring them to you. Perhaps you have seldom seen people with fewer sins, for they never think of God; their vices got the start of their reason; they have never known either their infirmity, or the Physician who can cure it: they have never thought of desiring the health of their soul, and still less of asking God to give it; so that they are still, according to M. Le Moine, as innocent as at their baptism. They have never once thought of loving God or being sorry for their sins; so that, according to Father Annat, they have never sinned, being devoid both of love and repentance. Their whole life is a continued search after pleasure of every sort, and their course has never been interrupted by the slightest remorse. All these excesses made me think their perdition certain; but you, father, teach me, that these excesses make their salvation secure. Blessings on you, father, for thus justifying people! Others teach how to cure souls by painful austerities, but you show that those whom we might have thought most desperately diseased, are in good health. O! the nice way of being happy in this world and in the next. I always thought that we sinned the more, the less we thought of God. But from what I see, when once one has so far gained upon one's self, as not to think of Him at all, all things in future become pure. None of your half sinners who have some lingering after virtue! They will all be damned, those half sinners. But for those rank sinners, hardened sinners, sinners without mixture, full and finished, hell does not get them; they have cheated the devil, by dint of giving themselves over to him!'

The worthy father, who clearly enough saw the connection of these consequences with his principles, adroitly evaded it, and without troubling himself, whether from meekness or prudence, simply said to me, 'That you may understand how we avoid these inconveniences, know, that we indeed say that the impious persons you refer to, would be without sin, if they had never had any thoughts of conversion, or desires of giving themselves to God. But then we maintain that they all have these thoughts, and that God has never allowed a man to sin without previously giving him a view of the evil which he is going to do, and a desire either to avoid the sin or at least to implore his assistance to enable him to avoid it. None but the Jansenists say the contrary.'

'What! father,' I rejoined, 'is it heresy in the Jansenists to deny that in every instance when a man commits sin, he has a feeling of remorse in his conscience, in spite of which he proceeds *to take the leap and pass beyond,* as father Bauni says! It is rather amusing to be a heretic for that. I always thought that men were damned for not having good thoughts: but that they are damned for not believing that every body has them, of a truth, never occurred to me. But father, I feel bound in conscience to disabuse you, and tell you that there are thousands of people who have no such desires, who sin without regret, sin gladly, and make a boast of it. Who can know this better than yourself? Do you not confess some such persons as I speak of, for it is among persons of high rank that they are most frequently met with? But beware, father, of the dangerous consequences of your maxim. Do you not perceive what effect it may have upon those libertines whose only wish is to be able to doubt the truth of religion? What a handle for this do you give when you tell them as an article of faith, that at every sin which they commit, they are warned, and feel an inward desire to abstain from it! For is it not obvious, that, their own experience assuring them of the falsehood of your doctrine on the point which you say is an article of faith, they will extend the inference to all the others? They will say that if you are not true in one article, you may be suspected in all; and thus you will oblige them to conclude either that religion is false, or that you are ill instructed in it.'

But my second, taking up my view, said to him, 'In order to preserve your doctrine, father, you will do well not to explain, so precisely as you have done to us, what you understand by *actual grace*. How could you, without losing all credit in the minds of men, declare openly that *nobody sins without previously having a knowledge of his infirmity and of the Physician, a desire of cure, and of asking God to grant it?* Will it be believed on your word, that those who are addicted to avarice, unchastity, blasphemy, duelling, revenge, theft, sacrilege, have really a desire to cultivate chastity, humility, and the other Christian virtues? 'Will it be thought that those philosophers who vaunted so highly of the power of nature, knew its infirmity and the Physician? Will you say that those who held as an indubitable maxim, that *God does not give virtue, and that no person ever asked it of him*, thought of asking it themselves? 'Who will believe that the Epicureans, who denied divine Providence, had inspirations inclining them to pray to God? men who said, *it was an insult to apply to him in our wants, as if he were capable of amusing himself with thinking of us.* 'In fine, is it imaginable, that idolators and atheists have, in all the temptations inclining them to sin, (that is, an infinite number of times during their life,) a desire to pray to the true God of whom they are ignorant, to give them the true virtues which they do not know?'

'Yes,' said the worthy father, with a determined tone, we will say it; and sooner than say that men sin without having a perception that they are doing evil, and a desire of the opposite virtue, we will maintain that the whole world, both wicked men and infidels, have these inspirations and desires on every temptation. For you cannot show me, at least from Scripture, that it is not so.

I here took speech to say to him, 'What! father, is it necessary to have recourse to Scripture to demonstrate so clear a matter? It is neither an article of faith, nor a fit subject of argument. It is a matter of fact. We see it, we know it, we feel it.'

But my Jansenist, taking up the father on his own terms, said to him, 'If you insist, father, on yielding only to Scripture, I consent, but at least do not resist it; and, seeing it is written that *God has not made known his judgments to the Gentiles*, and that *he has left them to wander in their own ways*, say not that God has enlightened those whom the Sacred Books declare to have been *left in darkness and the shadow of death*.

'To perceive that your principle is erroneous, is it not enough to see that St. Paul calls himself the *chief of sinners*, because of a sin which he had committed *through ignorance* and *with zeal*.

'Is it not enough to see from the Gospel that those who crucified Jesus Christ needed the pardon which he asked for them, although they knew not the full wickedness of the deed, and, according to St. Paul, would not have done it had they known?

'Is it not enough, when Jesus Christ warns us that there will be persecutors of the Church, who will think they are doing God service in striving to overthrow it, to remind us, that this sin which, according to the Apostle, is the greatest of all, may be committed by persons who, so far from knowing that they sin, would think it a sin not to do so? And, in fine, is it not enough that Jesus Christ himself has told us that there are two kinds of sinners—those who sin with knowledge, and those who sin without knowledge; and that they will all be punished, though in different degrees?

The worthy father, pressed by so many passages of Scripture to which he had appealed, began to give way, and, leaving the wicked to sin without inspiration, said: 'At least you will not deny that the righteous never sin without God giving them—' 'You are drawing back,' said I, interrupting him, 'you are drawing back, father; you are giving up the general principle; and, seeing that it wont hold in regard to sinners, you would fain compound the matter, and make it, at least, subsist in regard to believers. In that case, the use of it is greatly curtailed, very few will be able to avail themselves of it, and it is scarcely worth while contesting it with you.'

But my second, who, I believe, had studied the whole question that very morning, so much was he at home upon it, replied, 'This, father, is the last entrenchment into which those of your party who have been pleased to debate the point retire. But you are far from being safe in it. The example of believers is not a whit more favourable for you. Who doubts that they often fall into sins of surprise without perceiving it? Do we not learn from the saints themselves, how many secret snares concupiscence lays for them, and how frequently it happens, let them be temperate as they may, that they give to pleasure what they think they are only giving to necessity, as St. Augustine says of himself in his Confessions?

'How common is it in debate to see the most zealous give way to ebullitions of temper for their own interest, while the only testimony which their conscience gives at the time is, that they are are acting solely for the interests of truth, this erroneous impression sometimes continuing for a long time after?

'But what shall we say of those who engage with eagerness in things which are really bad, believing them to be really good, cases of which Ecclesiastical History furnishes examples, and in which, according to the Fathers, sin is nevertheless committed?

'But for this, how could believers have hidden sins? How could it be true that God alone knows the magnitude and the number of them? That no one knows whether he is deserving of love or of hatred, and that the greatest saints must always remain in fear and trembling, although they are not conscious of transgression, as St. Paul says of himself?

'Understand then, father, that the examples, both of the righteous and the wicked, equally disprove your supposed essential requisite to sin, namely., a knowledge of the evil and a love of the contrary virtue, since the passion which the wicked have for vice plainly testifies that they have no desire for virtue, and the love which the righteous have for virtue loudly proclaims that they are not always aware of the sins which, according to Scripture, they commit every day.

'So true is it that believers sin in this manner, that distinguished saints seldom sin otherwise. For how is it conceivable, that those pure souls who so carefully and earnestly eschew whatever may be displeasing to God the moment they perceive it, and who, nevertheless, sin repeatedly every day, should, previously to each lapse, have *a knowledge of their infirmity on that occasion, and of the Physician, a desire to obtain health, and to pray to God to succour them*; and, notwithstanding of all these inspirations, these zealous souls should *still pass beyond* and commit the sin?

'Conclude then, father, that neither the wicked nor even the righteous have always that knowledge, those desires, and all those inspirations every time they sin; in other words, to use your own terms, they have not *actual grace* on all the occasions on which they sin. No longer say with your new authors, that it is impossible to sin without knowing righteousness; but say rather with St. Augustine and the ancient Fathers, that it is impossible for any man not to sin who is ignorant of righteousness. *Necesse est ut peccet, a quo ignoratur justitia.*'

The worthy father, finding himself precluded from maintaining his opinion in regard to the righteous, as well as in regard to sinners, did not, however, lose courage. Pondering a little, he said, 'I am sure I am going to convince you;' and, taking up his Father Bauni at the place which he had shown us, 'See, see, the reason on which he founds his view. I know well that he had no lack of good proofs. Read his quotation from Aristotle, and you will see that after so express an authority, you must burn the books of this prince of philosophers, or be of our opinion. Listen then to the principles which Father Bauni establishes. He says, first, that *an act can not be imputed to sin when it is involuntary.* 'Admitted,' said my friend. 'This,' said

I, 'is the first time that I have seen you agree. Stay where you are, father, if you will take my word.' 'That were to do nothing,' said he, 'for we must ascertain what conditions are necessary to make an action voluntary.' 'I greatly fear,' replied I, 'that you will split upon that.' 'Fear not,' said he, 'the thing is sure. Aristotle is with me. Listen attentively to what Father Bauni says: *An action, to be voluntary, must be done by one who sees and knows, and thoroughly perceives the good and evil which is in it.* VOLUNTARIUM EST (*as is commonly defined by the philosopher.* You are aware,' said he, giving my hand a squeeze, 'he means Aristotle,) QUOD FIT A PRINCIPIO COGNO-SCENTE SINGULA IN QUIBUS EST ACTIO; *so much so that when the will at random, and without discussion, proceeds to will or dislike, to do or not do something, before the understanding has been able to see whether there is evil in willing or in shunning it, in doing it or leaving it undone, such action is neither good nor bad; in as much as, previous to this requisite, this view and reflection of the mind as to the good or bad qualities of the thing in question, the act which is done is not voluntary.*'

'Well,' said the father, 'are you satisfied?' 'It seems,' rejoined I, 'that Aristotle is of Father Bauni's opinion, but I am surprised at it. What! father, in order to act voluntarily, is it not enough to know what we do, and to do it because we please to do it? Must we moreover *see, know, and thoroughly perceive the good and evil that is in the action?* If so few actions of our lives are voluntary, for we seldom think of all that, what oaths at play, what excesses of debauchery, what irregularities during carnival, must be involuntary, and consequently neither good nor bad, from not being accompanied with those *reflections of the mind on the good or bad qualities* of what is done! But, father, is it possible that this can have been Aristotle's idea? I have always heard that he was a man of talent.' 'I will explain to you,' said my Jansenist, and, having asked the father for Aristotle's Ethics, he opened at the beginning of the third book, where Father Bauni has taken the words he quotes, and said to the worthy father, 'I forgive you for believing on Father Bauni's word, that this was Aristotle's opinion. You would have thought differently if you had read it for yourself. It is very true he teaches that *to make an action voluntary, it is necessary to know the particulars of the action;* SINGULA IN QUIBUS EST ACTIO. But what does he mean by this, except the particular circumstances of the action? This is clearly proved by his illustrations, which refer only to cases in which some one of those circumstances is unknown, as that of *a person who, in winding up a machine, sets free a dart, by which some one is hurt;* or of *Merope, who slew her son mistaking him for an enemy,* and so on.

'You thus see the kind of ignorance which renders actions involuntary; it is only that of the particular circumstances, which, as you, father, very well know, is called by theologians, *ignorance of fact.* But as to that of *right,* in other words, as to ignorance of the good or evil which is in the action, the only point here in question, let us see if Aristotle is of the opinion of Father Bauni. These are the philosopher's own words: *All wicked men are ignorant of what they ought to do, and of what they ought to shun. And this is the very thing which renders them wicked and vicious. Hence, we cannot say that because a man is ignorant of what it is expedient for him to do, in order to discharge his duty, his act is involuntary. For this ignorance in the choice of good and evil, does not make the act involuntary, but only makes it vicious. The same thing must be said of him who is ignorant in general of the rules of his duty, since ignorance makes man deserving of blame, and not of excuse.* And hence the ignorance which renders actions involuntary and excusable, is only that which regards the particular fact, and its special circumstances. In that case, we pardon the man and excuse him, considering him to have acted against his will.

'After this, father, will you still say that Aristotle is of your opinion? Who will not be astonished to see a heathen philosopher more enlightened than your doctors on a matter so important to morality in general, and even to the direction of souls, as a knowledge of the conditions which make actions voluntary or involuntary, and which, in consequence, exempt or do not exempt them from sin? Hope nothing then, father, from this Prince of Philosophers, and no longer resist the Prince of Theologians, who thus decides the point. (Retr. liv. 1, c. 15.) *Those who sin from ignorance, act only because they wish to act, although they sin without wishing to sin. And thus even the sin of ignorance can be committed only by the will of him who commits it, though by a will which disposes to the act and not to the sin. This, however, does not hinder the act from being a sin, because for this it is enough to have done what there was an obligation not to do.*

The father seemed surprised, and still more at the passage from Aristotle than at that from St. Augustine. But while he was thinking what to say, a message announced that the Countess of —— and the Marchioness of ——, were waiting for him. Taking a hasty leave he said, 'I will speak of it to our fathers. They will certainly find some answer. Some of ours here are very ingenious.' We perfectly understood him, and when I was alone with my friend, I expressed my astonishment at the revolution which this doctrine made in morals. He replied that he was very much astonished at my astonishment. 'Do you not then know that their corruptions in morals are much greater than in other matters?' He gave me some curious examples, and left the rest for another time. I hope to give you what I shall learn from him the first time I write.

I am, etc.

LETTER FIFTH.

DESIGN OF THE JESUITS IN ESTABLISHING A NEW MORALITY. TWO SETS OF CASUISTS AMONG THEM. MANY OF THEM LAX, SOME STRICT GROUND OF THIS DIVERSITY. DOCTRINE OF PROBABILITY EXPLAINED. HERD OF MODERN AND UNKNOWN AUTHORS SUBSTITUTED FOR THE HOLY FATHERS.

PARIS, 20*th March*, 1656.

SIR,—Here is what I promised you. Here you have the first specimens of the morality of the worthy Jesuit fathers, *those men eminent for learning and wisdom, who are all guided by Divine wisdom, which is much surer than any philosophy.* You perhaps think me in jest. I say it seriously, or rather they themselves say it in their book, entitled, *Imago Primi Sæculi.* I only copy their words, which thus continue the eulogium: *It is a company of men, or rather angels, which was foretold by Isaiah in these words, 'Go, angels, prompt and swift.* How clearly the prophecy applies! *They are eag'e spirits, a troop of phœnixes,* (an author having lately shown that there are more than one.) *They have changed the face of Christendom.* We must believe it since they say it. You will be fully persuaded of it by the sequel of this letter, which will acquaint you with their maxims.

I was desirous to have the best information. I did not trust to what our friend had told me. I was desirous to have it from them themselves. But I have found that he spake no more than the truth. I believe he never misrepresents. This you will see from the narrative of my interviews.

In the one which I had with him, he told me such strange things that I could scarcely believe him; but he showed them to me in the books of their fathers, so that I had nothing left to say in their defence, except that they were the sentiments of some individuals, which it was not fair to impute to the body. I, in fact, assured him that I knew some who are as strict as those he quoted to me are lax.

On this he exp'ained to me the spirit of the Company, which is not generally known, and you will, perhaps, be very glad to learn it. What he said to me was this:

'You think it a great deal in their favour, to show, that they have fathers as conformable to the maxims of the Gospel as the others are opposed to them, and you infer that those lax opinions belong not to the whole Company. I know it. For if it were so, they would not tolerate their purer teachers. But since they have some who teach this licentious doctrine, the inference is, that the spirit of the Company is not that of Christian severity. If it were, they would not tolerate what is so opposed to it.' 'How,' replied I, 'what object then can the entire body have? It must be that they have no definite object, and every one at liberty to say at a venture whatever he thinks.' 'That cannot be,' he replied; 'so large a body could not exist under random guidance, and without a spirit to govern and regulate all its movements. Besides, a special regulation forbids any to print without the permission of their superiors.' 'What,' said I, 'how can their superiors consent to such different maxims?' 'This I must tell you,' replied he.

'Know then, that their object is not to corrupt manners; that is not their intention. But neither is it their only aim to reform them; that were bad policy. Their view is this; they have a good enough opinion of themselves to believe that it is conducive, and in a manner necessary to the welfare of religion, that they should be every where in repute, and govern all consciences. And because strict Gospel maxims are fitted to govern some sorts of persons, they use them on the occasions to which they are suitable. But as these maxims are not in accordance with the views of most people, they, in those cases, abandon them, that they may be able to satisfy all and sundry. Hence it is, that having to do with persons of all classes, and with nations differing widely from each other, they require to have casuists assorted to this great diversity.

'From this principle, you can easily see, that if they had only lax casuists, they would defeat their principal object, which is to embrace the whole world, since those who are truly pious require a stricter guidance. But as this class is not numerous, they do not require many strict directors to guide them. They have few for the few, while the great crowd of lax casuists are ready for the crowd who desire laxity.

By this *obliging and accommodating* behaviour, as Father Petau terms it, they hold out their hand to all the world. Should any one come before them firmly resolved to restore ill-gotten gains, don't imagine they will dissuade him. They will praise him on the contrary, and confirm his holy resolution. But let another come who wishes to have absolution without restoring, the thing will be difficult indeed if they do not furnish him with means, the safety of which they will guarantee.

'In this way they preserve all their friends, and defend themselves against all their enemies. For, if they are charged with their extreme laxity, they forthwith produce to the public their austere directors, with some books which they have composed in the strict spirit of the Christian law; and the simple, and those who do not examine to the bottom of things, are satisfied with these proofs.

'They are thus provided for all sorts of persons, and meet the demand so completely, that when they happen to be in countries where a God crucified seems foolishness, they suppress the offence of the Cross, and preach only a triumphant, not a suffering Jesus; as they have done in the Indies and China, where they allowed the converts even to practise idolatry, by the subtle device of making them conceal under their dress an image of Jesus Christ, to which they were mentally to refer the public worship which they paid to the idol Cachinchoam, and their Keum-fucum, as they are charged by the Dominican Gravina, and as is attested by a memorial in Spanish, presented to Philip IV. of Spain by the Cordeliers of the Philippine Isles, and quoted by Thomas Hurtado in his treatise entitled, the Martyrdom of Faith, p. 427, so that the congregation of cardinals, *de propaganda fide*, was obliged specially to prohibit the Jesuits, under pain of excommunication, from permitting the worship of idols under any pretext, and concealing the mystery of the Cross from those whom they instruct in religion, expressly commanding them not to admit any to baptism without ascertaining their knowledge in this respect, and ordaining them to exhibit a crucifix in their churches, as is contained at large in the decree of the Congregation, dated July 9, 1646, and signed by Cardinal Capponi.

'In this way they have spread themselves over the whole earth by the aid of the doctrine of Probability, which is the source and basis of all this corruption. This you must learn from themselves. For they make no secret of it, any more than of what you have just heard, with this single difference, that they cloak their human and politic prudence with the pretext of a divine and Christian prudence, as if the faith and tradition which maintain the latter were not always one and invariable in all times and places; as if it were the rule that ought to bend in order to meet the subject, which should be conformable to the rule; and as if souls, in order to be purified from their stains, had only to corrupt the law of the Lord, whereas it is the law of the Lord, which is without spot and perfect, that should convert souls, and make them conformable to its salutary lessons.

'Go then, I beg of you, visit these worthy fathers, and I feel sure that, in the laxity of their morality, you will easily discover the cause of their doctrine concerning grace. You will see Christian virtues which are elsewhere unknown, and devoid of the charity which is their soul and life; you will see so many crimes palliated, and so many disorders permitted, that you will no longer see any thing strange in their maintaining that all men have always grace enough to live piously in the way they understand it. As their morality is wholly heathenish, nature is sufficient to observe it. When we maintain the necessity of effectual grace, we give it other virtues for its object—not merely to cure one set of vices by another, not merely to make men practise the external duties of religion, but a righteousness exceeding that of the Pharisees and the greatest sages of heathenism. For such righteousness as theirs, reason and the law give *sufficient grace*. But to disengage the soul from the love of the world, to withdraw it from all that is dearest to it, to make it die to itself, to carry it and attach it solely and invariably to God, is the work of an almighty hand. And it is as unreasonable to maintain that we have always full power to do so, as it would be unreasonable to deny that virtues devoid of love to God, which those worthy fathers confound with Christian virtues, are in our power.'

These were his words, and he spoke them in great sorrow, for he is seriously distressed at all these disorders. I, for my part, admired these worthy fathers for the skilfulness of their policy, and set off, as he advised me, to find a good casuist of the company. It was an old friend, whose acquaintance I desired to renew for the very purpose, and as I was instructed how to manage with them, I had no difficulty in putting matters in train. He at first hugged me a thousand times, for he always loves me, and, after some talk on indifferent subjects, I took occasion from its being the season of Lent, to learn something from him on fasting, in order to get insensibly into the subject. I signified to him that I was scarcely able to support fasting. He exhorted me to make an effort, but as I continued to complain, he felt for me, and began to search for some ground of dispensation. He, in fact, offered me several, which did not suit me, when at last it occurred to him to ask if I did not find it difficult to sleep without supping. 'Yes, father,' said I, 'and this often obliges me to lunch at noon and sup in the evening.' 'I am very glad,' he replied, 'at having found a way of relieving you without sin. Go to, your are not obliged to fast. I do not ask you to believe me, come to the library.' I went, and there, taking down a book, 'Here is a proof,' said he, 'and, God knows, good proof. It is Escobar.' 'Who is Escobar, father?' I asked. 'What, do you not know Escobar of our Society, who has compiled this Moral Theology from twenty-four of our fathers? He allegorises this in the preface, and likens his book to the Apocalypse, *which was sealed with seven seals.* He says that *Jesus offers it thus sealed to the four living creatures, Suarez, Vasquez, Molina, and Valentia, in*

presence of four-and-twenty Jesuits, who represent the elders.'
He read the whole of the allegory, which he considered very
exact, and thereby gave me a very high idea of the excel-
lence of the work. Having afterwards looked for the passage on fasting, 'Here it is,' said he, 'tr. i., ex. 13,
no. 67. *If a person cannot sleep unless he has supped, is he
obliged to fast?* No. Are you not satisfied?' 'Not quite,'
said I, 'for I can bear fasting if I lunch in the morning
and sup in the evening.' 'Look, then, to what follows,'
said he, 'for they have thought of every thing; *What, if he
can do it by taking a collation in the morning and supping in
the evening.* My very case! *No more is he obliged to fast,
for no man is obliged to change the order of his repasts.*
'An excellent reason,' said I. 'But, tell me, 'continued he,
' do you use much wine.' 'No, father,' said I, 'I cannot
bear it.' 'I asked,' replied he, ' to make you aware that
you might drink it in the morning, and when you please,
without breaking the fast; and this holds in every case.
Here is the decision at the same place, no. 75. *Can one,
without breaking the fast, drink wine at any hour he pleases,
and even in large quantities? He may, even hypocras.* I
had forgotten this *hypocras*,' said he, 'I must put it in my
note-book.' 'He is an honest man, this Escobar,' said I.
'Every body likes him,' replied the father, ' he puts such
pretty questions. Look at this one which is at the same
place, no. 38. *If a man doubts whether he is twenty-one, is
he obliged to fast?* No. *But if I am twenty-one complete,
an hour after midnight, and the fast is to-morrow, will I be
obliged to fast to-morrow?* No. *For you might eat as
much as you please from midnight till one o'clock, since
you would, till then, be under twenty-one, and thus, being
entitled to break the fast, you are not bound by it.'*
'How amusing that is,' said I. 'There is no getting
away from him,' replied he, ' I spend my days and nights
in reading him, I do nothing else.' The worthy father,
seeing me pleased, was delighted, and continued, 'See,
also,' said he, ' the tract of Filiutius, who is one of the
twenty-four Jesuits:' Tom. II. tr. 27, part 2, c. 6,
no. 143. *When one is fatigued in any way, as in running*

after a girl, is he obliged to fast? No. But if he has fatigued himself for the very purpose of being relieved from the fast, will he be bound by it? Though he should have done it of set purpose, he will not be obliged.' 'Well, would you have thought it?' said he. 'In truth, father,' I said, 'I scarcely believe it yet. What, is it not a sin, not to fast when one can do it? Is it lawful to seek occasions of sinning? Are we not rather obliged to shun them? That would be very convenient.' 'Not always obliged,' said he, 'according to—' 'According to whom?' I asked. 'Ho, ho,' rejoined the father. I asked 'Were any inconvenience suffered by shunning occasions, would there, in your opinion, be any obligation to shun them?' 'Father Bauni, at least does not think so. See p. 1084: *We must not refuse absolution to those who remain in proximate occasions of sin, if they are so situated that they cannot withdraw without giving occasion to the world to speak, or without subjecting themselves to inconvenience.*' 'I rejoice at it, father, all now wanted is to say, that we may of set purpose seek occasions, since it is permitted not to shun them.' 'Even that is sometimes permitted,' added he; 'the celebrated casuist, Basil Ponce, says so, and Father Bauni quotes and approves his opinion in his Treatise on Penitence, q. 4, p. 94. *One may seek an occasion directly, and for itself,* PRIMO ET PER SE, *when the spiritual or temporal welfare of ourselves or our neighbour determines us.*

'Truly,' said I, 'it looks as if I were dreaming when I hear men of the cloister speaking in this way. But, father, tell me in conscience, is that your opinion?' 'No, indeed,' said the father. 'You are speaking then,' I continued, 'against your conscience?' 'Not at all,' said he, 'I was not speaking according to my own conscience, but according to that of Ponce and Father Bauni; and you may follow them in safety, for they are men of ability.' 'What, father, because they have put these three lines in their books, can it have become lawful to seek occasions of sin? I thought the only rule to follow was Scripture and the tradition of the Church, but not your casuists.' 'Good God!'

exclaimed the father, 'you put me in mind of those Jansenists. Are not Father Bauni and Basil Ponce able to make their opinion probable?' 'Probability does not satisfy me,' said I, 'I want certainty.' 'I see well,' said the worthy father to me, 'that you know not the doctrine of probable opinions. You would speak otherwise if you knew it. Indeed I must make you acquainted with it. Your visit will not be lost time; without this, you cannot understand any thing. It is the foundation and the A B C of all our morality.' I was delighted at seeing him fall on what I wished, and saying I would be glad to learn, begged him to explain what was meant by a probable opinion. 'Our authors will tell you better than I can,' said he. 'Here is the way in which it is generally explained by all, and, among others, by our four-and-twenty in the beginning of Ex. iii. n. 8. "An opinion is called probable when it is founded on reasons of some weight; hence, it sometimes happens that a single very grave doctor may render an opinion probable. Here, too, is the reason. For a man specially devoted to study, would not adhere to an opinion if he were not drawn to it by a good and sufficient reason."' 'And thus,' said I, 'a single doctor may whirl consciences round, and tumble them over and over at his pleasure, and always in perfect safety.' 'You must not laugh,' said he, 'nor think to combat the doctrine. When the Jansenists tried it, they lost their time. It is too well established. Listen to Sanchez, who is one of the most celebrated of our fathers. Sum, L. i., n. 9, c. 7. "You doubt perhaps, if the authority of a single good and learned doctor can render an opinion probable. I answer yes. And this is confirmed by Angelus, Sylvius, Navarre, Emmanuel Sa,.etc. The way in which they prove it is this: A probable opinion is one which has a considerable foundation. Now, the authority of a learned and pious man is of no small weight, or rather is of great weight. "For," (listen well to this reason,) "if the testimony of such a man is of great weight to assure us that a thing has taken place, for example, at Rome, why should it not have the same weight in a dubious point of morals?"'

'Rather amusing,' said I, 'to compare the things of the world with those of conscience.' 'Have patience; Sanchez replies to that in the lines which immediately follow. "I do not approve of a qualification by certain authors, that the authority of such a doctor is sufficient in matters of human right, but not in those of divine right. For it is of great weight both in the one and the other."'

'Father,' said I frankly, 'I cannot make any use of this rule. What security have I, that in the liberty which your doctors take to examine things by reason, a point which appears sure to one will appear so to all? There is such diversity of judgment—' 'You do not understand it,' said the father interrupting me; 'they accordingly very often are of different opinions, but that is of no consequence. Each makes his own probable and safe. Verily, we know well that they are not all of one way of thinking. And so much the better. On the contrary, they seldom if ever agree. There are few questions on which you do not find that the one says Yes and the other says No. And, in all those cases, each of the opposing opinions is probable. This makes Diana say on a certain subject, Part 3, to. 4, r. 244. "Ponce and Sanchez take opposite views, but, as they were both learned, each makes his opinion probable."'

'Then, father,' said I, 'one must be very much at a loss how to choose.' 'Not at all,' said he, 'you have only to follow the opinion which you like best.' 'But what if the other is more probable?' 'No matter,' said he. 'And if the other is more safe?' 'No matter,' again said the father, 'here it is well explained by Emmanuel Sa of our company in his Aphorism *De dubio*, p. 183. *We may do what we think lawful according to a probable opinion, although the contrary may be more safe. The opinion of a grave doctor is sufficient.*' 'And if an opinion is at once both less probable and less safe, will it be lawful to follow it, to the exclusion of that which is believed to be more probable and more safe?' 'Yes; once more,' said he, 'listen to Filiutius, the great Jesuit of Rome. Mor. Quest., tr. 21, c. 4, n. 128. *It is lawful to follow the less probable opinion though it be the less safe. This is the common opinion of the new authors.*

Is not that clear?' 'We have, certainly, large scope, reverend father,' said I, 'thanks to your probable opinions. We have fine liberty of conscience. And you casuists, have you the same liberty in your answers?' 'Yes,' said he, 'we answer as we please, or rather, as pleases those who consult us. For here are our rules, taken from our fathers, Layman, *Theol. Mor.*, l. i., tr. i, c. 2, s. 2, n. 7; Vasquez, Dist. 62, c. 9, n. 47; Sanchez, Sum, l. i, c. 9, n. 23; and our four-and-twenty, *princ*, Ex. 3, n. 24. Here are the words of Layman, whom the book of the four-and-twenty has followed: "A doctor being consulted may give counsel not only probable according to his opinion, but contrary to his opinion, if it is esteemed probable by others, when this contrary opinion happens to be more favourable and more agreeable to the person consulting. SI FORTE ET ILLI FAVORABILIOR SEU EXOPTATIOR SIT. But I say, moreover, that it would not be unreasonable for him to give those who consult him, an opinion deemed probable by some learned person, even though he be fully convinced that it is absolutely false."'

'Very good, father, your doctrine is most convenient Only to answer yes, or no, at pleasure! One cannot sufficiently prize such an advantage. I now see clearly what you gain by the contrary opinions which your doctors have on every subject. The one is always of use, and the other never does any harm. If you do not find your gain on one side, you turn to the other, and always in safety.' 'True,' said he, 'and thus we can always say as Diana did, on finding Father Bauni for him, when father Lugo was against him: "Sæpe premente Deo, fert Deus alter opem." If one god presses, another brings relief.'

'I understand, said I, 'but a difficulty occurs to me. After consulting one of your doctors, and getting from him an opinion somewhat wide, we might, perhaps, be caught if we were to fall in with a confessor of a different temper, who might refuse absolution if we did not change our view. Have you not provided for this, father?' 'Do you doubt it?' replied he, 'confessors are obliged to give absolution to their penitents who have probable opinions, and under pain of mortal sin, that they might not fail to do so. This has been well shown by our fathers, among others, by father Bauni, Tr. 4, De Pœnit, Q. 13, p. 93. *When the penitent follows a probable opinion, the confessor must absolve him, though his opinion be contrary to that of the penitent.*' 'But he does not say it is a mortal sin not to absolve him?' 'How hasty you are,' said he, 'listen to what follows; he infers this in express terms: *To refuse absolution to a penitent who acts on a probable opinion, is a sin which is in its nature mortal.* In confirmation of this opinion, he quotes three of our most famous fathers, Suarez, tr. 4, d. 32, s. 5; Vasquez, disp. 62, c. 7; and Sanchez, num. 29.

'O, father,' said I, 'how very prudently this has been arranged. Now there is nothing to fear. No confessor would dare to refuse. I did not know that you had the power of ordaining under pain of damnation. I thought you only able to take away sins. I did not think you knew how to introduce them. But you have all power, from what I see.' 'You do not speak properly,' said he, 'we do not introduce sins, we only call attention to them. I have already observed, two or three times, that you are not a good logician.' 'Be this as it may, father, my doubt is fully solved. But I have still another to state, it is this: I cannot see what you are to do, when the Fathers of the Church are contrary to the opinion of some one of your casuists.

'You know very little of the matter,' said he. 'the Fathers were good for the morality of their day, but they are too remote for ours. Not they, but our new casuists now give the rule. Listen to our father Cellot, (de *Hier* l. 8, c. 16, p. 714,) who, in this, follows our famous father Reginald: "In questions of morality the new casuists are preferable to the ancient Fathers, although they were nearer the apostles." Proceeding on this maxim, Diana says, p. 5, tr. 8, r. 31, "Are the holders of benefices obliged to restore the revenue which they apply improperly? The ancients said yes, but the moderns say no; let us hold by this opinion which discharges the obligation to restore."'

'Fine sentiments,' said I, 'and full of consolation for numbers of people! 'We leave the Fathers,' said he, 'to those who deal in theory, but we who govern consciences read them seldom, and in our writings quote only the new casuists. See Diana who has written so much. At the beginning of his book, he gives a list of the authors quoted. There are 296, and not one more than eighty years old.' 'That is, since the existence of your Company?' 'About it,' he replied. 'That is to say, father, that on your arrival, St. Augustine, St. Chrysostom, St. Ambrose, St. Jerome, etc., so far as regards morality, disappeared. But at least let me know the names of their successors; who are those new authors?' 'They are very able and very celebrated persons,' said he; 'they are, Villalobos, Conink, Llamas, Achokier, Dealkozer, Dellacrux, Veracruz, Ugolin, Tambourin, Fernandez, Martinez, Suarez, Henriquez, Vasquez, Lopez, Gomez, Sanchez, De Vechis, De Grassis, De Grassalis, De Pitigianis, De Graphæis, Squilanti, Bizozeri, Barcola, De Bobadilla, Simancha, Perez de Lara, Aldretta, Lorca, De Scarcia, Quaranta, Scophra, Pedrezza, Cabrezza, Bishe, Dias, De Clavasio, Villagut, Adam à Manden, Iribarne, Binsfeld, Volfangi à Vorberg, Vosthery, Strevesdorf.' 'O father,' exclaimed I, quite frightened,' 'were all these people Christians?' 'How Christians,' replied he, 'did I not tell you that they are the only persons by whom we govern Christendom in the present day?' I felt pity, though I did not show it, and merely asked if all those authors were Jesuits. 'No,' said he, 'but no matter, they have said good things, notwithstanding. Not that the greater part have not taken or imitated them from us, but we do not stickle upon the point of honour; and, besides, they quote our fathers every hour and with eulogium. See Diana, who is not of our Company, when he speaks of Vasquez, he calls him *the Phœnix of minds*, and he sometimes says, that *to him, Vasquez alone is worth all the rest of men put together. Instar omnium.* Accordingly all our fathers make very frequent use of the worthy Diana; for, if you properly understand our doctrine of probability, you will see that his not being of our Company is of no consequence. On the contrary, we are quite willing that others besides Jesuits, should be able to render their opinions probable, in order that they may not all be imputed to us. Hence, when any author whatever has advanced one, we are entitled by the doctrine of probable opinions to take it if we choose, and we are not its guarantees when the author is not of our body.' 'I understand all that,' I said; 'I see that all comes well to you, except the ancient Fathers, and that you are masters of the field. All you have to do is to career in it.

'But I foresee three or four great inconveniences and formidable barriers, which you will have to encounter in your course.' 'And what are they?' said the father, quite amazed. 'They are,' I replied, 'the Holy Scriptures, Popes, and Councils, which you cannot gainsay, and which are all in strict accordance with the Gospel.' 'Is that all?' said he, 'you gave me a fright. Do you imagine that a thing so palpable was not foreseen, and has not been provided for? I really wonder at your thinking that we are opposed to Scripture, Popes, or Councils. I must make you understand the contrary. I would be very sorry you should think we fail in what we owe them. You have, no doubt, formed this notion from some opinions of our fathers, which seem to run counter to their decisions, though it is not so. But, to show their agreement, we must have more leisure. I wish you not to remain imperfectly informed concerning us. If you will be so good as return tomorrow I will give you the explanation.' Here ended our conference, which will also be the end of my discourse, and it is quite enough for one letter. Trusting you will be satisfied with it while waiting the sequel,

I am, etc.,

LETTER SIXTH.

ARTIFICES OF THE JESUITS TO EVADE THE AUTHORITY OF SCRIPTURE, COUNCILS, AND POPES. CONSEQUENCES OF THE DOCTRINE OF PROBABILITY. THEIR CORRUPTIONS IN FAVOUR OF BENEFICIARIES, PRIESTS, MONKS, AND DOMESTICS. HISTORY OF JOHN OF ALBA.

PARIS, 10*th April*, 1656.

SIR,—I told you at the end of my last letter, that the worthy Jesuit had promised to instruct me how the casuists reconcile the contrariety between their opinions and the decisions of Popes, Councils, and Scripture. He did so instruct me on my second visit, of which I now give you an account.

The worthy father spoke to me as follows: 'One of the ways in which we reconcile these apparent contradictions, is by the interpretation of some particular term. For example, Pope Gregory XIV. has declared that assassins are not entitled to the benefit of asylum in churches, and ought to be taken out of them by force. Notwithstanding, our four-and-twenty elders say, tr. 6, ex. 4, n. 27, *That all who murder treacherously should not incur the pains of this Bull.* This seems to you a contradiction, but we reconcile it by interpreting the word *assassin* as they do in these terms. *Are not assassins unworthy of the privilege of asylum in churches? Yes. By the Bull of Pope Gregory XIV. But we understand the term assassin to mean those who have received money to murder treacherously. Hence it follows, that those who murder without receiving any sum, and merely to oblige their friends, are not called assassins.* In the same way it is said in the Gospel, *Give alms out of your superfluity.* Notwithstanding, several casuists have found means to discharge the most wealthy from the obligation of giving alms. This also seems to you a contradiction; but it is easily reconciled by interpreting the word *superfluity* in such a way, that it seldom or ever happens that a person has it. This has been done by the learned Vasquez in his treatise on Alms, c. 4. *What men of the world keep to raise their own condition and that of their kindred, is not called superfluity, and this is the reason why superfluity is seldom if ever to be found in men of the world, and even in kings.*

'Diana also, after quoting this passage from Vasquez, (for he usually founds on our fathers), very properly infers that *in the question whether the rich are obliged to give alms of their superfluity, although the affirmative were true, it would never, or almost never, become obligatory in practice.*'

'I see plainly, father, that that follows from the doctrine of Vasquez. But what answer would be given to the objection, that in order to secure salvation, it would, according to Vasquez, be as safe not to give alms, provided one has ambition enough to leave no superfluity, as according to the Gospel it is safe to be without ambition, in order to have a superfluity out of which to give alms?' 'It would be necessary to answer,' said he, 'that both methods are safe according to the same Gospel; the one according to the Gospel in the most literal and obvious acceptation, and the other according to the same Gospel interpreted by Vasquez. This shows you the utility of interpretation.'

'But when the terms are so clear that they admit of none, we make use of the consideration of favourable circumstances, as you will see by an example. The popes have excommunicated monks for laying aside their habit, and yet our four and twenty elders speak in this way, tr. 6. ex, 7. n. 103. *On what occasions may a monk change his dress without incurring excommunication?* He mentions several, among others the following: *If he changes it to go and thieve, or to go incognito into houses of bad fame, intending shortly to resume it.* Indeed it is clear that the bulls do not speak of such cases.'

I could scarcely believe this, and prayed the father to show it to me in the original: and I saw that the chapter in which the words occur is headed, *Praxis ex Societatis Jesu Schola: Practice according to the school of the Company of Jesus.* Here I saw the words: *Si habitum dimittat ut furetur occulte, vel fornicetur.* He showed me the same thing in Diana in these terms: *Ut eat incognitus ad lupanar.* 'How comes it, father, that they have freed them from excommunication in this instance?' 'Do you not comprehend,' said he? 'Do you not see what scandal it would give to surprise a monk in this state with his religious dress? And have you never heard,' continued he, 'how the first bull, *contra sollicitantes,* has been met, and in what way our four-and-twenty, in a chapter which is also in the *Practice of the School of our Company,* explain the bull of Pius V., *contra clericos,* etc.?' 'I know nothing of all this,' said I. 'You seldom read Escobar then,' said he. 'I only got him yesterday, father, and with difficulty. I don't know what has happened lately to set every body on the search for him.' 'What I told you,' rejoined the father, 'is at tr. 1. ex. 8. n. 102. Look for it in your copy. It will give you a fine specimen of the mode of interpreting bulls favourably.' I did see it that very evening; but I dare not give it to you: it is frightful.

The worthy father then continued. "You now understand the use which is made of favourable circumstances. But the bulls are sometimes so precise that contradictions cannot be reconciled in this way. In such cases you might well suppose that the contradictions would be real. For example: three popes have decided that monks, bound by a particular vow to a perpetual Lent, are not dispensed from it by becoming bishops. And yet Diana says that *notwithstanding of this decision, they are dispensed.*' 'And how does he reconcile it?' said I. 'By the most subtle of all the new methods,' replied the father: 'by the greatest finesse of Probability. I am going to explain it to you. The principle is that of which you heard the other day, namely, that the affirmative and negative of most opinions have each some probability, in the judgment of our doctors; indeed, enough to be followed with safety of conscience. Not that the *pro* and the *con* are both true in the same sense: that is impossible; but only that they are both probable, and consequently safe.'

'On this principle Diana our good friend speaks thus in Part 5, tr. 13, r. 39. "I reply to the decision of these three popes, which is contrary to my opinion that they have spoken in this way from fixing on the affirmative, which in fact is probable even in my judgment; but it does not follow that the negative has not also its probability. And in the same treatise, r. 65, on another subject, in which he is again of a contrary opinion to a pope, he speaks thus: "That the Pope may have said it as head of the Church, I admit; but he has only done it to the extent of the sphere of the probability of his sentiment." Now you see plainly that this is not to go counter to the sentiments of the popes: it would not be tolerated at Rome, where Diana is in such high credit. For he does not say that what the popes have decided is not probable; but leaving their opinion in the full sphere of Probability, he yet says that the contrary is also probable.' 'That is very respectful,' said I. 'And it is more subtle,' added he, 'than the reply which Father Bauni made when his books were censured at Rome; for in writing against M. Hallier, who was then persecuting him furiously, the words slipped from him, *What has the censure of Rome in common with that of France?* You now see plainly enough how, either by the consideration of favourable circumstances, or in fine, by the double probability of the *pro* and the *con*, we always reconcile these pretended contradictions which previously astonished you, and always as you see without running counter to Scripture, councils, or popes.' 'Reverend father, said I, 'how happy the world is to have you for masters! How useful these probabilities are! I did not know why you had been so careful to establish that a single doctor, *if he is grave*, may render an opinion probable; that the contrary may be so also, and that we may choose the *pro* or the *con*, as best pleases us, although not believing it true, and with such safety of conscience, that a confessor who should refuse to give absolution on the faith of these casuists would be in a state of damnation. Hence I understand that a single casuist can at pleasure make new rules of morality, and dispose according to his fancy of every thing that regards the conduct of manners.' 'What you say,' said the father, 'must be taken with some limitation. Attend well to this. Here is our method, in which you will see the progress of a new opinion from birth to maturity.

'At first the *grave* doctor who has discovered it exhibits it to the world, and casts it like a seed to take root. It is still weak in this state, but time must mature it by degrees. And hence Diana, who has introduced several, says in one place: "I advance this opinion, but because it is new, I leave it to be matured by time." Thus we see it for a few years insensibly gaining strength, till after a considerable period it becomes authorised by the tacit approbation of the Church, according to this great maxim of Father Bauni: "An opinion being advanced by some casuists, and the Church not opposing it, is evidence that she approves it." And, in fact, it is by this principle he sanctions one of his sentiments in his treatise 6, p. 312.' 'What, father!' said I, ' the Church will at that rate approve of all the abuses which she suffers, and all the errors in the books which she does not censure?' 'Dispute,' said he, 'against Father Bauni. I give you a statement, and you debate with me. There is no disputing upon a fact. I said then that when time has thus ripened an opinion, it is quite probable and safe. Hence the learned Caramuel, in the dedication of his Fundamental Theology to Diana, says, that this great Diana " has rendered several opinions probable which were not so before; *quæ ante non erant*; and that thus there is no longer any sin in following them, though there was sin before; *jam non peccant, licet ante peccaverint.*"'

'Of a truth, father,' said I, ' it is a mighty advantage to be beside your doctors. Of two persons doing the same things, the one who does not know their doctrine sins, and the other who know it does not sin! Is it then at once both instructive and justifying? The law of God according to St. Paul, made transgressors; yours makes almost all men innocent. I entreat you, father, to inform me fully on the subject. I will not leave you until you have told me the principal maxims which your casuists have established.

'Alas!' said the father, 'our principal aim should have been to establish no other maxims than those of the Gospel in all their strictness. And it is plain enough from the correctness of our own manners, that if we suffer any laxity in others it is rather from complaisance than from design. We are forced to it. Men are now-a-days so corrupted, that being unable to make them come to us, we must of course go to them. Otherwise, they would leave us; they would do worse, they would become utterly regardless. With a view to retain them, our casuists have considered the vices to which all ranks are most disposed, thus to be able, without however injuring the truth, to establish maxims so mild that one must be strangely constituted not to be satisfied; for the capital design which our Company has formed for the good of religion is to rebuff none, to beware of driving people to despair.'

'Accordingly, we have maxims for all classes of persons; for holders of benefices, for priests, for monks, for gentlemen, for servants, for the rich, for persons in trade, for those whose affairs are in disorder, for pious women, and such as are not pious, for married people, for libertines. In short, nothing has escaped their foresight.' 'In other words,' said I, 'you have them for clergy, lords, and commons. I am very desirous to hear them.'

'Let us begin,' said the father, 'with the holders of benefices. You know what traffic is now carried on in benefices, and that if we were to proceed on what St. Thomas and the ancients have written on the subject, there would be a vast number of Simonists in the Church. Hence, it was most necessary for our fathers to temper things by their prudence, as the following passage of Valentia, one of Escobar's four living creatures, will inform you. It is the conclusion of a long discourse in which he furnishes several expedients; but this in my opinion is the best. It is at p. 2039 of vol. iii. "Where a temporal good is given for a spiritual good, (in other words, money for a benefice,) and the money is given as the price of the benefice, it is manifest simony; but if it is given as a motive which disposes the patron to bestow it, it is not simony, although he who bestows it considers and expects the money as the principal inducement." Tannerus, who is also of our Company, says the same thing in his vol. iii, p. 1519, although he admits that " St. Thomas is against him, inasmuch as he teaches absolutely that it always is simony to give a spiritual good for a temporal, if the temporal is the end." By this means we prevent an infinitude of simonies. For who would be so wicked while giving money for a benefice, as to refuse to make it his intention to give it as a *motive* which disposes the holder of the benefice to resign it? No man can be so far left to himself.' 'I agree,' said I, 'that all men have sufficient grace to take such a step.' 'Not a doubt of it,' rejoined the father.

'Thus have we softened matters in regard to the holders of benefices. As to priests we have several maxims, which are very favourable to them. For example, that of No. xxiv, tr. 1, ex. 11, n. 96: "May a priest who has been paid to say mass, receive money a second time for the same mass? Yes," says Filiutius, " by applying the part of the sacrifice, which belongs to him as priest, to the person who makes the second payment, provided he do not receive full payment for a whole mass, but only for a part, *e. g.* a third of the mass." '

'Assuredly, father, this is one of the cases in which the *pro* and *con* are very probable. Your last statement cannot but be so, on the authority of Filiutius and Escobar. But, while leaving it in the sphere of its probability, the contrary might, methinks, be also said and supported on these grounds. When the Church permits priests who are poor to take money for their masses, because it is very just that those who serve the altar live by the altar, it does not therefore mean, that they are to barter the sacrifice for money, still less deprive themselves of all the grace which they should be the first to draw from it. I would say, moreover, that according to S. Paul, priests are obliged to offer sacrifice *first for themselves and then for the people*, and that thus while it is lawful for them to allow others to participate in the benefit of the sacrifice, they may not voluntarily renounce the whole benefit of it for themselves, and give it to another for the third of a mass; that is, for four or five sous. Indeed, father, how far soever I might be from being *grave*, I could render this opinion probable.' 'You would have no great difficulty,' said he. 'It is visibly so. The difficulty was to find probability in the opposite of opinions which are manifestly good. And this is only the privilege of great minds. Father Bauni excels in it. It is a pleasure to see this learned casuist penetrating into the *pro* and *con* of the following question, which also respects priests, and finding reason every where; he is so ingenious and so subtle.

'He says in one place, (it is in tr. 10, p. 474,) "A law could not be passed obliging curates to say mass every day; because such a law would expose them indubitably (*haud dubie*) to the peril of sometimes saying it in mortal sin." Nevertheless in the same tract, 10, p. 441, he says that "priests who have been paid to say mass daily, ought to say it daily, and cannot excuse themselves on the ground of not being always properly prepared, because they can always perform an act of contrition, and if they fail it is their own fault, and not his who makes them say the mass." To obviate the great difficulties which might prevent them, he, in the same tract (qu. 32, p. 457,) thus solves the question: "May a priest, the same day he has committed a mortal sin, and one of the most heinous, say mass, by confessing previously? No, says Villalobos, because of his impurity; but Sanchez says yes, and without any sin; and I hold that his opinion is safe, and should be followed in practice. *Et tuta et sequenda in praxi.*"'

'What, father, this opinion is to be followed in practice! Would a priest who had fallen into such a state dare, the same day, to approach the altar on the word of Father Bauni? Ought he not to show deference to the ancient laws of the Church, which excluded from the sacrifice for ever, or at least for a long period, priests who had committed sins of this description, rather than adopt the new opinions of your casuists, who admit them to it the very day they have fallen?' 'You have no memory,' said the father; 'did I not formerly instruct you that in morality we were to follow not the ancient Fathers, but the new casuists.' 'I remember well,' replied I. 'But there is more in this. There are here laws of the Church.' 'You are right,' said he, 'but you do not yet know the fine maxim of our fathers, "that the laws of the Church lose their force when no longer observed, *cum jam desuetudine abierunt*," as Filiutius says, tom. 2, tr. 25, n. 33. We see the present necessities of the Church better than the ancients. If we were to be so strict in excluding priests from the altar, you can easily perceive that there would not be so great a number of masses. Now multiplication of masses brings so much glory to God, and advantage to men, that I would venture to say with our father Cellot, in his Treatise on the Hierarchy, p. 611, printed at Rouen, "that there would not be too many priests, though not only all men and women, if that were possible, but also inanimate things, and the very brutes, (*bruta animalia*) were changed into priests, to celebrate mass."' I was so struck at the oddness of the idea, that I was unable to speak, so he continued thus:

'But, enough on the subject of priests, I might become tedious; let us proceed to monks. As their greatest difficulty is the obedience which they owe to their superiors, listen to the softening which it has received from our fathers. Castro Palao of our Company says, Op. Mor. p. 1, disp. 2, p. 6; "It is beyond dispute that the monk who has a probable opinion in his favour is not bound to obey his superior, although the opinion of the superior is the more probable. For, in that case, the monk is at liberty to adopt the one which is most agreeable to him, (*quae sibi gratior fuerit*,)" as Sanchez says. "Moreover, though the command of the superior be just, that does not oblige you to obey him: For it is not just in all points and in all modes, (*non undequaque juste praecipit*,) but only probably, and thus you are only bound probably to obey him, and you are probably not bound. *Probabiliter obligatus et probabiliter deobligatus.*' 'Certainly, father, we cannot too highly value this fine fruit of double probability!' 'It is of great use,' said he, 'but let us abridge. I will not speak of the treatise of our celebrated Molina, in behalf of monks who have been expelled from their convents for misconduct. Our father Escobar refers to it, tr. 6, ex. 7, n. 111, in these terms, "Molina affirms that a monk expelled from his monastery, is not obliged to reform, in order to be re-admitted, and is no longer bound by his vow of obedience."'

'Now then, father,' said I, 'ecclesiastics are very much at their ease. I see well that your casuists have treated them favourably. They have acted in the matter as if for themselves. I much fear that other classes of persons will not be so well treated. Every one must look to himself.' 'They could not have done better for themselves;' rejoined the father, 'all have been treated with equal charity, from the highest to the lowest. And this leads me to prove it, by telling you our maxims concerning servants.

'With regard to them, we have considered the difficulty which those of them, who are conscientious, must feel in serving debauchees. For, if they do not execute all the messages on which they are sent, they lose their livelihood, and if they do, they feel remorse. To solace them, our four-and-twenty fathers (tr. 7, ex. 4, n. 223,) have specified the services which they may perform with a safe conscience. Here are some of them: "to carry letters and presents, to open doors and windows, to assist their master in getting up to the window, to hold the ladder while he mounts; all this is permitted and indifferent. It is true that in the latter case they must be threatened more than usual if they refuse. For it is an injury to the master of the house to get in at the window."'

'You see how very judicious this is.' 'I expected no less,' said I, 'from a book compiled from four-and-twenty Jesuits.' 'But,' added the father, 'our father Bauni has well instructed servants how to perform all these services for their masters, innocently, by taking care to direct their attention, not to the sins in which they become art and part, but to the profit which accrues from them. This he has well explained in the Sum of Sins, p. 710, 1st ed. "Let confessors observe carefully that they cannot give absolution to valets who carry dishonest messages, if they consent to the sins of their masters; but the contrary must be said if they do it for their temporal advantage." And that is very easily done; for why should they persist in consenting to sins, of which they have only the trouble?'

'Father Bauni has likewise established a grand maxim in favour of those who are not content with their wages. It is in the Sum, pp. 213, 214, 6th ed. "May servants who complain of their wages increase them of their own accord, by fingering as much of the property of their masters as they imagine necessary to equal said wages to their work? They may on some occasions, as when they are so poor and out of place, that they are obliged to accept of any offer that is made to them, and other valets of their class receive much more."'

'Father,' said I, 'that is exactly the case of John of Alba.' 'What John of Alba,' said the father, 'what do you mean?' 'What, father! have you forgotten what took place in this town in the year 1647? Where were you then?' 'I was teaching cases of conscience,' said he, 'in one of our colleges a good way from Paris.' 'I see, then, father, that you do not know this story. I must tell it you. A person of rank told it the other day where I was. He said that this John of Alba, being in the service of your fathers of the College of Clermont, in St. James street, and not being satisfied with his wages, stole something by way of compensation. Your fathers having discovered it, put him in prison, charging him with domestic theft. The case came into Chatelet, 6th April, 1647, if my memory serves me right. For he mentioned all those particulars without which they would scarcely have been credited. The culprit being interrogated, confessed that he had taken some tin plates from your fathers; but he maintained for all that that he had not stolen them, founding his justification on this doctrine of father Bauni, which he presented to the judges with a writing of one of your father's who had taught him the same thing. On which M. de Monrouge, one of the most distinguished members of the Court, gave his opinion, "that he did not think that in consequence of writings by these fathers containing a doctrine which was illegal, pernicious, and opposed to all laws, natural, human, and divine, capable of upsetting all families, and authorising all domestic thefts, the panel ought to be acquitted. But his opinion was, that this too faithful scholar should be whipped in front of the college gate by the hand of the executioner, who should at the same time burn the writings of those fathers on the subject of larceny, prohibiting them at the peril of their lives henceforth to teach any such doctrine."

'While waiting the result of this opinion, which was very much approved, an incident happened which caused the process to be remitted. But in the meantime the prisoner disappeared, it is not known how, and the affair was no more heard of, so that John of Alba got off without giving back his plate. He told us this, and added that the opinion of M. de Monrouge is among the records of the Chatelet, where any one may see it. We were amused with the story.'

'Why do you trifle so,' said the father, 'what does all that signify? I am speaking to you of the maxims of our casuists; I was preparing to speak to you of those which concern gentlemen, and you interrupt me with stories out of place.' 'I only told it to you in passing,' said I, 'and also to call your attention to an important point of the subject, which I find you have forgotten in establishing your doctrine of probability.' 'What,' said the father, 'what can have been missed after so many gifted men have dealt with it?' 'It is this,' I replied. 'You have indeed made those who follow your opinions secure as regards God and conscience; for from what you say, they are safe in those quarters when they follow a grave doctor. You have also made them secure in regard to confessors, for you have obliged priests to absolve them on a probable opinion under pain of mortal sin. But you have not secured them in regard to judges, and hence they find themselves exposed to the lash and the gibbet in following your probabilities. This is a capital defect.' 'You are right,' said the father, "you give me pleasure. But that is because we have not so much power over judges as over confessors, who are obliged to apply to us in cases of conscience in which we are supreme judges.' 'I understand,' said I. 'But if on the one hand you are the judges of confessors, are not you on the other the confessors of judges? Your power is of great extent: compel them to acquit criminals who have a probable opinion under pain of exclusion from the sacraments, that it may not turn out to the great contempt and scandal of probability, that those whom you render innocent in theory are whipped and hung in practice. Without this, how will you find disciples?' 'It will be necessary to think of it,' said he; 'the thing is not to be overlooked. I will mention it to our father Provincial. Still you might reserve your advice for another time, and not interrupt what I have to tell you of the maxims which we have established in favour of gentlemen. I will not instruct you unless you promise not to tell me any more stories.'

This is all you shall have to-day, for more than one letter will be required to acquaint you with all I learned at a single interview.

Meanwhile, I am, etc.

LETTER SEVENTH.

THE METHOD OF DIRECTING THE INTENTION ACCORDING TO THE CASUISTS. OF THEIR PERMISSION TO KILL IN DEFENCE OF HONOUR AND PROPERTY. THIS EXTENDED TO PRIESTS AND MONKS. CURIOUS QUESTION PROPOSED BY CARAMUEL: MAY THE JESUITS LAWFULLY KILL THE JANSENISTS?

Paris, 25*th April*, 1656.

Sir,—After appeasing the worthy father, whom I had somewhat disturbed by the story of John of Alba, he resumed, on my assuring him that I would not tell any more of the same kind, and spoke to me of the maxims of his casuists respecting gentlemen, nearly in these terms:

'You know,' said he, 'that the ruling passion of persons of this class is the point of honour, which hourly involves them in violent proceedings, very much opposed to Christian piety, so that it would be necessary to exclude almost the whole of them from our confessionals, had not our fathers somewhat relaxed the strictness of religion in accommodation to human weakness. But, as they wished to remain attached to the Gospel by doing their duty towards God, and to the men of the world by practising charity towards their neighbour, we had need of all our talents to devise expedients which might temper things so nicely, that honour might be maintained and redressed by the means ordinarily used in the world, without, however, offending conscience; thus at once preserving two things, apparently so opposite, as piety and honour.

'But, in proportion to the utility of this design, was the difficulty of executing it. For I believe you are fully aware of the magnitude and laborious nature of the enterprise.' 'It astonishes me,' said I, with some coolness. 'Astonishes you?' said he, 'I believe it; it would astonish many others. Are you ignorant that on the one hand the law of the Gospel enjoins us not to render evil for evil, and to leave vengeance to God; and that, on the other, the laws of the world forbid any one to suffer an injury without taking satisfaction for it, often by the death of an enemy? Have you ever seen any thing that appears more contradictory? And yet, when I tell you that our fathers have reconciled these things, you simply say it astonishes you?' 'I did not fully explain myself, father. I would hold the thing impossible if, after what I have seen of your fathers, I did not know that they can easily do what is impossible to other men. It is this which makes me believe that they have certainly found some method which I admire without knowing it, and which I beg you to unfold to me.'

'Since you take it thus,' said he, 'I cannot refuse you. Know, then, that this marvellous principle is our grand method of *directing the intention*, the importance of which is so great in our moral system that I would venture almost to compare it to the doctrine of probability. You have seen some traces of it in passing, in certain maxims which I have mentioned to you. For, when I showed you how valets may, in conscience, execute certain disagreeable messages, did you not observe that it was merely by turning away their intention from the evil in which they are act and part to the gain which accrues from it? This is what is meant by *directing the intention*. In like manner, you have seen how those who give money for benefices would be real simonists without a similar diversion. But I wish now to show you this great method, in all its lustre, on the subject of homicide, which it justifies on a thousand occasions, in order that, by its effect here, you may be able to judge what it is capable of effecting.' 'I already see,' said I, that by means of it every thing will be permitted, nothing will escape.' 'You are always going from the one extreme to the other,' replied the father, 'correct that. For, in order to show you that we do not permit every thing, know, for example, that we never permit any one to have a formal intention of sinning for the mere sake of sinning, and that when any one whatever persists in having no other end in evil than evil itself, we break with him; the thing is diabolical; this holds without exception of age, sex, or quality. But when one is not in this unhappy disposition, we endeavour to put in practice our method of *directing the intention*, which consists in making a lawful object the end of our actions. Not that we do not, as far as we can, dissuade from things forbidden; but when we cannot prevent the act we at least purify the intention, and thus correct the vice of the means by the purity of the end.

'In this way our fathers have found a method of permitting the violence which is practised in defending honour. It is only to turn away the intention from the desire of revenge, which is criminal, to direct it to the desire of defending honour, which, according to our fathers, is lawful. Thus they fulfil all their duties towards God and towards men. For they please the world by permitting actions, and they satisfy the Gospel by purifying intentions. This the ancients did not know; this is due to our fathers. Do you now comprehend it?' 'Very well,' said I, 'you bestow on men the external and material effect of the action, and you give God this internal and spiritual movement of the intention; and, by this equitable division, you bring human laws into unison with the divine. But, father, to tell you the truth, I am somewhat distrustful of your promises, and I doubt if your authors say as much as you.' 'You do me wrong,' said the father; 'I advance nothing which I do not prove, and, by so many passages, that their number, their authority, and their reasons, will fill you with admiration.'

'To show you the alliance which our fathers have made between the maxims of the Gospel and those of the world, by this direction of intention, listen to our father Reginald, in his Proxies, l. 21, n. 62, p. 260. "It is forbidden to individuals to avenge themselves; for St. Paul says, Rom. xii, Render to no man evil for evil; and Eccl. xxviii, He who would avenge himself will bring down the vengeance of God, and his sins will not be forgotten; besides, all that is said in the Gospel about forgiving offences, as Matthew, vi, 18."' 'Certainly, father, if after that he says any thing else than is in Scripture, it will not be for want of knowing. What then, is his conclusion?' 'Here it is,' said he,

"From all these things it appears, that a military man may, on the instant, pursue him who has wounded him, not indeed with the intention of rendering evil for evil, but with that of preserving his honour. *Non ut malum pro malo reddat, sud et conservet honorem.*"

'Do you see how careful they are to forbid the intention of rendering evil for evil, because Scripture condemns it? They have never allowed it. See Lessius de Just., l. 2, c. 9, d. 12, n. 79: "He who has received an injury may not have the intention of avenging himself, but he may have that of avoiding infamy, and for this may, on the instant, repel the injury, and that with the sword: *etiam cum gladio.*" We are so far from allowing them to take vengeance on their enemies, that our fathers will not even allow them to wish death from a movement of hatred. See our father Escobar, tr. 5, n. 145: "If your enemy is disposed to hurt you, you ought not to wish his death from a movement of hatred, but you may do so in order to avoid loss." For that, accompanied with this intention, is so lawful, that our great Hurtado de Mendoza says, "that we may pray God for the speedy death of those who are disposed to persecute us, if we cannot otherwise avoid them." It is in his Treatise De Spe, vol. 2, d. 15, s. 4, sec. 48.

'Reverend father, the Church has surely forgotten to insert a petition to this effect, among its prayers.' 'Everything,' said he, 'has not been inserted that God might be asked to grant. Besides the thing could not be, for this opinion is later than the breviary. You are not a good chronologist. But, without quitting this subject, listen to this passage from our father Gaspar Hurtado, de Sub. pecc. diff. 9, quoted by Diana, p. 5, tr. 14, r. 99. He is one of Escobar's twenty-four fathers. "A beneficed person may, without mortal sin, desire the death of him who has a pension, from his benefice, and a son that of his father, and rejoice when it happens, provided it is only for the advantage which accrues from it, and not from personal hatred."'

'O, father!' said I, 'this is a lovely fruit of the direction of intention. I see plainly that it is of great extent. But, nevertheless, there are certain cases, the solution of which would still be difficult, although very necessary for gentlemen.' 'State them, that we may see,' said the father. 'Show me,' said I, 'that with all this direction of intention it is lawful to fight a duel.' 'Our great Hurtado de Mendoza,' said the father, 'will satisfy you instantly, in the passage which Diana quotes, p. 5, tr. 14, r. 99: "If a gentleman who is challenged in a duel is known not to be devout, and the sins which he is seen committing every hour without scruple, make it easily be judged, that if he refuses to fight it is not from the fear of God, but from cowardice, and it is hence said that he is a chicken and not a man, *gallina, et non vir,* he may, to preserve his honour, be at the place assigned, not indeed with the express intention of fighting a duel, but only with that of defending himself, if he who has called him out comes there to attack him unjustly. And his act will be quite indifferent in itself. For what harm is there in going into a field to walk in it, while waiting for a man, and defending one's self, if there attacked? And thus he does not sin in any manner, since he does not at all accept a duel, his attention being directed to other circumstances. For the acceptance of a duel consists in the express intention of fighting, which he has not.'"

'You have not kept your word, father; that is not properly to permit duelling. On the contrary, he thinks it so strongly forbidden that, to make it lawful, he avoids calling it a duel.' 'Ho, ho,' said the father, 'you begin to penetrate, I am delighted at it. I might say, nevertheless, that in this he permits all that is asked by those who fight a duel. But, since it is necessary to answer you precisely, our father Layman will do it for me, by permitting the duel in express terms, provided the intention is directed to accept it solely to preserve honour or fortune. It is at l. 3, c. 3, n. 2, 3. "If a soldier in the army or a gentleman at court, finds himself so situated that he must lose his honour or his fortune if he does not accept a duel, I do not see how we can condemn him who accepts it in self-defence." Peter Hurtado says the same thing as reported by our celebrated Escobar, tr. 1, ex. 7, n. 96, 98; when he gives us Hurtado's words, "That one may fight a duel even in defence of one's property, if that is the only means of preserving it, because every man is entitled to defend his property, and that even by the death of his enemies.'" At these passages I wondered, to think how the piety of the king employs his power to prohibit and abolish duelling in his dominions, and the piety of the Jesuists tasks their subtlety in permitting and sanctioning it in the Church. But the worthy father was in such trim that it would have been wrong to stop him, so he continued thus: 'In fine,' said he, 'Sanchez, (see what persons I quote to you,) goes farther. For he makes it lawful not only to accept but to send a challenge, by properly directing the intention. And in this our Escobar follows him at the same place, n. 97.' 'Father,' said I, 'I hold him quit if it is so. But I will never believe that he wrote it till I see it.' 'Read him then, yourself,' said he, and I, in fact, read those words in the Moral Theology of Sanchez, l. 2, c. 39, n. 7. "It is very reasonable to hold that a man may fight a duel to save his life, his honour, or his property to a considerable amount, when an attempt is made to wrest them from him by lawsuits and chicanery, and this is the only means of preserving them. And Navarre says very well, that on this occasion, it is lawful to accept and to send a challenge: *Licet acceptare et offerre duellum.* And also that one may waylay his enemy and slay him; and, even in those rencounters, when the method of duelling cannot be used, one may waylay and kill his enemy, and so get out of the affair. For, by this means, we avoid at once both exposing our life in combat, and partaking of the sin which our enemy would commit in a duel."

'Behold, father,' said I, 'a pious assassin, but though pious, he is always assassin, because permitted to kill his enemy treacherously.' 'Have I said to you,' said the father, 'that any one may kill treacherously? God forbid! I tell you that any one may kill in ambush, and you thence conclude, that one may kill treacherously, as if it was the same thing. Learn from Escobar, tr. 6, ex. 4, n. 26, what is meant by killing treacherously, and then you may speak. "A man is said to kill treacherously when he kills a person who does not at all suspect him. And this is why one who kills his enemy is not said to kill treacherously, though it be from behind, and in ambush: *Licet per insidias aut a tergo percutiat.*" And, in the same treatise, n, 26; " He who kills his enemy, with whom he had been reconciled on a promise of not again attempting his life, is not absolutely said to kill in treachery, unless the friendship between them was very close. *Arctior amicitia.*"

'You see from this that you do not even know the meaning of terms, and yet you speak as if you were a doctor.' 'I confess,' said I, 'that that is new to me, and I learn from this definition that it is impossible to kill in treachery. For people seldom think of assassinating any but their enemies. But be this as it may, we may, according to Sanchez, kill boldly, I no longer say in treachery, but from behind or in ambuscade, any person pursuing us before a court of justice.' 'Yes,' said the father, 'but by carefully directing the intention; you always forget the principal thing. And this is what Molina also maintains, tom. 4, tr. 3, disp. 12. And, even according to our learned Reginald, l. 21, cap. 5, n. 57, " We may also kill the false witnesses whom he suborns against us." And, in fine, according to our great and celebrated fathers, Tanneras and Emmanuel Sa, we may even kill both the witnesses and the judge, if he is in concert with them. Here are his words, tr. 3, disp. 4, q. 8, n. 83: " Sotus," he says, "and Lessius hold that it is not lawful to kill false witnesses and the judge who are leagued to put an innocent man to death, but Emmanuel Sa and other authors are right in disapproving of that view, at least, as regards conscience." And he moreover assures us at the same place that we may kill both witness and judge.'

'Father,' said I, ' I now understand your principle of directing the intention well enough, but I desire much, also, to understand the consequences of it, and all the cases in which this method gives power to kill. Let us go over those which you have told me, for fear of mistake; ambiguity here would be dangerous. First, we must take care to kill seasonably, and on a good probable opinion. You have next assured me, that by carefully directing our intention, we may, according to your fathers, in order to preserve our honour, and even our property, accept a challenge, and occasionally send it, waylay and kill a false accuser and his witnesses along with him; and, moreover, the corrupt judge who favours them; and you have also told me, that he who has received a blow, may, but without taking revenge, take redress by the sword. But, father, you have not told me to what extent.' 'There can scarcely be a mistake,' said the father, 'for you may go the length of killing him. This is verily well proved by our learned Henriquez, l. 14, c. 10, n. 3, and others of our fathers, reported by Escobar, tr. 1, ex. 7, n. 48, in these words: "We may kill him who has given a blow though he is in flight, provided we avoid doing it from hatred or revenge, and do not thereby occasion excessive murders hurtful to the State. And the reason is, that we may thus run after our honour as after stolen property; for, although your honour is not in the hands of your enemy, as stolen clothes would be, it may, nevertheless, be recovered in the same manner, by giving proofs of magnanimity and authority, and thereby acquiring the esteem of men. And, in fact, is it not true that he who has received a blow, is reputed to be without honour, until he has killed his enemy?'"

This appeared to me so horrible, that I could scarcely restrain myself, but to know the rest I allowed him to continue thus: 'We may even,' said he, 'to prevent a blow, kill him who means to give it, if that is the only means of avoiding it. This is commonly held by our fathers. For example, Azor. Inst. Mor., p. 3, p. 105, (he also is one of the four-and-twenty elders,) "Is it lawful for a man of honour to kill him who wishes to give him a blow with the fist or with a stick? Some say no, and their reason is, that the life of our neighbour is more precious than our honour; besides, that it is cruelty to kill a man merely to avoid a blow. But others say it is lawful, and I certainly find it probable when it cannot otherwise be avoided. For without that the honour of the innocent would be continually exposed to the malice of the insolent." The same is said by our great Filiutius, tom. 2, tr. 29, c. 3, n. 50; and father Hereau in his writings on Homicide, t. 2, disp. 170, s. 16, sec. 137; and Bechan, Som., t. 1, q. 64; de Homicid. And our fathers Flahaut and Le Court, in their writings which the University in their Third Request quoted at some length, with the view of discrediting them, but without success; and Escobar at the same place, n. 48, all say the same thing. In short, it is so generally maintained, that Lessius decides it as a point which is not disputed by any casuist, l. 2, c. 9, c. 76. For he adduces a great number who are of this opinion, and none who opposes it, and he even claims, n. 77, Peter Navarre, who, speaking generally of affronts of which there is none worse to bear than a blow, declares, that according to the opinion of all the casuists; *ex sententia omnium, licet contumeliosum occidere, si aliter ea injuria arceri nequit.* Do you wish any more?'

I thanked him, for I had only heard too much. But, in order to see how far this damnable doctrine would go, I said to him, 'But, father, is it not lawful to kill for somewhat less? Cannot we so direct our intention, as to be able to kill any one for giving us the lie?' 'Yes,' said the father, 'according to our father Baldelle, l. 3, disp. 24, n. 24, quoted by Escobar at the same place, n. 49; "It is lawful to kill him who says to you, You have lied, if you cannot repress him otherwise." And we may kill in the same way for slander, according to our fathers. For Lessius, whom father Hereau, among others, follows word for word, says, at the place already quoted; "If you try, by calumnies, to ruin my reputation with persons of honour, and I cannot avoid it otherwise than by killing you, may I do it? Yes, according to modern authors, and even though the crime which you publish be true; if, however, it is secret, so that you cannot discover it in course of justice. And here is the proof. If you would rob me of my honour by giving me a blow, I may prevent you by force of arms. The same defence, therefore, is lawful when you would injure me with the tongue. Besides, we may prevent insults, therefore we may prevent evil speaking. In fine, honour is dearer than life; now we may kill to defend our life, therefore we may kill to defend our honour." Here are arguments in form. This is not to discover, but to prove. And, in fine, this great Lessius shows at the same place, n. 78, that we may kill for a simple gesture, or expression of contempt. "We may," says he, "assail and destroy honour in several ways, in which defence appears very just, as when one would strike with a stick or the fist, or affront us by words or signs. *Sive per signa.*"'

'O father,' said I, 'we have here every thing that can be wished to put honour in safety; but life is much exposed, if for evil speaking merely, or offensive gestures, we may kill in conscience.' 'That is true,' said he, 'but as our fathers are very circumspect, they have deemed it proper to forbid the doctrine to be put in practice on slight occasions. For they say, at least, that *it scarcely should be practised.* And this was not without reason; here it is.' 'I know it,' said I, 'it is because the law of God forbids to kill.' 'That is not the view they take of it,' said the father, 'they find it allowable in conscience, and considering the truth merely in itself.' 'And why, then, do they forbid it.' 'Listen,' said he, 'It is because a State would be depopulated in no time, were all evil speakers in it slain. Learn from our Reginald, l. 21, n. 63, n. 260: "Although this opinion that we may kill for evil speaking, is not without probability in theory, the contrary must be followed in practice. For we must always avoid doing damage to the State by our mode of self defence. Now, it is clear that by killing all persons of this description, there would be too great a number of murders." Lessius speaks in the same way, at the place already quoted: "It is necessary to take heed that the practice of this maxim be not hurtful to the State. For, then, it must not be permitted. *Tunc enim non est permittendus.*"'

'What, father! then it is only a prohibition of policy, and not of religion? Few people will be stopped by it, especially when in passion. For it might be probable enough that no harm was done to the State by ridding it of a wicked man.' 'Accordingly,' says he, 'our father Filiutius joins to this a much more weighty reason, tr. 29, c. 3, no. 51. It is, *that we would be punished criminally for killing in this way.*'

'I was right in saying to you, father, that you would never do any thing to the purpose, so long as you have not the judges on your side.' 'The judges,' said the father, 'not penetrating to the conscience, only judge the outward action; whereas, we look principally to the motive, and hence it is, that our maxims are at times somewhat different from theirs.' 'Be this as it may,' said I, 'it follows very clearly from yours, that, damage to the State avoided, we may kill evil speakers with a safe conscience, provided we can do it with a safe person.'

'But, father, after having provided so well for honour, have you done nothing for property? I know that it is of less importance, but no matter. It seems to me, that we might properly direct our intention so as to kill in preserving it.' 'Yes,' said the father, 'and I have touched on a matter which may have given you this hint. All our casuists agree, and even permit it, "Although we no longer dread any violence from those who rob us of our property as when they are in flight." Azor, of our Society, proves it, p. 3, l. 2, c. 1, q. 20.'

'But, father, what must the value of a thing be to carry us to this extremity?' 'It is necessary, according to Reginald, l. 21, c. 5, n. 66; and Tanneras, in. 22, disp. 4, q. 8, d. 4, n. 69; "that the thing be of great service in the judgment of a man of skill." Layman and Filiutius speak in the same way.' 'That is saying nothing, father; where will we go to look for a man whom it is so rare to meet, in order to make this valuation? Why do they not determine the sum exactly?' 'How,' said the father, 'was it so easy a matter, in your opinion, to estimate the life of a man, and a Christian in money? Here I wish to make you feel the necessity of our casuists. Search in all the ancient Fathers for how much it is lawful to kill a man. What will they say, *non occides; thou shalt not kill.*' 'And who, then, has been bold enough to determine this sum?' rejoined I. 'Our great and incomparable Molina, the glory of our Company, who, by his inimitable prudence, has valued it "at six or seven ducats, for which he affirms that it is lawful to kill, though he who is carrying them off is in flight." It is in his t. 4, tr. 3, disp. 16, d. 6. And he says, moreover, at the same place, that "he would not presume to condemn a man as guilty of any sin who kills one, wishing to rob him of a thing of the value of a crown or less: *unius aurei, vel minoris adhuc valoris.*" Which has led Escobar to lay down this general rule, n. 44, that "regularly we may kill a man for the value of a crown, according to Molina." '

' Dear father, where can Molina have been enlightened to determine a thing of this importance, without any aid from Scripture, Councils, or Fathers? I see plainly that on the subject of murder, as well as that of grace, he must have had special light, and light of a very different kind from St. Augustine. I am now very learned on this chapter, and I know perfectly, that none but churchmen will henceforth abstain from slaying those who injure them, either in their honour or their goods.' 'What do you mean,' replied the father? ' would it, in your opinion, be reasonable that those whom we ought to respect most of all, should alone be exposed to the insolence of the wicked? Our fathers have provided against this irregularity. For Tanneras, tom. 2, d. 4, q. 8, d. 4, n. 76, says, " that it is lawful for ecclesiastics and even monks to kill, in defending not only their life but also their property, or that of their community." Molina, as reported by Escobar, n. 43; Becan, in 2, 2, t. 2, q. 7; de Hom. concl. 2, n. 5; Reginald, l. 2, c. 5, n. 68; Layman, l. 3, tr. 3, p. 3, c. 3, n. 4; Lessius, l. 2, c. 9, d. 11, n. 72; and others, all use the same words.'

' And, even according to our celebrated father L'Amy, it is lawful for priests and monks to be beforehand with those who would blacken them by calumnies, by killing them as a means of prevention; but always by carefully directing the intention. Here are the terms, t. 5, disp. 36, n. 118; "It is lawful for an ecclesiastic, a monk, to kill a calumniator, who threatens to publish scandalous charges against his community or himself, when this is the only means of preventing it, as when he is ready to circulate his slanders if not promptly despatched. For, in this case, as the monk might lawfully kill, on wishing to deprive him of life, it is also lawful to kill him who would rob him or his community of honour, in the same way as men of the world might."'

'I did not know that,' said I, 'but I merely believed the contrary without thinking, from having heard say, that the Church is so abhorrent of blood, that it does not even permit ecclesiastical judges to officiate in criminal trials.' 'Do not rest upon that,' said he, 'our father L'Amy proves this doctrine very well, although with a feeling of humility becoming this great man, he submits it to prudent readers. And Caramuel, our illustrious defender, who refers to it in his Fundamental Theology, p. 543, thinks it so certain as to maintain that *the contrary is not probable;* and he draws admirable inferences from it, for instance, this one which he calls *the conclusion of conclusions, conclusionum conclusio:* "that a priest not only may, on certain occasions, kill a calumniator, but that there are occasions in which he ought to do it; *etiam aliquando occidere.*" On this principle he examined several new questions, for example the following, WHETHER THE JESUITS MAY KILL THE JANSENISTS? 'That, father,' exclaimed I, 'is a wonderful point of theology, and I hold the Jansenists dead already by the doctrine of father L'Amy.' 'There you are caught,' said the father, 'Caramuel infers the contrary from the same principles.' 'How so, father?' 'Because,' said he, 'they do not hurt reputation. Here are his words, n. 1146, 1147, pp. 547, 548. "The Jansenists call the Jesuits Pelagians; might we kill them for that? No, inasmuch as the Jansenists no more obscure the lustre of our company, than an owl that of the sun; on the contrary they have heightened it, though contrary to their intention; *occidi non possunt, quia nocere non potuerunt.*"'

'Eh, father? then the lives of the Jansenists depend only on whether or not they hurt your reputation? If so, I consider them far from safe. For, if it becomes probable in any degree, however small, that they injure you, from that moment they may be slain without scruple. You will make an argument of it in form, and then, with a direction of intention, nothing more is necessary for despatching a man with a safe conscience. Happy the people who are unwilling to suffer injuries, in being instructed in your doctrine! But how unhappy those who offend them! In truth, father, it would be as well to have to do with people of no religion, as with those who have learned it to the extent of this direction. For, after all, the intention of him who wounds is no comfort to him who is wounded; he does not perceive this secret direction, and he only feels that of the blow which smites him. I even know not whether it would not be less galling to be brutally murdered by an infuriated man, than to feel one's self poignarded conscientiously by a devotee.

'In good sooth, father, I am somewhat surprised at all this; and those questions of fathers L'Amy and Caramuel do not please me.' 'Why,' said the father, 'are you Jansenist?' 'I have another reason,' said I; 'from time to time, I give one of my friends in the country an account of what I learn of the maxims of your fathers. And, though I only simply report and faithfully quote their words; I know not, nevertheless, but some odd fellow might be met with, who, imagining that this does you harm, might draw from your principles some wicked conclusion.' 'Go to,' said the father, 'no mischief will happen you; I will be caution. Know, that what our fathers have printed themselves, and with the approbation of their superiors, it is neither bad nor dangerous to publish.'

I write you, then, on the word of this worthy father; but what always fails me is paper, not quotations. The latter are so many and so strong, that, to give all, would require volumes.

I am, etc.

LETTER EIGHTH.

CORRUPT MAXIMS OF THE CASUISTS CONCERNING JUDGES, USURERS, THE CONTRACT MOHATRA, BANKRUPTS, RESTITUTION, ETC. VARIOUS EXTRAVAGANCES OF THE CASUISTS.

Paris, 28*th May*, 1656.

Sir,—You did not think there would be any curiosity to know who we are, and yet people are trying to guess at it, but with littl¹ success. Some take me for a doctor of Sorbonne. Others give my letters to three or four individuals, who, like myself, are neither priests nor ecclesiastics. All these false guesses only tell me that I have tolerably succeeded in my intention of being known only to yourself, and the worthy father, who always tolerates my visits, and whose harangues I always tolerate, though with great difficulty. I am obliged to keep myself in check, for he would not continue were he to perceive that I am shocked, and I should thus be unable to keep my promise of acquainting you with their system of morality. I assure you you should give me some credit for the violence which I do to my own feelings. It is very painful to see Christian morality completely overthrown by these monstrosities without daring openly to contradict them. But, after having borne so much for your satisfaction, I believe I shall break out at last for my own, when he has no more to tell me; meanwhile, I will use as much self-restraint as possible; for the less I say, the more he tells me. He told me so much the last time, that I shall have great difficulty in repeating the whole of it. You will find principles very convenient for avoiding restitution. For, whatever be the mode in which he glosses his maxims, those which I am about to explain go in effect to favour corrupt judges, usurers, bankrupts, thieves, prostitutes, sorcerers, who are all very liberally discharged from restoring what they gain in their different lines. This is what I learned from the worthy father on this occasion.

At the commencement of our interview, he said, 'I engaged to explain the maxims of our authors, in regard to all classes of society. You have already seen those relating to beneficed persons, priests, monks, servants, and gentlemen; let us now extend our survey to others, and begin with judges.

'I will, in the first place, acquaint you with one of the most important and advantageous maxims which our fathers have taught in their favour. It is from our learned Castro Palao, one of our four-and-twenty elders. Here are his words. "May a judge, in a question of law, decide according to a probable opinion, while abandoning the most probable? Yes, and even against his own conviction. *Imo contra propriam opinionem.*" This is also referred to by our father Escobar, tr. 6, ex. 6, n. 45.' 'O father,' said I, here is a fine beginning; the judges are much obliged to you; and I consider it very strange that they oppose your probabilities as we have sometimes observed, since they are so favourable to them. For you thereby give them the same power over the fortunes of men that you have given yourselves over consciences.' 'You see,' said he, 'that we do not act from interest; we have had regard only to the quiet of their consciences; and it is here that our great Molina has laboured so usefully on the subject of presents made to them. To remove the scruples which they might have in taking them on certain occasions, he has been careful to enumerate all the cases in which they can conscientiously receive them, unless there be some special law prohibiting it. It is in his t. 1, tr. 2, d. 88, n. 6. Here they are, "Judges may receive presents from parties when they give them either from friendship or gratitude for the justice which has been done them, or to dispose them to render it in future, or to oblige them to take a particular care of their business, or to engage them to give it quick despatch.' Our learned Escobar also speaks of it in this way, tr. 6, ex. 6, n. 43. "If there are several persons, none of whom is more entitled to despatch than the others, would it be wrong in the judge to take a present from one on condition, *in pacto,* of despatching his case first? Certainly not, according to Layman, for he does no injury to the others, according to natural law, when he grants to the one in consideration of his present what he might have granted to any one he pleased, and even being under equal obligation towards all, from the equality of their right, he becomes more obliged towards him who makes the gift, which binds him to prefer him to others, and this preference seems to admit of being estimated by money. *Quæ obligatio videtur pretio æstimabilis."* '

'Reverend father,' said I, 'I am surprised at this permission which the first magistrate of the kingdom does not yet know. For the first chief President brought a bill into Parliament to prevent certain officers of court from taking money for this sort of preference. This shows he is far from thinking that judges may lawfully do so, and this reform, so useful to all parties, has been universally applauded.' The good father, surprised at my language, replied, 'Is that true? I knew nothing of it. Our opinion is only probable, the contrary is probable also.' 'Indeed, father,' said I, 'it is considered that the President has more than probably done right, and that he has thereby arrested a course of corruption which was well known, and had been too long permitted.' 'I think so, too,' said the father, 'but let us pass this, let us leave the judges.' 'You are right,' said I, 'besides, they are not duly grateful for what you do for them.' 'It is not that,' said the father, 'but there is so much to say upon all, that it is necessary to be brief upon each.

'Let us now speak of men of business. You know that the greatest difficulty which we have with them is to dissuade them from usury, and it is of this accordingly that our fathers have taken a particular care, for such is their detestation of this vice, that Escobar says, tr. 3, ex. 5, n. 1: *To say that usury is not a sin would be heresy.* And our father Bauni in the Sum of Sins, ch. 14, fills several pages with the penalties due to usurers. He declares them *infamous during life, and unworthy of burial after their death.*' 'O father, I did not

think him so severe.' 'He is when he ought,' said he, 'but this learned casuist having also observed, that men are enticed to usury merely by the desire of gain, says at the same place, "It would be no small obligation to the world, if, while guaranteeing them from the bad effects of usury, and, at the same time, from the sin which is the cause of it, we were to furnish them with the means of drawing as much and more profit from their money, by some good and legitimate employment, than they draw from usury."'
'No doubt, father, there would be no usurers after that.'
'And this is the reason,' said he, 'why he has furnished a general method for all classes of persons, gentlemen, presidents, counsellors, etc., and one so easy that it consists merely in the use of certain words, which are to be pronounced when lending money, in consequence of which, they may draw profit from it without fear of its being usurious, which, doubtless, it would otherwise be.' 'What are these mysterious terms, father?' Here they are, and in the very words, for you know that he has written his Sum of Sins in French, *to be understood by all the world*, as he says in his Preface. "He from whom money is asked, will answer in this way; I have no money to lend, though I have to lay out for honest and lawful profit. If you wish the sum you ask, to turn it to account by your industry, half gain, half loss, I may perhaps agree. It is true, indeed, that as there might be too much difficulty in arranging about the profit, if you would secure me in a certain amount, and in the principal also, which is to run no risk, we might more easily come to an agreement, and I will let you have the money forthwith." Is not this a very easy method of gaining money without sin? And is not father Bauni right when, concluding his explanation of this method, he says: "Here, in my opinion, is a method by which a vast number of persons in the world, who, by their usury, extortion, and illicit contracts, provoke the just indignation of God, may save themselves while drawing full, fair, and lawful profits."'

'O father,' said I, 'these are very potent words? Doubtless, they have some hidden virtue to drive away usury, which I do not understand; for I have always thought that this sin consisted in getting back more money than was lent.' 'You know very little of this matter,' said he, 'Usury, according to our fathers, consists almost entirely in the intention of drawing this profit as usurious. And this is why our father Escobar makes it practicable to avoid usury by a simple change of intention. It is at t. 3, ex. 5, n. 4, 33, 34. "It would be usurious, he says, to take profit from those to whom we lend, if it were demanded as due in strict justice; but if it is demanded as due from gratitude, it is not usury." And at n. 3; "It is lawful not to intend direct profit from money lent, but to claim it through the medium of the good will of him to whom it was lent. *Media benevolentia* is not usury."

'These are subtle methods, but one of the best, in my opinion, (for we have a choice of them,) is that of the contract Mohatra.' 'The contract Mohatra, father!' 'I see,' said he, 'you don't know what it is. There is nothing strange but the name. Escobar will explain it to you, tr. 3, ex. 3, n. 36. "The contract Mohatra is that by which goods are purchased dear, and on credit, with the view of selling them back to the seller ready money and cheap." This is the contract Mohatra, from which you see that a certain sum is received in hand while you remain bound for a larger sum.' 'But I suppose, father, nobody but Escobar has ever used the term; do any other books speak of it?' 'How little you know of things,' said the father, 'the last book of Moral Theology, printed at Paris this very year, speaks of the Mohatra, and learnedly. Its title is *Epilogus Summarum,* and is, as the title page bears, "an abridgement of all the Sums of Theology, taken from our fathers Suarez, Sanchez, Lessius, Hurtado, and other celebrated casuists." You will see them at p. 54. "The Mohatra is: when a man who is in want of twenty pistoles, purchases goods from a merchant for thirty pistoles, payable in a year, and sells them back to him on the spot for twenty pistoles, cash." You see from this, that the Mohatra is not a term that has never been heard of.' 'Well, father, is this contract lawful?' 'Escobar,' replied the father, 'says at the same place, *that there are laws which prohibit it under very strict penalties.*' 'It is useless, then, father.' 'Not at all,' said he, 'for Escobar at the same place, gives expedients for making it lawful, "Although the principal intention of him who sells and buys back is to make profit, provided always that in selling he does not take more than the highest price of goods of this sort, and in buying back, does not go below the lowest price, and that there is no previous agreement in express terms or otherwise." But Lessius, de Just., l. 2, c. 21, d. 16, says, that "though the sale may have been made with the intention of buying back cheaper, there never is any obligation to return the profit, unless, perhaps from charity, in the case where the other party is in poverty, and also, provided it can be returned without inconvenience; *si commode potest.*" After this, there is no more to be said.' 'In fact, father, I believe greater indulgence would be sinful.' Our fathers,' says he, 'know well where to stop. From this you plainly see the utility of the Mohatra.

'I have many other methods which I might teach you; but these are sufficient, and I have to speak to you of those whose affairs are in disorder. Our fathers have thought how to solace them, in the state in which they are. For, if they have not means enough to subsist decently, and, at the same time, pay their debts, they are permitted to put away a part from their creditors and declare themselves bankrupt. This is what our father Lessius has decided, and Escobar confirms, tr. 3, ex. 2, n. 163. "Can he who becomes bankrupt, retain with a safe conscience as much of his effects as may be necessary for the respectable maintenance of his family; *ne indecore vivat?* I say yes, with Lessius, and even though he may have gained them by injustice and crimes notorious to all the world; *ex injustitia et notorio delicto;*" although, in this case, he may not retain so large a quantity as he might otherwise have done."
'How, father, by what strange charity will you have these effects to remain with him who has gained them by thievish tricks, for his respectable subsistence, rather than with his creditors, to whom they legitimately belong?' It is im-

possible,' said the father, 'to please every body, and our fathers have thought particularly of solacing these poor wretches. In favour of the indigent also, our great Vasquez, quoted by Castro Palao, tom. i, tr. 6, d. 6, p. 6, n. 12, says, that "when we see a thief resolved and ready to steal from a poor person, we may dissuade him, by calling his attention to some particularly wealthy individual to steal from instead of the other." If you have not Vasquez or Castro Palao, you will find the same thing in your Escobar; for, as you know, almost every thing is taken from twenty-four of the most celebrated of our fathers. It is tr. 5, ex. 5, n. 120. *The practice of our Society in regard to charity towards our neighbour.*'

'It is a very extraordinary charity, father, to prevent the loss of the one by the injury of the other. But I think the thing should be made complete, and that he who gives the counsel should be obliged, in conscience, to restore to the rich man what he may have made him lose.' 'Not at all,' said he, 'for he did not steal from him himself; he only counselled the other to do it. Now, listen to this sage solution of our father Bauni, on a case which will astonish you still more, and in which you would think yourself much more obliged to restore. It is at ch. 13 of his Sum. Here are the words in his own French. "Some one entreats a soldier to beat his neighbour, or to set fire to the granary of a person who has offended him, and it is asked if, failing the soldier, the one who asked him to do the outrage, should, out of his own substance, repair the evil which has ensued. My opinion is no. For no man is bound to restitution who has not violated justice. Is it violated by asking a favour of another? Whatever request we make, he is always free to grant or deny it. To whatever side he inclines, it is his will that determines him; nothing obliges him to do it, but kindness, civility, and a facile temper. Should the soldier, then, not repair the evil which he does, it would not be right to compel him at whose entreaty he injured the innocent."' This passage well nigh put an end to our colloquy, for I was on the point of bursting into a fit of laughter at the *kindness* and *civility* of the firer of a barn, and at the strange arguments for exempting the prime and true culprit in fire-raising from restitution, whom the judges would not exempt from death; but if I had not checked myself, the good father would have been offended; for he spoke seriously, and afterwards said to me with the same air:

'You ought to see by all these proofs how vain your objections are, and yet they divert us from our subject. Let us return, then, to persons uncomfortably situated, for whose comfort our fathers, among others Lessius, l. 2, c. 12, n. 12, affirms that it is *lawful to steal not only in an extreme necessity, but also in a grave necessity, though not extreme.* Escobar also quotes him tr. 1, ex. 9, n. 29. 'This is surprising, father; there are few people in the world who do not consider their necessity grave, and to whom you do not thus give power to steal with a safe conscience. And, though you should confine the permission only to persons who are actually in this state, you open the door to an infinite number of petty thefts, which the judges would punish notwithstanding of this grave necessity, and which you are bound *a fortiori* to repress; you who ought not only to maintain justice among men, but also charity, which this principle destroys. For, do we not violate it, and injure our neighbour when we cause him to lose his property that we may ourselves profit by it? So I have hitherto been taught.' 'It is not always so,' said the father, 'for our great Molina has taught us, t. 2, tr. 2, disp. 328, n. 8, that " the rule of charity does not require us to deprive ourselves of a profit in order thereby to save our neighbour from an equal loss." This he shows in order to prove, as he had undertaken at that place, that " we are not obliged in conscience to restore the goods which another might have given us to defraud his creditors." And Lessius, who maintains the same view, confirms it by this same principle, l. 2, c. 20, n. 168.

'You have not pity enough for those who are ill at ease; our fathers have had more charity than that. They render justice to the poor, as well as to the rich. I say much more; they render it even to sinners. For, although they are very much opposed to those who commit crimes, they nevertheless teach that the goods gained by crime may be lawfully retained. This Lessius teaches generally, l. 2, c. 14, d. 8. "We are not obliged, says he, "either by the law of nature or positive law, in other words, no law obliges us to restore what we have received for committing a criminal act, as adultery, although this act be contrary to justice." For, as Escobar, quoting Lessius, says, tr. 1, ex. 8, n. 59; "the property which a wife acquires by adultery is truly gained by an unlawful means; but, nevertheless, the possession is lawful; *Quamvis mulier illicite acquirat, licite tamen retinet acquisita.*" And this is the reason why the most celebrated of our fathers formally decide, that what a judge takes from a party with a bad cause, to give an unjust decree in his favour, and what a soldier receives for murdering a man, and what is gained by infamous crimes, may be lawfully retained. This, Escobar collects out of our authors, and brings together, tr. 3, ex. 1, n. 23, where he lays down this general rule: "Property acquired by shameful methods, as by murder, an unjust sentence, a dishonest action, etc., is possessed lawfully, and there is no obligation to restore it." And again, tr. 5, ex. 5, n. 53; "We may dispose of what we receive for murder, unjust sentences, infamous sins, etc., because the possession is just, and we acquire the dominion and property of things which are so gained."' 'O dear, father,' said I, 'I never heard of this mode of acquiring, and I doubt if any court of justice will sanction it, and regard assassination, injustice, and adultery, as good titles.' 'I know not,' said the father, 'what books of law may say, but I know that ours, which are the true regulators of conscience, speak as I do. It is true they except one case in which they make restitution obligatory. It is, "when money has been received from those who have not the power of disposing of their property, as children in family, and monks." For our great Molina excepts them, de Just., t. 1, tr. 2, disp. 94; *nisi mulier accepisset ab eo qui alienare non potest, ut a religioso et filio-familias.* For then the money must be restored. Escobar quotes this passage, tr. 1, ex. 8, n. 59, and he confirms the same thing, tr. 3, ex. 1, n. 23.'

'Reverend father,' said I, 'I see monks better treated here than others.' 'Not at all,' said the father, 'Is not as much done for minors generally, and monks are minors all their lives? It is just to except them. But, with regard to all others, there is no obligation to restore what is received from them for a bad action. Lessius proves it at large, de Just. l. 2, c. 14, d. 8, n. 52. "For," says he, "a wicked action may be estimated in money, considering the advantage received by him who causes it to be done, and the trouble taken by him who executes it; and this is the reason why there is no obligation to restore what is received for doing it, be its nature what it may, murder, unjust sentence, filthy action," (for these are the examples which he uniformly employs on this subject,) "unless it has been received from those who have not power to dispose of their property. You may say, perhaps, that he who receives money for giving a wicked stroke sins, and thus can neither take it nor retain it; but I reply, that, after the thing is executed, there is no longer any sin either in paying or receiving payment." Our great Filiutius enters still more into practical detail, for he observes, "that we are obliged in conscience, to pay acts of this sort differently, according to the different conditions of the persons who commit them, and as some are worth more than others." This he establishes on solid ground, tr. 31, c. 9, n. 231; *occultæ fornicariæ debetur pretium in conscientia, et multo majore ratione, quam publicæ. Copia enim quam occulta facit mulier sui corporis, multo plus valet quam ea quam publica facit meretrix; nec ulla est lex positiva quæ reddat eam incapacem pretii. Idem dicendum de pretio promisso virgini, conjugatæ, moniali, et cuicumque alii. Est enim omnium eadem ratio.*'

He afterwards showed, in his authors, things of this nature so infamous that I dare not report them, and at which he himself would have been horrified, for he is a worthy man, but for the respect he has for his fathers, which makes him venerate every thing that comes from that quarter. Meanwhile I was silent, less from any intention to make him continue this subject than from surprise, at seeing the writings of monks full of decisions at once so horrible, unjust, and extravagant. He therefore continued his discourse at freedom, and concluded thus: 'Hence our illustrious Molina (after this I believe you will be satisfied) thus decides the question: "When a man has received money for doing a wicked action, is he obliged to restore it? We must distinguish," says this great man; "if he has not done the act, for which he has been paid, the money must be restored; but if he has done it, there is no such obligation;" *si non fecit hoc malum, tenetur restituere; secus, si fecit.* This is what Escobar relates, tr. 3, ex. 2, n. 138.

'Such are some of our principles touching restitution. You have been well instructed in them to-day. I wish now to see how far you have profited. Answer me, then: "Is a judge who has received money from one of the parties, to give decree in his favour, obliged to restore it?"' 'You have just told me no, father.' 'I suspected as much, said he: 'did I say generally? I told you that he is not obliged to restore if he has given decree in favour of the party who is in the wrong. But, if he is in the right, would you have him to pay for gaining what he was lawfully entitled to? You do not reason. Do you not perceive that the judge *owes* justice, and therefore cannot *sell* it, but that he does not owe injustice, and therefore may take money for it. Accordingly, all our principal authors, as Molina, disp. 94, 99; Reginald, l. 10, n. 84, 184, 185, 187; Filiutius, tr. 31, n. 220, 228; Escobar, tr. 3, ex.1, n. 21, 23; Lessius, lib. 2, c. 14, d. 8, n. 52; uniformly teach, "that a judge is indeed obliged to restore what he has received for doing justice, if it has not been given him out of liberality, but is never obliged to restore what he has received from a man in whose favour he has given an unjust decree."'

I was struck dumb by this fantastic decision, and whilst I was considering the pernicious consequences of it, the father prepared another question for me, and said: 'Answer this time with more circumspection.' I now ask you, *Is a man who deals in divination obliged to restore the money which he has gained by practising it?* 'Just as you please, reverend father,' said I. 'How as I please? Truly you are strange! It would seem from your way of speaking that truth depends on our will. I see plainly you never could discover this one of yourself. See Sanchez then solve the difficulty, who indeed but Sanchez! First he distinguishes in the Sum, l. 2, c. 38, n. 94, 95, 96: "where the diviner has used only astrology and other natural means, and where he has employed diabolic art." He says that he is obliged to restore in one of the cases, and in the other not. Will you now say in which?' 'There is no difficulty there,' said I. 'I see plainly what you mean,' replied he, 'you think he ought to restore in the case where he has used the intervention of demons; but you do not understand the matter at all, it is the very opposite. Here is Sanchez' solution at the same place: "If the diviner has not taken the trouble and the care to know by means of the devil what he could not know otherwise; *si nullam operam apposuit ut arte diaboli id sciret*, he must restore, but if he has taken the trouble, he is not obliged."' 'And how is that, father?' 'Do you not understand?' said he. 'It is because we may truly divine by the art of the devil, whereas astrology is a false method.' 'But, father, if the devil does not answer truly, for he is seldom more true than astrology, the diviner must then, for the same reason, restore.' 'Not always,' said he. "*Distinguo*," says Sanchez, upon that; "For if the diviner is ignorant in the diabolic art, *si sit artes diabolicæ ignarus*, he is obliged to restore; but if he is a skilful sorcerer, and has done his utmost to know the truth, he is not obliged, for then the diligence of such a sorcerer may be estimated in money. *Diligentia a mago apposita est pretio æstimabilis*."' 'That is sound sense, father,' said I, 'for here is a means of inducing sorcerers to become learned and expert in their art, from the hope of gaining wealth legitimately, according to your maxims, by faithfully serving the public.' 'I believe you are jesting,' said the father, 'that is not right; for, were you to speak thus in places where you are not known, there might be persons who would take your words in bad part, and charge you with turning the things of religion into derision.' 'I would easily defend myself from the charge, father; for I believe that if care is taken to ascertain the true meaning of my words, not one will be found that does not completely show the contrary; and, perhaps in the course of our interviews an opportunity will one day occur of making this fully appear.' 'Ho, ho,' said the father, 'you are not now laughing.' 'I confess to you,' said I, 'that this suspicion of mocking sacred things would touch me deeply, as it would be very unjust.' 'I did not say so, altogether,' rejoined the father, 'but let us speak more seriously.' 'I am quite disposed if you wish it, father; it depends on you. But I acknowledge to you, that I have been surprised at seeing that your fathers have so far extended their care to all classes, that they have been pleased even to regulate the legitimate gains of sorcerers.' 'It is impossible,' said the father, 'to write for too many people, or to be too particular with the cases, or to repeat the same things too often in different books. You will see it plainly from this passage of one of the greatest of our fathers, as you may suppose him to be, since he is at present our Father Provincial. It is the Reverend Father Cellot in his Hierarchy, l. 8, c. 16, sec. 2. "We know," says he, "that a person who was carrying a large sum of money to restore it by order of his confessor, having stopped by the way at a bookseller's, and asked if there was nothing new, *num quid novi*, was shown a new book of Moral Theology; and, while carelessly turning over the leaves without thinking, fell upon his own case, and learned that he was not obliged to restore, so that, being disencumbered of the burden of his conscience, and still remaining burdened with the weight of his money, he returned home greatly lightened: *abjecta scrupuli sarcina, retento auri pondere, levior domum repetiit.*"'

'After this, tell me whether it is useful to know our maxims? Will you now laugh at them? Will you not rather, with Father Cellot, make this pious reflection on the fortunate coincidence? "Coincidences of this sort are in

God, the effect of his providence; in the guardian angel, the effect of his guidance; and in those to whom they happen, the effect of their predestination. God, from all eternity, was pleased that the golden chain of their salvation should depend on such an author, and not on a hundred others, who say the same thing because they do not happen to meet with them. If the one had not written, the other would not have been saved. Let us then beseech those by the bowels of Christ, who blame the multitude of our authors, not to envy them the books which the eternal election of God and the blood of Jesus Christ has procured for them." Such are the fine words in which this learned man so solidly proves the proposition which he had advanced, namely, "the utility of having a great number of writers on Moral Theology. *Quam utile sit de Theologia Morali multos scribere.*" '

'Father,' said I, 'I will defer to another time declaring what my sentiment is in regard to this passage, and at present will say no more than this, that if your maxims are useful, and it is important to publish them, you ought to continue to instruct me. For I assure you, that the person to whom I send them, shows them to a vast number of people. Not that we have any intention of using them ourselves, but because, in fact, we think, it useful that the world should be fully informed of them.' 'Accordingly,' said he, 'you see that I do not conceal them; and, in continuing, I will speak to you next occasion on the comforts and conveniences of life, which our fathers permit, in order to make salvation easy, and devotion pleasant. Thus, after having learned what regards particular conditions, you will learn what applies generally to all, and thus nothing will be wanting to make your instruction complete.' The father, after he had thus spoken, left me.—I am, etc.

I have always forgotten to tell you that there are Escobars of different editions. If you purchase, select those of Lyons, with the frontispiece of a lamb on a book sealed with seven seals, or those of Brussels, of date 1651. As these are the latest, they are better and fuller than those of the previous editions of Lyons, of date 1644 and 1646.

LETTER NINTH.

OF SPURIOUS DEVOTION TO THE BLESSED VIRGIN INTRODUCED BY THE JESUITS. DIFFERENT EXPEDIENTS WHICH THEY HAVE DEVISED TO SAVE THEMSELVES WITHOUT PAIN, AND WHILE ENJOYING THE PLEASURES AND COMFORTS OF LIFE. THEIR MAXIMS ON AMBITION, ENVY, GLUTTONY, EQUIVOCATION, MENTAL RESERVATION, FREEDOM ALLOWABLE IN GIRLS, FEMALE DRESS, GAMING, HEARING MASS.

PARIS, 3rd *July*, 1656.

SIR,—I will present my compliments in no higher strain than the worthy father did to me the last time I saw him. As soon as he perceived me, he came up, and, with his eye on a book which he held in his hand, said: " Would not he who should open paradise to you do you an infinite service? Would you not give millions of gold to have the key to it, and to go in whenever you pleased? You need not be at so great expense; here is one worth a hundred more costly." I knew not whether the good father was reading or speaking from himself, but he removed my doubt by saying, ' These are the first words of a fine work, by Father Barri of our Society; for I never say any thing of myself.' ' What work, Father?' said I. ' Here is its title,' said he: ' Paradise opened to Philagio, by a Hundred Devotions to the Mother of God, of easy practice.' ' What, father! does each of these easy devotions suffice to open heaven?' ' Yes,' said he; look at the sequel of the words which you have heard, " The devotions to the Mother of God, which you will find in this book, are so many heavenly keys, which will completely open paradise, provided you practise them;" and, therefore, he concludes with saying, " that he is satisfied if one only is practised."

' Teach me, then, father, some of the most easy.' ' They are all so,' he replied; ' for example, " to bow to the blessed Virgin on meeting any image of her: to say the little chaplet of the ten pleasures of the Virgin: frequently to pronounce the name of Mary: to give commission to the angels to present our respects to her: to wish to build more churches to her than all monarchs together have built: to bid her good day every morning, and good evening late at night: daily to say the *Ave Maria*, in honour of the heart of Mary." And he says that this devotion is sure, moreover, to win the heart of the Virgin. "But, father,' said I, ' that is, provided we also give her ours.' 'That is not necessary,' said he, ' when one is too much attached to the world.' Listen to him: " Heart for heart; this, indeed, is what ought to be, but yours is somewhat too much tied, clings somewhat too much to the creature. Owing to this I dare not invite you at present, to offer this little slave whom you call your heart." And thus he contents himself with the *Ave Maria* which he had requested. These are the devotions in pp. 33, 59, 156, 172, 258, 420, first edition. 'This is quite convenient,' said I, 'and I don't think any body will be damned after this.' 'Alas!' said the father, 'I see plainly you know not how heard the hearts of some people are. There are some who would not take the trouble of daily saying *Good day, Good evening*, because that cannot be done without some effort of memory. Hence, it was necessary for Father Barri to furnish them with practices still more easy, as " to keep a chaplet night and day on the arm, in the form of a bracelet, or to carry about one's person a rosary, or image of the Virgin.' These are the devotions at pp. 14, 326, 447. " Say now that I do not furnish you with easy devotions to acquire the good graces of Mary," as Father Barri expresses at p. 106. 'This, father,' said I, ' is extremely easy.' 'Accordingly,' said he, ' it is all that could be done; and I believe it will be sufficient. A man must be a poor wretch, indeed, if he will not spend a moment of his whole life in putting a chaplet on his arm, or a rosary in his pocket, and thereby secure his salvation with such certainty, that those who try it were never deceived by it, in whatever way they may have lived; though we still counsel them to live well. I will only give you, at p. 34, the instance of a woman who, while daily practising the devotions of bowing to the images of the Virgin, lived all her life in mortal sin, and died at last in this state, but was, nevertheless, saved through the merit of this devotion. 'How so?' exclaimed I. 'Because,' said he, ' our Lord raised her from the dead, for the very purpose. So certain is it, that we cannot perish while we practise some one of these devotions.'

' In truth, father, I know that devotions to the Virgin are a powerful means of salvation, and that the least have great merit when they proceed from feelings of faith and charity, as in the saints who have practised them; but to persuade those who use them without changing their bad lives, that they will be converted at death, or that God will raise them again, seems to me far more fitted to support sinners in their misconduct, by the false peace which this rash confidence gives, than to turn them from it by the true conversion which grace alone can effect.' "What matters it," said he " how we get into paradise, provided we do get in?" as was said on a similar subject, by our celebrated Father Binnet, who was once our Provincial, in his excellent treatise, On the Marks of Predestination, n. 31, p. 130, of the fifteenth edition. "Whether by leaping or flying, what matters it, provided we take the city of glory," as this father says, also, at the same place. 'I confess,' said I, 'that it is of no consequence; but the question is, whether we shall so enter?' 'The Virgin,' says he, ' guarantees it. See the last lines of Father Barri's treatise; "Suppose that at death the enemy had some claim upon you, and that there was sedition in the little republic of your thoughts, you have only to say that Mary is your surety, and that it is to her he must apply."

'But, father, any one who chose to push that, would puzzle you. Who assures us that the Virgin answers for us?' 'Father Barri,' said he, 'answers for her,' p. 465. "For the profit and happiness which will accrue to you, I answer, and become surety for the blessed Mother." ' But, father, who is to answer for Father Barri?' ' How?' said the father, ' he is one of our Company?' and do you not know, moreover, that our Society guarantees all the writings of our fathers? I must explain this; it is right you should know it. By an order of our Society all sorts of booksellers

are prohibited from printing any work of our fathers without
the approbation of the theologians of our Company, or without the permission of our superiors. This regulation was
made by Henry III., 10th May, 1583, and confirmed by
Henry IV., 20th December, 1603, and by Louis XIII., 14th
February, 1612; so that our whole body is responsible for
the writings of each of our fathers. This is a peculiarity
of our Company. And hence it is that no work comes out
among us without having the spirit of the Society. It was
apropos to inform you of this.' 'Father,' said I, ' you have
done me a service, and I am only sorry I did not know it
sooner, for this knowledge obliges one to pay much more
attention to your authors.' ' I would have done it,' said he,
if the opportunity had occurred, but profit by it in future,
and let us continue our discourse.'

' I believe I have unfolded to you means of securing salvation; means easy enough, safe enough, and in sufficient
number; but our fathers would fain have people not to rest
at this first degree, in which nothing is done but what is
strictly necessary for salvation. As they aim constantly at
the greatest glory of God, they would wish to raise men to
a more pious life; and because men of the world usually
feel repugnant to devotion from the strange idea which
is given them of it, we have thought it of the last importance to remove this first obstacle; and it is for this that
Father Le Moine has acquired great reputation by his treatise
of Easy Devotion, composed with this view. In it he draws
a charming picture of devotion. It was never so well described before. Learn this from the first sentences of the
book: " Virtue has never yet shown herself to any one; no
portrait of her has been made that resembles her. It is
not strange that so few have been in a haste to scramble up
her rock. She has been represented as peevish, loving
only solitude; she has been associated with pain and toil;
and, in fine, she has been made the enemy of diversion and
sport, which are the bloom of joy and seasoning of life."
This he says, p. 92.

'But, father, I know well that there are great saints
whose life was extremely austere.' True,' said he, ' but

besides these there have *always been polite saints and civilized devotees*, as this father says, p. 191, and you will see, p. 86, that the difference in their manners is owing to that of their humours. Listen to him: " I deny not that we see devout men of a pallid and melancholy hue, who ove silence and retreat, have only phlegm in their veins and earth in their countenance. But many others are seen of a happier complexion, with an overflow of that soft and warm temperament, that benign and rectified blood which inspires joy."

'You see from this that the love of retreat and silence is not common to all devout persons, and that, as I told you, it is more the result of their complexion than of their piety; whereas, those austere manners of which you speak, are properly the characteristics of a wild and savage nature. Accordingly, you will see them classed with the ridiculous and brutish manners of melancholy madness in the description which father Le Moine gives in the seventh book of his Moral Portraits. Here are some of the features. "He is without eyes for the beauties of nature and art. He would think himself burdened with a heavy load if he had taken any enjoyment for its own sake. On festival days he retires among the dead; he likes himself better in the trunk of a tree, or in a grotto, than in a palace or on a throne. As to affronts and injuries, he is as insensible to them, as if he had the eyes and ears of a statue. Honour and glory are idols which he knows not, and to which he has no incense to offer. A lovely person is to him a spectre; and those imperious and commanding features, those agreeable tyrants which every where make voluntary and enchained slaves, have the same power over his eyes that the sun has over those of owls."'

'Reverend father, I assure you that if you had not told me that M. Le Moine is the author of this picture, I would have said that it was some infidel who had drawn it for the purpose of turning the saints into ridicule. For, if it is not the representation of a man completely estranged from the feelings which the Gospel requires us to renounce, I confess I understand nothing of the matter.' 'See, then,' said he, 'how little you do know of it, for these *are marks of a weak and savage spirit, which has none of the honest and natural affections which it ought to have*, as father Le Moine says at the end of this description. It is by this means *he teaches virtue and Christian philosophy*, agreeably to the design which he had in this work, as he declares in the advertisement. And, indeed, it cannot be denied that this method of treating devotion is far more acceptable to the world than that previously in use.' 'There is no comparison,' said I, 'and I begin to hope you will keep your word to me.' 'You will see it far better in the sequel,' said he; 'I have yet spoken only of piety in general. But to show you in detail how much our fathers have relieved matters, is it not most consolatory for the ambitious to learn that they can preserve a true devotion with an excessive love of grandeur?' 'What, father, whatever excess they may display in the search?' 'Yes,' said he, 'for it would always be no more than a venial sin, unless grandeur should be desired as a more effectual means of offending God or the State. Now venial sins are not incompatible with a devout spirit, since the greatest saints are not exempt from them. Listen then to Escobar, tr. 2, ex. 2, n. 17: "Ambition, which is an irregular appetite for place and station, is in itself a venial sin; but when elevation is desired as a means of hurting the State, or having more opportunity of offending God, these external circumstances make the sin mortal."'

'That is convenient enough, father.' 'And is it not, moreover,' continued he, ' a very pleasant doctrine for misers to say, as Escobar does, tr. 5, ex. 5, n. 253, "I know that the rich do not sin mortally in not giving alms of their superfluity, in the great necessities of the poor. *Scio in gravi pauperum necessitate divites non dando superflua non peccare mortaliter*."' 'In truth,' said I, 'if that is so, it is plain that I have little knowledge of my sins.' 'To show you the thing still better, do you not think that a good opinion of ourselves and complacency in our own works, is one of the most dangerous sins? And will you not be much surprised if I let you see that even should this good opinion be without foundation, it is so little of the nature of sin, that it is on the contrary a gift of God? ' Is it possible, father?' 'Yes, said he, ' and this our great father Garasse has taught us in his French work, entitled, *Summary of the leading truths of Religion*, p. 2, p. 419. "One effect of commutative justice is, that all honest labour is rewarded either with praise or satisfaction. When men of ability compose an excellent work, they are justly rewarded by the public applause. But when a person of mean intellect labours much in doing nothing worth while, and thus cannot obtain public applause, still, that the work may not go unrewarded, God gives him a personal satisfaction, which he cannot be envied without injustice more than barbarous. Thus God, who is just, makes frogs feel satisfaction in their own music.'

'These,' said I, ' are fine decisions in favour of vanity, ambition, and avarice? Will not envy, father, be more difficult to excuse?' 'It is a delicate subject,' said the father. ' It is necessary to use father Bauni's distinction in his Sum of Sins. For his opinion, c. 7, p. 123, fifth and sixth edition, is that " envy of the spiritual good of our neighbour is mortal, but envy of his temporal good only venial.' ' And for what reason, father?' ' Listen,' said he; " for the good found in temporal things is so meagre and of so small consequence for heaven, that it of no importance before God and his saints." ' But, father, if this good is so *meagre*, and of so little consequence, how do you allow men to be killed in order to preserve it?' ' You mistake matters,' said the father, ' we tell you that the good is of no importance in the view of God, but not in the view of men.' ' I did not think of that,' said I, ' and I hope that through these distinctions, there will no longer be any mortal sins in the world.' ' Do not think so,' said the father, ' for some are always mortal in their nature, laziness for example.'

'O father,' said I, ' then all the conveniences of life are gone?' ' Wait,' said the father, ' till you know the definition of this vice by Escobar, tr. 2, ex. 2, n. 81. " Laziness is regret that spiritual things are spiritual, just as if one were sorry that the sacraments are a source of grace. And it is a mortal sin." 'O, father! I don't think that ever any body thought of being lazy in that way.' 'Accordingly,' said the father, 'Escobar adds, n. 105: "I confess it is very rare for any one to fall into the sin of laziness." Do you perceive clearly from this how important it is to define things properly?' "Yes, father,' said I, 'and on this I remember your other definitions of assassination, ambush, and superfluity. Whence comes it, father, that you do not extend this method to all sorts of cases, so as to define all sins after your manner, that men might no longer sin in gratifying their desires?'

'It is not always necessary for that,' said he, 'to change the definitions of things. You are going to see this in regard to good cheer, which passes for one of the greatest pleasures in life, and which Escobar, in the Practice according to our Society, permits in this way, n. 102. "Is it lawful to eat and drink one's full without necessity, and from mere voluptuousness? Yes, certainly, according to Sanchez, provided it is not hurtful to health, because natural appetite may lawfully enjoy the acts which are natural to it: *An comedere et bibere usque ad satietatem absque necessitate ob solam voluptatem, sit peccatum? Cum Sanctio negative respondeo, modo non obsit valetudini, quia licite potest appetitus naturalis suis actibus frui.*"' 'O, father,' said I, 'that is the most complete passage, and the most finished principle in all your morality: from it also we may draw convenient inferences. Then gluttony is not even a venial sin?' 'No,' said he, 'in the way which I have just stated, but it would be a venial sin according to Escobar, n. 56, "if, without any necessity, one were to gorge himself with meat and drink even to vomiting: *Si quis se usque ad vomitum ingurgitat.*"'

'Enough on this subject. I will now speak to you of the facilities which we have introduced for avoiding sins in worldly conversation and intrigue. One of the most embarrassing of all things is to avoid falsehood, especially when one wishes to accredit something false. This object is admirably gained by our doctrine of equivocation, which "allows ambiguous terms to be used, by causing them to be understood in a sense different from that in which we ourselves understand them," as Sanchez says, Op. mor., p. 2, l. 3, c. 6, n. 13.' 'I know that, father,' said I.' 'We have published it so much,' continued he, 'that at length every body is acquainted with it. But do you know how to act when equivocal terms are not to be found?' 'No, father.' 'I doubted as much,' said he;' 'that is new: it is the doctrine of mental reservations. Sanchez gives it at the same place: " A man," says he, " may swear that he has not done a thing, although he has really done it, understanding in himself that he did not do it on a certain day, or before he was born, or internally adding some other similar circumstance, without using words which may let the meaning be known. And this is very convenient on many occasions, and is always very just when necessary or useful for health, honour, or estate."'

'How, father; is it not a lie, and even perjury?' 'No,' said the father; 'Sanchez proves it at the same place, and our Filiutius also, tr. 25, c. 11, n. 331; "because," says he, "it is the intention that regulates the quality of the act." He also gives (n. 328,) another surer means of avoiding falsehood: It is after having said loud out, *I swear that I did not do it*, we add, in a whisper, *to-day;* or, after saying loud out, *I swear*, we whisper, *that I say*, and afterwards continue aloud *that I did not do it*. You see plainly that this is to speak the truth.' 'I admit it,' said I; 'but perhaps we would find that it is to speak the truth in a whisper and falsehood loud out: besides, I should fear that many people would not have sufficient presence of mind to use these methods.' 'Our fathers,' said he, 'have at the same place for the sake of those who cannot use these reservations, taught that to avoid the lie it is sufficient for them to say simply, that *they did not do* what they did, provided that *they have a general intention to give their language the meaning which a man of ability would give it.*

'Tell the truth: many a time have you been thrown into embarrassment for want of this knowledge?' 'Occasionally,' said I. 'And will you not likewise admit that it would often be very convenient to be dispensed in conscience from keeping certain promises which you may have made?'

'Father,' said I, 'it would be the most convenient thing in the world.' 'Listen then to Escobar, tr. 3, ex. 3, n. 48, where he gives this general rule: "Promises do not oblige when we have no intention of obliging ourselves by making them. Now it seldom happens that we have this intention, at least without confirming them by oath or contract, so that when we simply say, I will do it, we mean that we will do it unless we change our intention. For we mean not thereby to deprive ourselves of our liberty." He gives other rules which you may see for yourself, and he says at the end: "all this is taken from Molina and our other authors: *Omnia ex Molina et aliis.*" So that there can be no doubt on the subject.'

'Father,' said I, 'I did not know that the direction of intention was of force to make promises null.' 'You see,' said the father, 'that great facility is here given to the intercourse of society. But what gave us the greatest trouble was to regulate conversation between men and women; for our fathers are more reserved in regard to chastity. Not that they do not handle curious enough questions and give sufficient indulgence, especially to married persons, or persons betrothed.' On this I was instructed in the most extraordinary questions that can be imagined. He gave me materials to fill several letters, but I will not so much as note the passages, because you show my letters to all classes of persons, and I should not like to furnish such reading to those who would only seek it for diversion.

The only thing he showed me in the books, even in French, which I can point out to you, is what you may see in father Bauni's Sum of Sins, p. 165, as to certain little freedoms which he there explains, provided the intention is properly directed, as in *passing for a gallant*; and you will be surprised to find at p. 148, a principle of morality concerning the power which he says daughters have to dispose of their virginity without their parents' consent. Here are his words: "when this is done with the daughter's consent, though the father has cause to complain, nevertheless, it is not because the said daughter, or he who has corrupted her, has done him any wrong, or has, as regards him, violated ustice; for the daughter is as much in possession of her virginity as of her body, which she may do with as seems to her good, with the exception of killing or dismembering it." By this, judge of the rest. This brought to my mind a passage in a heathen poet, who was a better casuist than these fathers, since he says that "a daughter's virginity does not belong entirely to herself, but partly to her father and partly to her mother, without whom she cannot even dispose of it by marriage." I doubt if there is a judge who would not lay down a rule the reverse of this maxim of father Bauni.

This is the utmost I can tell you of all which I heard on this subject, on which the father dwelt so long, that I was obliged at last to beg him to change it. He did so, and spoke to me of their regulations as to female dress in the following terms. 'We shall not speak of those females,' said he, 'whose intentions are impure, but in regard to others, Escobar says, tr. 1, ex. 8, n. 5. "If they dress with no bad intention, and only to gratify the natural inclination to vanity, *ob naturalem fastus inclinationem*, it is either only a venial sin, or no sin at all." And father Bauni in his Sum of Sins, c. 46, p. 1094, says, that though "the woman should be aware of the bad effect which her attention to dress would produce both on the body and soul of those who should behold her adorned in rich and costly attire, she nevertheless would not sin in using it." He quotes our Sanchez among others, as being of the same opinion.'

'But, father, what answer do your fathers give to the passages of Scripture which so vehemently denounce the least approach to any thing of this sort?' 'Lessius,' said the father, 'answered learnedly, de Just. l. 4, c. 4, d. 14, n. 114, where he says, "that those passages were binding only on the women of that time, that they might by their modesty give an edifying example to the heathen."' 'And where did he get that, father?' 'No matter where he got it; it is enough that the opinions of those great men are always probable in themselves. But father Le Moine has in one respect modified this general permission, for he will not on any account allow old women to use it, as appears from his Easy Devotion, at *inter alia*, pp. 127, 157, 163. "Youth," says he, has a natural right to be decked. A female may be permitted to deck herself at an age when life is in its bloom and verdure; but there it must stop: it would be strangely out of place to seek for roses among snow: only to the stars does it belong to be always in full dress, because they have the gift of perpetual youth. The best course then in this matter would be to take counsel of reason and a good mirror, to yield to decency and necessity, and withdraw as night approaches."' 'That is quite judicious,' said I. 'But,' continued he, 'that you may see how our fathers have attended to every thing, I must tell you that after giving permission to women to indulge in play, and seeing that this permission would often be of no use to them if they did not also give them wherewith to play, they have established another maxim in their favour, which is seen in Escobar in the chapter on larceny, tr. 1, ex. n. 13. "A woman," says he, "may play and take her husband's money for the purpose."'

'Indeed, father, that is very complete.' 'There are many other things besides,' said the father, 'but we must leave them to speak of the most important maxims for facilitating the use of holy things, for instance, the manner of attending at mass. Our great theologians, Gaspar Hurtado, de Sacr. t. 2, d. 5, dist. 2, and Coninck, q. 83. a. 6, n. 197, teach on this subject, that "it is sufficient to be bodily present at mass though absent in spirit, provided the countenance is kept externally decent." Vasquez goes farther, for he says that "the injunction to hear mass is satisfied even though the intention has nothing to do with it." All this is also in Escobar, tr. 1, ex. 11, n. 74, 107, and also tr. 1, ex. 1, n. 116, where he explains it by the example of those who are forcibly taken to mass, and have the express intention not to hear it.' 'Truly,' said I, 'I would never believe this if another did not tell me.' 'In fact,' said he, 'this stands somewhat in need of the authority of these great men, as well as what Escobar says, tr. 1, ex. 11, n. 31, "that a wicked intention, such as looking at women with a lustful eye during the hearing of mass, properly does not hinder the injunction from being satisfied: *Nec obest alia prava intentio, ut aspiciendi libidinose feminas.*"

There is also a convenient thing in our learned Turrianus, Select. 2. d. 16, dub. 7. "You may hear the half of a mass from one priest, and then the other half from another; and you may even hear the end first from one, and then the beginning from another." 1 must tell you, moreover, that it is lawful "to hear two halves of a mass at the same time, from two different priests, the one beginning the mass when the other is at the elevation; because we may have our attention on these two sides at once, and two halves of a mass make an entire mass: *duæ medietates unam missam constituunt.*" So have decided our fathers, Bauni, tr. 6, q. 9, p. 312; Hurtado, de Sacr. t. 2, Missa, d. 5, diff. 4; Azorius, p. 1, l. 7, c. 3, q. 3, Escobar, tr. 1. ex. 11. n. 73, in the chapter *on the rule for hearing mass according to our Society.* And you will see the inferences which he draws in this same book, editions of Lyons, 1644 and 1645. The words are: "Hence I conclude that you can hear mass in very little time: if for example you fall in with four masses at once, which are so arranged that when one begins, another is at the Gospel, another at the consecration, and the last at the communion."' 'Certainly, father, we shall in this way hear mass in an instant at Notre Dame.' 'You see then that better could not be for facilitating the mode of hearing mass.

'I wish now to show you how they have softened down the use of the sacraments, and especially that of penitence. For herein you will see the highest proof of benignity in the conduct of our fathers, and you will wonder how the devotion which fills every one with awe could have been handled by our fathers with so much prudence, that "having struck down the obstacle which demons had placed at its entrance, they have rendered it easier than vice and more pleasant, so that mere living is incomparably more difficult than good living," to use the words of father Le Moine, pp. 244, 291, of his Easy Devotion. Is not this a marvellous change?' 'In truth, father,' said I, 'I cannot help telling you my mind. I fear that your measures are ill chosen, and that this indulgence is capable of offending more people than it can attract. The mass, for example, is so venerable and holy that nothing more would be necessary to discredit them in the minds of many persons than to show in what manner they speak of it.' 'That is very true,' said the father, 'with regard to certain people, but do you not know that we accommodate ourselves to all sorts of persons. It seems you have lost sight of what I have so often told you on this subject. I mean, then, to treat of it our first leisure time, deferring for that purpose our consideration of the mitigations of confession. I will make you understand it so thoroughly that you never will forget it.' On this we separated, and thus I imagine that the subject of our next interview will be their policy.

I am, etc.

LETTER TENTH.

HOW THE JESUITS HAVE SOFTENED DOWN THE SACRAMENT OF PENITENCE, BY THEIR MAXIMS TOUCHING CONFESSION, SATISFACTION, ABSOLUTION, PROXIMATE OCCASIONS OF SIN, CONTRITION, AND THE LOVE OF GOD.

PARIS, *2nd August*, 1656.

SIR,—I do not yet give you the policy of the Society, but one of its greatest principles. You will here see the mitigations applied to confession, certainly the best means which these fathers have discovered to attract all and repulse none. It was necessary to know it before going further; for this reason, the father judged it proper to instruct me in it as follows:

'You have seen,' said he, 'from all I have hitherto told you, with what success our fathers have laboured to discover, by the light given to them, that many things are permitted which were supposed to be forbidden; but because there are still sins remaining which cannot be excused, and the proper cure for them is confession, it becomes necessary to smooth the difficulties by the methods which I have now to explain. Hence having pointed out in our previous conversations, how the scruples which troubled the conscience have been relieved by showing that what was thought to be bad is not so, it remains at this time to point out a simple mode of expiating what is truly sinful, by rendering confession as easy as it was formerly difficult.' 'And by what means, father?' 'By those admirable subtleties,' said he, 'which are peculiar to our Company, and which our fathers in Flanders call, in the 'Image of our first Century,' l. 3, or. 1, p. 401, and l. 1, c. 2, "Pious and holy finessing, and a holy artifice of devotion. *Piam et religio-*

sa *calliditatem, et pietatis solertiam,"* l. 3, c. 8. By means of these inventions, "crimes are expiated in the present day, *alacrius,* with more alacrity and eagerness than they were formerly committed, so that many persons efface their stains as quickly as they contract them: *Plurimi vix citius maculas contrahunt, quam eluunt,*' as is said in the same place.' 'Pray, father, do teach me this salutary finessing.' 'There are several heads of it,' said he, 'for as there are many painful things in confession, so particular mitigations have been applied to each. And because the principal difficulties which men feel, are shame at confessing certain sins, particularly in detailing the circumstances, penance to be inflicted, resolutions not to relapse, avoiding the immediate occasions which lead to this, and regret for having committed them, I hope to show you to-day, that there is now scarcely any annoyance in all this, so careful have we been to remove all that is bitter and all that is sharp, in this necessary remedy.

'To begin with the difficulty which is felt in confessing certain sins, as you are not ignorant that it is often very important to preserve a confessor's esteem, so is it very convenient to permit, as do our fathers, and among others, Escobar, who also quotes Suarez, tr. 7, c. 4, n. 135, "The having of two confessors, the one for mortal, and the other for venial sins, so as to remain in good repute with the ordinary confessor: *Uti bonam famam apud ordinarium tueatur,* provided it is not made a handle for remaining in mortal sin." And he afterwards gives another subtle method of confessing a sin even to an ordinary confessor, without his perceiving that it has been committed since the last confession. "It is," says he, "to make a general confession, and throw this sin in among the others which are confessed in the slump." He again states the same thing at the beginning of ex. 2, n. 73, and you will admit, I am sure, that the shame felt in confessing relapses is much relieved by this decision of father Bauni, Theol. Mor. tr. 4, q. 15, p. 137: "Except on certain occasions which occur but seldom, the confessor is not entitled to ask whether the sin confessed is habitual, and there is no obligation to answer such a question, because he has no right to inflict on his penitent the shame of acknowledging frequent relapses." '

'How, father, I would as soon say that a physician has no right to ask his patient if he has long had fever. Are not sins very different according to their different circumstances, and should not the purpose of a true penitent be to expose the state of his conscience to his confessor, fully with as much sincerity and openness of heart as if he were speaking to Jesus Christ, whose place the priest occupies? Now is not a man very far from being in this disposition when he conceals his frequent relapses in order to conceal the greatness of his sin?' This, I saw, puzzled the worthy father, who accordingly tried to evade the difficulty rather than to solve it, by informing me of another of their rules, which merely sanctions a new irregularity, without at all justifying this decision of father Bauni, which is, in my opinion, one of their most pernicious maxims, and one of the fittest to encourage the vicious in their bad practices. 'I am free to admit,' said he, 'that habit adds to the heinousness of the sin, but it does not change its nature, and this is the reason why there is no obligation to confess it according to the rule of our fathers, to whom Escobar refers at the beginning of ex. 2, n. 39, " One is only obliged to confess the circumstances which change the species of sin, and not those which only aggravate it."

'Proceeding on this rule, our father Granados says, part 5, cont. 7, t. 9, d. 9, n. 22, that "one who has eaten flesh in Lent, does enough by confessing a breach of the fast, without saying whether it was in eating flesh or taking two meagre repasts." And according to father Reginald, tr. 1, l. 6, c. 4, n. 14, " A diviner who has used diabolic art, is not obliged to declare the circumstance: it is sufficient to say that he has intermeddled with divination, without saying whether by chiromancy or compact with the devil." Fagundez, of our Society, also says, p. 2, l. 4, c. 3, n. 17, " Ravishing is not a circumstance which one is bound to discover, when the girl has consented." Our father Escobar refers to all this at the same place, n. 41, 61, 62, with several other curious enough decisions on circumstances which there is no obligation to confess. You may there see them for yourself.' These *artifices of devotion*,' said I, ' are very accommodating.'

' Nevertheless,' said he, ' all this would be nothing if we had not mitigated penance, which, more than any thing else, produces the greatest repugnance to confession. But the most fastidious cannot now feel any apprehension, since we have maintained in our Theses at the College of Clermont, that if the " confessor enjoins a suitable penance, *convenientem*, and the penitent is, notwithstanding, unwilling to accept it, he may retire, renouncing absolution and the penance enjoined." Escobar moreover says, in the Practice of Penance according to our Society, tr. 7, ex. 4, n. 188, " If the penitent declares that he wishes to put off his penance till the next world, and suffer in purgatory all the pains due to him, the confessor, for the integrity of the sacrament, should impose a very light penance, and especially if he sees that a greater would not be received."' ' I believe,' said I, ' if that were so, confession should no longer be called the sacrament of penance.' ' You are wrong,' said he, ' for we always give one at least in form.' ' But father, do you deem a man worthy of absolution who refuses to do any thing painful, in order to expiate his offences? And when persons are in this condition, ought you not rather to retain their sins than to remit them? Have you a true idea of the extent of your ministry? Do you not know that you there exercise the power of binding and loosing? Do you think it lawful to give absolution indifferently to all who ask it, without previously ascertaining that Christ looses in heaven those whom you loose on earth?' ' Eh!' said the father, ' do you think we don't know that " the confessor must constitute himself judge of the disposition of the penitent, as well because he is obliged not to dispense the sacraments to those who are unworthy of them, Jesus Christ having enjoined him to be a faithful steward, and not to give holy things to dogs, as because he is judge, and it is the duty of a judge to judge justly, by loosing those who are worthy of it, and binding the unworthy, and also because he must not absolve those whom Jesus Christ condemns?"' 'Whose words are these, father?' 'Those of father Filiutius,' he replied, ' to. 1, tr. 7, n. 354.' 'You surprise me,' said I, 'I took them to be from one of the Fathers of the Church. But, father, this passage must greatly perplex confessors, and make them very circumspect in dispensing the sacrament in order to ascertain whether the sorrow of their penitents is sufficient, and whether the promises they give to sin no more in future are receivable.' 'There is nothing at all embarrassing in this,' said the father; 'Filiutius took good care not to leave confessors in this difficulty, and therefore, after the above words, he gives them the easy method of getting out of it: " The confessor may easily set himself at rest touching the disposition of his penitent: if he does not give sufficient signs of sorrow, the confessor has only to ask him if he does not in his soul detest sin, and if he answers yes, he is obliged to believe him. The same must be said of his resolution for the future, unless there be some obligation to restore, or to abandon some proximate occasion."' 'This passage, father, I see plainly, is from Filiutius.' 'You are mistaken, for he has copied it, word for word, from Suarez, in 3 par. to. 4, disp. 32, s. 2, n. 2.' 'But father, this last passage of Filiutius destroys what he had laid down in the first. For confessors will no longer be able to constitute themselves judges of the dispositions of their penitents since they are obliged to believe them on their word, even though they do not give any sufficient sign of sorrow. Is it because there is such a certainty of their word being true, that it alone is a convincing sign? I doubt whether experience has taught your fathers that all who give these promises keep them: I am mistaken if they do not often experience the contrary.' 'It matters not,' said the father, 'we always oblige confessors to believe them. For father Bauni, who has gone to the bottom of this question in his Sum of Sins, c. 46, p. 1090, 1091, 1092, concludes, that " whenever those who frequently relapse without showing any amendment, present themselves to the confessor, and tell him that they are sorry for the past, and mean well in future, he must believe them on their word, although there is reason to presume that such resolutions go no farther than the lips. And though they afterward persist with more freedom and excess than ever in the same faults, absolution must, nevertheless, be given, according to my opinion." I am confident all your doubts are now solved.'

'But, father,' said I, 'you seem to impose a great burden on confessors, in obliging them to believe the opposite of what they see.' 'You do not,' said he, 'understand it; it is only meant that they are obliged to act and absolve as if they believed the resolution to be firm and steadfast, although they do not believe it in fact. This is explained by our fathers, Suarez and Filiutius, in the sequel of the above passages. For, after saying that "the priest is bound to believe his penitent on his word," they add that "it is not necessary for the confessor to be persuaded that the resolution of his penitent will be executed, or even to judge it probable; it is difficult to think that at the instant he has the intention generally, although he is to relapse in a very short time. This all our authors teach: *ita docent omnes autores.*" Will you doubt the truth of what our authors teach?' 'But, father, what then will become of this which Father Petau is obliged to acknowledge in his preface to Pen. Pub., p. 4: "Holy fathers, doctors, and councils agree as in an infallible truth, that the penitence which prepares for the eucharist must be true, steady, bold, not lax and sleepy, not liable to relapses, subject to fits and starts."' 'Don't you see,' said he, 'that father Petau is speaking of the *ancient Church?* But that is now so *little in season*, to use the expression of our fathers, that according to Father Bauni, the very opposite is true: tr. 4, q. 15, p. 95: "There are authors who say that we ought to refuse absolution to those who often relapse into the same sins, and especially when, after having been repeatedly absolved, there appears no amendment; others say no. The only true opinion is, that absolution must not be refused; and that although they profit not by all the advices which have repeatedly been given them, though they have not kept the promises they made to change their life, though they have not laboured to purify themselves, no matter; whatever others say, the true opinion, and that which ought to be followed is, that even in all these cases absolution is to be given." And tr. 4, q. 22, p. 100, " We ought neither to refuse nor defer to absolve those who are addicted to habitual sins against the law of God, of nature, and of the Church, although we see no prospect of amendment: *etsi emendationis futuræ nulla spes appareat.*" '

'But, father, this certainty of always obtaining absolution may well incline sinners—' 'I understand you,' said he, interrupting me, 'but listen to Father Bauni, q. 15: " We may absolve him who acknowledges that the hope of being absolved has disposed him to sin more readily than but for this hope he would have done." And Father Caussin, defending this proposition, says, p. 211 of his Resp. ad Theol. Mor., " that if it was not true, the greater part of mankind would be interdicted from confession, and the only remedy left to sinners would be the branch of a tree and a rope." ' 'O father, what numbers of people these maxims will attract to your confessionals!' 'Accordingly,' said he, 'you cannot think how many come; " we are weighed down, and, as it were, oppressed under the numbers of our penitents; *poenitentium numero obruimur,*" as it is expressed in 'The Image of our First Century,' l. 3, c. 8. " I know,' said I, ' an easy means of relieving you of this pressure. You have only to oblige sinners to abandon proximate occasions; in this device alone you would find complete relief.' 'We do not want this relief,' said he; ' quite the contrary; for, as is said in the same book, l. 3, c. 7, p. 374, " the aim of our Society is to labour in establishing virtue, in warring upon vice, and in serving a great number of souls." And as few are willing to quit proximate occasions, we have been obliged to define a proximate occasion, as is seen in Escobar, in the Practice of our Society, tr. 7, ex. 4, n. 226: " By proximate occasion we do not mean that in which a man sins but seldom, as with his landlady, from sudden transport, three or four times a-year," or, according to Father Bauni, in his French work, " once or twice a-month," p. 1082; and also 1089, where he asks, " What is to be done in the case of masters and servants, male and female cousins, who live together, and from so doing are mutually disposed to sin."' 'Separate them,' said I.' 'He also says so, "if the relapses are frequent, and almost daily; but if they but seldom offend together as once or twice a-month, and they cannot separate without great inconvenience and damage, we may absolve them according to those authors, among others Suarez, provided they promise fairly to sin no more, and are truly sorry for the past." I thoroughly understood him, for he had already taught me what ought to satisfy a confessor in judging of this sorrow. 'And Father Bauni,' continued he, p. 1084, 'permits those who are living in proximate occasions, "to continue, when they cannot quit them without giving occasion to the world to talk, or without suffering inconvenience."' He likewise says, Theol. Mor., tr. 4, de Pœnit. q. 14, p. 94, and q. 13, p. 93, "that we may and must absolve a woman who has a man in her house with whom she often sins, if she cannot make him leave reputably, or if she has some cause for retaining him, *si non potest honeste ejicere, aut habeat aliquam causam retinendi,* provided she indeed purposes to sin no more with him."'

'O, dear father,' said I, ' the obligation to shun occasions of sin is greatly softened if we are exempted the moment we should suffer inconvenience; but I presume we are at least obliged to do it when there is no difficulty?' 'Yes, said the father, 'though that is not, however, without exception. For Father Bauni says, at the same place, "all sorts of persons may go into infamous houses, to convert prostitutes, though it is very probable that they will fall into sin, as where they have already often experienced that they have been led into sin by the appearance and cajolery of these women. And although there are doctors who do not approve this opinion, and think it is not lawful voluntarily to endanger our own salvation in helping our neighbour, I still very willingly embrace the opinion which they combat."' 'Behold, father, a new sort of preachers! But on what does Father Bauni found in giving them this mission?' 'It is,' said he, ' on one of his principles which he gives at the same place after Basil Ponce. I formerly spoke of it to you, and

I think you remember it. It is, "that we may seek an occasion directly and for itself, *primo et per se*, for the temporal or spiritual welfare of ourselves or our neighbour."' These quotations so horrified me, that I was on the point of breaking with him; but I checked myself, in order to let him go his full length, and contented myself with saying: 'What resemblance is there, father, between this doctrine and that of the Gospel, which enjoins us to "pluck out an eye, or part with the things most necessary to us, when they are injurious to our salvation?" How can you conceive that a man who voluntarily continues in occasions of sin, detests it sincerely? Is it not visible, on the contrary, that his feelings, in regard to it, are not what they ought to be, and that he has not yet attained to that true conversion of heart which makes us love God as much as we have loved the creature?'

'How?' said he; 'that would be genuine contrition. It seems you do not know that, as Father Pintereau says, in the second part of the Abbé du Boisic, p. 50, "all our fathers teach, with one accord, that it is an error, and almost a heresy, to say that contrition is necessary, and that attrition by itself alone, and produced *solely* by a dread of future punishment, which excludes any wish to offend, is not sufficient with the sacrament."' 'What, father! it is almost an article of faith, that attrition, produced by the mere dread of punishment, is sufficient with the sacrament? I believe this is peculiar to your fathers; for others who believe that attrition with the sacrament suffices, insist on its being accompanied with at least some love of God. And, besides, it seems to me that your authors themselves, did not formerly hold the doctrine to be so certain; for your Father Suarez speaks of it in this way, de Pœnit., q. 90, art. 4, disp. 15, n. 17: "Although it is a probable opinion that attrition is sufficient with the sacrament, it is not, however, certain, and it may be false; *non est certa, et potest esse falsa.* And if it is false, attrition is not sufficient to save a man. He, then, who dies knowingly in this state, voluntarily exposes himself to moral risk of eternal damnation. For this opinion is neither very ancient nor very common; *nec valde antiqua, nec multum communis.*" No more did Sanchez consider it so certain, since he says in his Sum, l. 1, c. 9, n. 34, "that the sick man and his confessor, who should content themselves with attrition and the sacrament at death, would sin mortally, because of the great risk of damnation to which the penitent would be exposed if the opinion that attrition is sufficient with the sacrament should prove not to be true;" nor Comitolus, also, when he says, Resp. Mor. l. 1, q. 32, n. 7, 8, "that he is not altogether sure that attrition is sufficient with the sacrament."'

The worthy father here stopped me. 'And so,' said he, 'you read our authors? You do well; but you would do still better were you not to read them without some one of us. Do you not see, that from having read them by yourself you have concluded, that these passages contradict those which now maintain our doctrine of attrition? whereas it could have been shown you that there is nothing which does them higher honour. For what an honour is it to our fathers of the present day, to have, in less than no time, spread their opinion every where so generally, that with the exception of theologians, every body imagines that what we now hold on the subject of attrition has always been the belief of the faithful? And thus, when you show by our fathers themselves, that a few years ago *this opinion was not certain*, what else do you than just give our latest authors all the honour of establishing it?

'Hence Diana, our intimate friend, thought he would do us a pleasure by pointing out the different steps in its progress. This he does, p. 5, tr. 13, where he says, "formerly, the old schoolmen maintained that contrition was necessary as soon as we had committed a mortal sin; then the belief came to be, that we are obliged to this only on festivals; and, at a later period, when some great calamity threatened the kingdom; according to others, the obligation was not to delay it long when death was approaching. But our fathers, Hurtado and Vasquez, have excellently refuted all these opinions, and fixed that we are obliged to it only when we cannot obtain absolution in any other way, or are *in articulo mortis.*" To continue the marvellous progress of this doctrine, I will add, that our fathers, Fagundez, præc. 2, t. 2, c. 4, n. 13, Granados, in 3 p., cont. 7, d. 3, s. 4, n. 17, and Escobar, tr. 7, ex. 4, n. 88, in the Practice of our Society, have decided that "contrition is not necessary even at death; because," say they, "if attrition with the sacrament was not sufficient at death, it would follow that attrition would not be sufficient with the sacrament." And our learned Hurtado, de Sacr. d. 6, quoted by Diana, part 5, tr. 4, Miscell., r. 193, and by Escobar, tr. 7, ex. 4, n. 91, goes still farther. Listen to him: "Is regret for having sinned when produced only by the temporal evil resulting from it, as the loss of health or money, sufficient? It is necessary to distinguish. If the sinner does not think that the evil is sent by the hand of God, this regret is not sufficient; but if he believes that this evil is sent of God, as, indeed, all evil," says Diana, "except sin, comes from him, this regret is sufficient." Thus Escobar speaks in the Practice of our Society. Our father Francis L'Amy also maintains the same thing, t. 8, dis. 3, n. 13.'

'You surprise me, father; for I see nothing in all this attrition but what is natural; and thus a sinner might make himself deserving of absolution without any supernatural grace. Now, every body knows that this is a heresy condemned by the Council.' 'I would have thought like you,' said he; 'and yet that cannot be, for our fathers of the College of Clermont have maintained in their Theses of 23rd May and 6th June, 1644, col. 4, n. 1, that 'an attrition may be holy and sufficient for the sacrament, though it be not supernatural;" and in that of August, 1643, "that an attrition which is only natural, is sufficient for the sacrament, provided it be honest:" *Ad sacramentum sufficit attritio naturalis, modo honesta.*

'This is the utmost that can be said, unless we add an inference, easy deduced from these principles, namely, that contrition, so far from being necessary to the sacrament, might be injurious to it, by wiping away sins itself, and thus leaving nothing for the sacrament to do. So says our father Valentia, the celebrated Jesuit, tom. 4, disp. 7, q. 8, p. 4, "Contrition is not at all necessary to obtain the principal effect of the sacrament, but, on the contrary, is rather an obstacle:" *Imo obstat potius quominus effectus sequatur.* No more can be desired in behalf of attrition.' 'I believe it father, but allow me to tell you my opinion, and to show you the excess to which this doctrine leads. When you say that *attrition produced by the mere fear of punishment*, is sufficient with the sacrament to justify sinners, does it not follow that we might, during our whole life, expiate sins in this way, and thus be saved without having once loved God? Now would your fathers dare to maintain this?

'I see plainly from what you say, that you require to be told the doctrine of our fathers respecting the love of God. This is the last trait of their morality, and the most important of all. You must have perceived this from the passages I quoted respecting contrition. But here are others more precise on the love of God; do not interrupt me, then, for the result is of great importance. 'Listen to Escobar, who gives the different opinions of our authors on this subject in the Practice of the love of God according to our Society, tr. 1, ex. 2, n. 21, and tr. 5, ex. 4, n. 8, in answer to this question, "When are we obliged to have in reality a love of God? Suarez says, It is enough if we love him before the hour of death, without specifying any time. Others, when we receive baptism; others, on festival days. But our father Castro Palao combats all these opinions, and rightly, *merito*. Hurtado de Mendoza maintains that we are obliged to do it every year, and that we are moreover very favourably dealt with in not being obliged to it oftener. But our father Coninck thinks we are obliged to it in three or four years. Henriquez every five years. And Filiutius says, it is probable we are not strictly obliged to it every five years. When then? He leaves it to the judgment of the wise."' I allowed all this trifling to pass, in which the wit of man sports so insolently with the love of God.

'But,' continued he, 'father Antony Sirmond who writes triumphantly on this subject, in his admirable work on the Defence of Virtue, *in which he speaks French in France*, as he tells his reader, thus discourses, tr. 2, s. 2, p. 12, 13, 14, etc.: "St. Thomas says that we are obliged to love

God as soon as we attain the use of reason. This is rather soon. Scotus, every Sunday. On what founded? Others, when we are grievously tempted. Yes, if this were the only way of avoiding temptation. Sotus, when we receive a favour from God. Right, to thank him for it. Others, at death; this is very late. No more do I think it is each time we receive some sacrament: attrition is here sufficient with confession, if we have opportunity. Suarez says that we are obliged to it at one time. But what time? He makes you the judge, and knows nothing about it. Now what this doctor knew not, I know not who knows." He concludes that in strictness we are not obliged to ought else than to observe the other commandments without any love for God, and without giving him our heart, provided we do not hate him. This he proves throughout his second treatise; you will see it in every passage, and among others, 16, 19, 24, 28, where he says, God, though commanding us to love him, is satisfied with our obeying him in his other commandments. Had God said, I will destroy you, whatever be the obedience which you render, if your heart, moreover, is not mine; would such a motive, in your opinion, have been properly proportioned to the end which God ought to have had, and must have had? It is said then that we love God by doing his will, as if we loved him with affection, as if the motive of charity disposed us to it. If that really happens, so much better; if not, we shall nevertheless strictly obey the commandment of love by doing works, so that (here see the goodness of God) we are not so much commanded to love as not to hate.

'Thus have our fathers discharged men from the *painful* obligation of loving God actually; and this doctrine is so advantageous, that our fathers, Aunat, Pintereau, Le Moine, and even A. Sirmond, defended it vigorously when it was attacked. You have only to see it in their answers to moral theology, while that of father Pintereau in the 2nd p. of the Abbé de Boisic, p. 53, will enable you to judge of the value of this dispensation, by the price which he says it has cost, namely, the blood of Jesus Christ. This crowns the doctrine. You see then that this dispensation from the *troublesome* obligation of loving God, is a privilege of the Gospel law over the Jewish law. "It was reasonable," says he, "that under the law of grace of the New Testament, God should remove the troublesome and difficult obligation contained in the law of rigour, of exerting an act of perfect contrition in order to be justified, and that he should institute sacraments to supply the defect by the aid of a simple arrangement. Otherwise assuredly, Christians, who are children, would not now have more facility in regaining the good graces of their Father than the Jews, who were slaves, in obtaining mercy from their master."'

'O father,' said I, 'no patience can stand this. It is impossible to listen without horror to things which I have just heard.' 'They are not mine,' said he. 'I know it well, father, but you have no aversion to them, and, very far from detesting the authors of these maxims, you esteem them. Are you not afraid that your consent will make you a partaker of their sin? And can you be ignorant that St. Paul declares *worthy of death* not only those who do the evil thing, but those who *take pleasure in them that do it?* Was it not enough to have allowed men to do so much that is forbidden, by the palliations you have introduced? Was it necessary, moreover, to give them the means of committing those very crimes which you have not been able to excuse, by the facility and certainty of absolution which you offer them, by destroying for this purpose the power of the priest, and obliging them to give absolution rather as slaves than judges, to the most hardened sinners, without change of life or any sign of sorrow, except promises a hundred times violated, without penance, *if they choose not to accept of it,* and without forsaking the occasions of sin, *if they thereby suffer inconvenience.*

'But they do not stop here: the licence which they have taken to shake the holiest rules of Christian conduct proceeds the length of entirely subverting the law of God! They violate the great commandment which comprehends the law and the prophets; they attack piety in the heart; they take away the spirit which gives life; they say that the love of God is not necessary to salvation; they even go so far as to pretend that "this dispensation from loving God is the advantage which Jesus Christ brought into the world." It is the height of impiety to say that the price of Christ's blood is to obtain for us a dispensation from loving him! Before the incarnation, men were obliged to love God; but since God has "so loved the world as to give his only begotten Son," the world which he has redeemed is discharged from loving him! Strange theology of our days! We dare to take off the *anathema* which St. Paul pronounces against those who "love not the Lord Jesus Christ!" We overthrow what St. John says, "he that loveth not abideth in death," and what Jesus Christ himself says, "whoso loveth not, keepeth not his commandments." Thus those are made worthy to enjoy God in eternity, who never once loved him on earth! Behold the mystery of iniquity accomplished. Open your eyes at last, father, and if you have not been touched by the other errors of your casuists, let these last extravagances induce you to withdraw. This is the wish of my heart, both for yourself and all your fathers, and I pray God that he would deign to make them know how false the light is which has led them to such precipices, and fully infuse his love into the breasts of those who presume to dispense others from loving.'

After some discourse of this nature, I left the father, and see no likelihood of returning. But do not regret it; for were it necessary to continue the subject, I am well enough read in their books to be able to tell you nearly as much of their morality, and at least as much of their policy, as he himself would have done.

I am, etc.

LETTER ELEVENTH.

TO THE REVEREND FATHER JESUITS.

RIDICULOUS ERRORS MAY BE REFUTED BY RAILLERY PRECAUTIONS TO BE USED. THESE OBSERVED BY MONTALTE: NOT SO BY THE JESUITS. IMPIOUS BUFFOONERY OF FATHER LE MOINE AND FATHER GARASSE.

18th August, 1656.

REVEREND FATHERS,—I have seen the letters you are circulating against those which I wrote to a friend, on the subject of your morality, in which one of the leading points of your defence is, that I have not spoken with due seriousness of your maxims: this you repeat in all your writings, and push so far as to say that "I have turned sacred things into ridicule."

This charge, fathers, is very surprising, and very unjust. In what place find you that I have turned sacred things into ridicule? Do you refer particularly to the "contract Mohatra," and "the story of John of Alba?" Is this what you mean by sacred things? Think you the Mohatra a thing so venerable, that it is blasphemy not to speak of it with respect? Are father Bauni's lessons on larceny, which disposed John of Alba to put it in practice against yourselves, so sacred that you are entitled to bring a charge of impiety against those who ridicule them?

What, fathers! are the fancies of your authors to pass for articles of faith, and cannot we scoff at passages from Escobar, and the fantastic and unchristian decisions of your other authors, without being accused of laughing at religion? How can you possibly have presumed so often to repeat a thing so unreasonable? Do you not fear that in blaming me for having derided your errors, you are giving me new subject of derision in this charge, and enabling me to retort it upon yourselves, by showing that the only subject of my laughter is what is laughable in your books; and that thus in ridiculing your morality, I have been as far from ridiculing sacred things, as the doctrine of your casuists is far from the holy doctrine of the Gospel?

In truth, fathers, there is a vast difference between laughing at religion, and laughing at those who profane it by their extravagances. It would be impiety to fail in respect for the truths which the Spirit of God has revealed; but it would be another form of impiety not to feel contempt for the falsehoods which the spirit of man opposes to them.

For, fathers, since you oblige me to enter into this subject, I pray you to consider, that as Christian truths are deserving of love and respect, so the errors which contradict them are deserving of contempt and hatred: because, there are two things in the truths of our religion; a divine beauty which makes them lovely, and a holy majesty which makes them venerable: and there are also two things in error; impiety, which makes it disgusting, and impertinence, which makes it ridiculous. Hence it is, that as the saints always regard truth with these two feelings of love and fear; and their wisdom is wholly comprised in fear, which is its principle, and love, which is its end; so, the saints regard error with these two feelings of hatred and contempt, and their zeal is employed alike in forcibly repelling the malice of the wicked, and pouring derision on their extravagance and folly.

Think not, then, fathers, to persuade the world that it is unbecoming a Christian to treat error with derision, since it is easy to convince those who know not, that this course is just, is common with the Fathers of the Church, and is authorised by Scripture, by the example of the greatest saints, and by that of God himself.

For, do we not see that God at once hates and despises sinners to such a degree, that at the hour of their death, the time when their state is most deplorable and wretched, Divine Wisdom will join mockery and laughter to the vengeance and fury which will doom them to eternal punishment? *In interitu vestro ridebo et subsannabo.* And the saints, acting in the same spirit, will do likewise, since, according to David, when they shall see the punishment of the wicked, "they shall tremble, and, at the same time, laugh: *videbunt justi et timebunt, et super eum ridebunt.*" Job speaks in the same way: *Innocens subsannabit eos.*

One very remarkable circumstance connected with this subject is, that in the first words which God spoke to man after the fall, there is, according to the Fathers, the language of mockery and a cutting irony. For, after Adam had disobeyed, hoping, as the devil had suggested, to be like God, it appears from Scripture that God, in punishment, made him subject to death; and after reducing him to this miserable condition due to his sin, mocked him in this state in these derisive words: "Behold, the man is become like one of us! *Ecce, Adam quasi unus ex nobis!* a deep and cutting irony, with which," according to St. Jerome and the commentators, God "cut him to the quick." "Adam," says Rupert, "deserved to be derided thus ironically, and was made to feel his folly by this ironical expression much more acutely than by a serious expression." And Hugo de St. Victor, after saying the same thing, adds, that "this irony was due to his sottish credulity, and that this species of ridicule is an act of justice, when he towards whom it is used deserves it."

You see, then, fathers, that mockery is sometimes the best means of bringing men back from their wanderings, and it is then an act of justice; because, as Jeremiah says, "the actions of those who err are deserving of laughter, because of their vanity: *vana sunt et risu digna.*" And so far is it from being impiety to laugh, that it is the effect of divine wisdom, according to the expression of St. Augustine: "The wise laugh at the foolish, because they are wise, not in their own wisdom, but that divine wisdom which will laugh at the death of the wicked."

Accordingly, the prophets, who were filled with the Spirit of God, have used this mockery, as we see by the example of Daniel and Elijah. In fine, instances of it occur in the discourses of Jesus Christ himself; and St. Augustine observes, that when he wished to humble Nicodemus, who thought himself a proficient in the law, "as he saw him inflated with pride in his capacity of Jewish doctor, he tests and confounds his presumption by the depth of his questions; and after reducing him to an utter inability to answer, asks, What! art thou a master in Israel, and knowest not these things? just as if he had said, Proud chief, acknowledge that thou knowest nothing." And St. Chrysostom and St. Cyril say on this, that "he deserves to be sported with in this manner."

You see, then, fathers, that if in the present day persons playing the masters towards Christians, as Nicodemus and the Pharisees towards the Jews, should happen to be ignorant of the principles of religion, and should maintain, for example, that "men can be saved without having once loved God during their whole life," it would only be following the example of Jesus Christ to make sport with their vanity and ignorance.

I feel confident, fathers, that these sacred examples suffice to make you understand that there is nothing contrary to the conduct of the saints, in laughing at the errors and extravagances of men; otherwise it would be necessary to blame the greatest doctors of the Church, who practised it; as St. Jerome, in his letters and his writings against Jovinian, Vigilantius, and the Pelagians; Tertullian, in his Apology against the follies of idolaters; St. Augustine against the monks of Africa, whom he calls *the hairy men;* St. Irenæus against the Gnostics; St. Bernard, and the other Fathers of the Church, who, having been the imitators of the apostles, should be imitated in all after ages, since they are set forth, let men say what they will, as the true models of Christians, even in the present day.

I did not think, therefore, I could go wrong in following them; and, as I believe I have sufficiently proved this, I will only add on this subject an excellent quotation from Tertullian, which justifies my whole procedure: "What I have done is only a mock before a real combat. I have rather shown the wounds which can be given you, than inflicted them. If there be passages which provoke a laugh, it is because the subjects themselves disposed to it. There are many things which deserve to be mocked and jeered at in this way, for fear of giving them weight by combating them seriously. Nothing is more due to vanity than laughter; to Truth properly does it belong to laugh, because she is joyous; and to make sport with her enemies, because she is sure of victory. It is true, care must be taken that the raillery is not low, and unbecoming the truth; but, with this exception, when it can be used with dexterity, it is a duty to use it." Do you not find this quotation, fathers, very pertinent to our subject? "The letters I have hitherto written are only a mock before a real combat." I have done nothing yet but play, and "shown you rather the wounds which can be given you than inflicted them." I have simply exhibited your passages, almost without making them the subject of remark. "If laughter has been excited, it is because the subjects themselves disposed to it;" for what more proper to excite laughter than to see a grave subject like Christian morality filled with such grotesque fancies as yours? Our expectation in regard to these maxims is raised so high when Jesus Christ is said to "have revealed them to fathers of the Society," that on finding "that a priest who has been paid to say a mass, may, besides, take payment from others by yielding up to them all the share he has in the sacrifice; that a monk is not excommunicated for laying aside his dress, when he does it to dance, pick pockets, or go incognito into houses of bad fame; and that the injunction to hear mass is satisfied by listening at once to the different parts of four masses, by different priests;" when I say we hear these and such like decisions, it is impossible that surprise should not make us laugh, because nothing tends more to excite laughter than a ridiculous disproportion between what is expected and what appears. And how could the greater part of these matters be treated otherwise, since, according to Tertullian, "to treat them seriously would be to give them weight?"

What! must the power of Scripture and tradition be employed to show, that you kill an enemy in treachery, if you stab him from behind and in ambuscade; that you purchase a benefice if you give money as a motive to make another resign it. These are matters, then, which must be despised, and which deserve to *be derided and sported with.* In fine, the remark of this ancient author, that *nothing is more due to vanity than laughter,* and the rest of the passage, apply here so exactly and with such convincing force as to leave no room for doubt, that we may well laugh at error without offending propriety.

I will tell you, moreover, fathers, that we may laugh at it without offending charity, although this is one of the charges which you still bring against me in your writings: " For charity sometimes obliges us to laugh at men's errors, in order to induce themselves to laugh at them and shun them;" so says St. Augustine: *Hæc tu misericorditer irride, ut eis ridenda ac fugienda commendes."* And the same charity, also, sometimes obliges us to repel them with anger, according to the saying of St. Gregory of Nazianzen: " the spirit of charity and meekness has its emotions and passions." In fact, as St. Augustine says, " Who would dare to maintain that truth should remain disarmed against falsehood, and that the enemies of the faith should be permitted to frighten believers with strong words, or delight them with pleasing displays of wit, while the orthodox must only write with a coldness of style which sets the reader asleep?"

Is it not obvious that by so acting we should allow the most extravagant and pernicious errors to be introduced into the Church, without being permitted to express contempt lest we should be charged with offending propriety, or vehemently to confute them lest we should be charged with want of charity?

What, fathers! you shall be allowed to say that *a man may kill to avoid a blow or an injustice,* and we shall not be permitted publicly to refute a public error of such moment? You shall be at liberty to say that *a judge may in conscience retain what he has received for doing injustice,* and we shall not be at liberty to contradict you? You shall print with privilege and the approbation of your doctors, that *we may be saved without ever having loved God,* and then shut the mouths of those who would defend the true faith, by telling them they will violate brotherly charity, by attacking you, and Christian moderation, by laughing at your maxims? I doubt, fathers, if there are any persons in whom you have been able to instil this belief; but, nevertheless, if there should be any who are so persuaded, and who think that I have violated the charity which I owe you, I wish much they would examine what it is within them that gives birth to this sentiment; for, although they imagine it to proceed from zeal, which will not allow them to see their neighbour accused without feeling offended, I would beg them to consider it as not impossible that it may have another source; that it is by no means improbable that it may be owing to a secret dislike, often unconscious, which our corrupt nature never fails to excite against those who oppose laxity of morals. To furnish them with a rule which may enable them to detect the true principle, I will ask them, whether, while they complain that monks have been so treated, they do not complain still more that monks should have so treated the truth. If they feel irritated, not only against the letters, but still more against the maxims therein referred to, I will admit it to be possible that their resentment proceeds from some degree of zeal, though a zeal by no means enlightened; and, in this case, the passages quoted above will suffice to enlighten them. But if they are indignant only against the censure, and not against the things censured, verily, fathers, I will not hesitate to tell them that they are grossly mistaken, and that their zeal is very blind.

Strange zeal, which feels irritated against those who expose public faults, and not against those who commit them! Strange charity, which is offended when it sees manifest errors confuted, and not offended at seeing morality overthrown by these errors! Were these persons in danger of assassination, would they be offended at being warned of the ambuscade which is being laid for them; and, instead of turning out of their way, to avoid it, would they go forward amusing themselves with complaints of the little charity displayed in discovering the criminal design of the assassins? Are they irritated when told not to eat of a dish which is poisoned, or not to go into a town, because the plague is in it?

Whence comes it, then, that they think it a want of charity to expose maxims injurious to religion; and, on the contrary, would think it a want of charity not to warn them of things injurious to their health and life, but just that the love they have for life makes them give a favourable reception to whatever tends to preserve it, while the indifference which they feel for truth causes them not only to take no part in its defence, but even to regret any effort to put down falsehood?

Let them consider, then, as before God, to what an extent the morality which your casuists diffuse on every side is insulting and pernicious to the Church; how scandalous and unmeasured the licence which they introduce into morals; how obstinate and fierce your effrontery in defending them. And if they do not think it time to rise against such disorders, their blindness will be as much to be pitied as your own, fathers, since you and they have like cause to dread the woe which St. Augustine adds to that of our Saviour, in the Gospel: Woe to the blind who lead! woe to the blind who are led! *Væ cœcis ducentibus! væ cœcis sequentibus!*

But, in order that you no longer may have any pretext for giving these impressions to others, nor adopting them yourselves, I will tell you, fathers, (and I am ashamed at your obliging me to tell you what I ought to learn from you,) I will tell you what test the Church has given us to judge whether reproof proceeds from a spirit of piety and charity, or from a spirit of impiety and hatred.

The first of these rules is, that the spirit of piety always disposes us to speak with truth and sincerity; whereas envy and hatred employ falsehood and calumny: *Splendentia et vehementia, sed rebus veris,* says St. Augustine. Whosoever makes use of falsehood is actuated by the spirit of the devil. No direction of intention can rectify calumny; and though the object were to convert the whole earth, it would not be lawful to blacken the innocent, because we must not do the least evil to secure the success of the greatest good; and, as Scripture says, "the truth of God has no need of our lie." "It is incumbent on the defenders of truth," says St. Hilary, "to advance only what is true." Accordingly, fathers, I can declare before God, that nothing do I detest more than to offend truth in any degree however small, and that I have always been particularly careful, not only not to falsify it (which would be horrible), but not to alter or give the slightest colour to the meaning of any passage; so, that if I presumed on this occasion to appropriate the words of the same St. Hilary, I might well say with him, "If the things I say are false, let my discourse be held infamous; but if I show that the things alleged are public and manifest, I do not exceed the bounds of modesty and liberty in reproving them."

But it is not enough to say only what is true; it is necessary, moreover, to abstain from saying all that is true, because we ought only to state what is useful, and not what can only hurt, without conferring any benefit. And thus, as the first rule is to speak truly, the second is to speak discreetly. "The wicked," says St. Augustine, "persecute the good, in blindly following the passion which animates them; whereas the good persecute the wicked with a wise discretion, just as surgeons are careful when they cut, while murderers care not where they strike." You know well, fathers, that in quoting the maxims of your authors, I have not produced those to which you would have been most sensitive, though I might have done it without sinning against discretion, as learned and orthodox men have done it before. All who have read your authors know as well as yourselves, how much I have spared you in this respect; besides, I have not spoken a word with reference to the concerns of any individual among you; and I should be sorry to have adverted to secret and personal faults, whatever proof I might have had of them, for I know that this is the characteristic of hatred and enmity, and ought never to be done unless the good of the Church imperatively demand it. It is plain, then, that I have in no respect acted without discretion, in what I have been obliged to say respecting the maxims of your morality; and that you have more cause to congratulate yourselves on my reserve than to complain of my severity.

The third rule, fathers, is: That when we are obliged to use ridicule, the spirit of piety will dispose us to use it only against error, and not against holy things; whereas the spirit of buffoonery, impiety, and heresy, laughs at all that is most sacred. I have already justified myself on this point;

and besides, it is a vice into which there is very little danger of falling when one has only to speak of the opinions which I have quoted from your authors.

In fine, fathers, to abridge these rules, I will further mention only this one, which is the principle and end of all the others, namely, That the spirit of charity will dispose us to have a heartfelt desire of the salvation of those against whom we speak, and to offer up prayers to God at the same time that we administer reproof to men. "We must always," says St. Augustine, "preserve charity in the heart, even when outwardly we are obliged to do what men may think rude, and strike with a harsh, but benign severity, their advantage being to be preferred to their satisfaction." I believe, fathers, that nothing in my letters indicates that I have not had this desire on your account, and thus charity obliges you to believe that I have had it in effect when you see nothing to the contrary. From this, then, it appears you cannot show that I have sinned against this rule, or against any of those which charity obliges us to follow; and therefore you have no right to say that I have violated it in what I have done.

But, fathers, if you would now have the pleasure of seeing a brief description of a conduct which sins against each of these rules, and really bears the characteristics of the spirit of buffoonery, envy, and hatred, I will furnish you with examples; and that they may be the better known, and more familiar to you, I will take them from your own writings.

To begin with the unworthy manner in which your authors speak of sacred things, whether in their ridicule, their gallantry, or their serious discourse, do you consider the many ridiculous tales of your Father Binet in his 'Consolation to the Sick,' well adapted to his professed design of giving Christian consolation to those whom God afflicts? Will you say, that the profane and coquettish manner in which your 'Father Le Moine has spoken of piety, in his 'Easy Devotion,' is better fitted to produce respect than contempt for the idea which he forms of Christian virtue? Does his whole volume of 'Moral Portraits,' both in its prose and verse, breathe anything but a spirit filled with vanity and worldly folly? Is there ought worthy of a priest in the ode of the seventh book, entitled, 'Praise of Modesty, in which it is shown that all pretty things are red, or given to blush?' He composed it for a lady, whom he calls Delphine, to console her for her frequent blushing. Accordingly, in each stanza he says that some of the things most esteemed are red, as roses, pomegranates, the lips, the tongue. With this gallantry, disgraceful to a monk, he has the insolence to introduce the blessed spirits who officiate in the presence of God, and of whom Christians should always speak with veneration:

> Les chérubins, ces glorieux,
> Composés de tête et de plume,
> Que Dieu de son esprit allume,
> Et qu'il éclaire de ses yeux;
> Ces illustres faces volantes
> Sont toujours rouges et brûlantes,
> Soit du feu de Dieu, soit du leur,
> Et dans leurs flammes mutuelles
> Font du mouvement de leurs ailes
> Un éventail à leur chaleur.
>
> Mais la rougeur éclate en toi,
> DELPHINE, avec plus d'avantage,
> Quand l'honneur est sur ton visage
> Vêtu de pourpre comme un roi, etc.*

What say you to this, fathers? Does this preference of Delphine's blush to the ardour of those spirits, who have no other ardour than that of charity, and the comparison of a fan to their mysterious wings, appear to you very Christian-like in lips which consecrate the adorable body of Jesus Christ? I know he only said it to play the gallant, and for fun; but this is what we call laughing at sacred things. And, is it not true, that if justice were done him, nothing could save him from censure? although, in defence, he should urge a reason which is itself not less censurable, and is stated in book first, namely, "that Sorbonne has no jurisdiction on Parnassus, and that the errors of that land are not subject either to censures or to the Inquisition," as if it were only forbidden to be an impious man, and a blasphemer, in prose. But at least this would not ward off censure from the following passage in the advertisement to the book: "The water of the stream on whose banks he composed his verses, is so well fitted to make poets, that were it converted into holy water, it would not drive away the demon of poesy." No more would it secure your Father Garasse, who, in his 'Summary of the Leading Truths of Religion,' joins blasphemy with heresy, by speaking of the sacred mystery of the Incarnation in this manner: "The human personality was grafted, or rode, as if on horseback, upon the personality of the Word!" In another passage from the same author, p. 510, without quoting many others, it is said, on the subject of the name of Jesus, usually printed thus, I.H̄.S. "Some have taken away the cross, and used the letters merely thus, I. H. S., which is a Jesus with his clothes off."

In this unworthy manner do you treat the truths of religion, contrary to the inviolable rule which obliges us always to speak of them with reverence. But you sin no less against the rule which obliges always to speak with truth and discretion. What is more usual in your writings than calumny? Are those of Father Brisacier candid? And does he speak with truth, when he says, part 4, pp. 24, 25, "that the nuns of Port Royal do not pray to the saints, and have no images in their church?" Are not these very bold falsehoods, seeing the contrary is manifest to the view of all Paris? And does he speak with discretion when he slanders the innocence of those daughters, whose lives are so pure and so austere, calling them *impenitent, unsacramentary, non-communicating nuns, foolish virgins, fantastical, Calagan, desperate; any thing you please;* and blackening them by the many other calumnies, which brought down upon him the censure of the late Archbishop of Paris; when he calumniates priests of irreproachable manners, so far as to say, part 1, p. 22, "that they practise novelties in confession, to entrap the fair and innocent, and that it would horrify him to relate the abominable crimes which they commit?" Is it not insufferable hardihood, to advance such black impostures, not only without proof, but without the least shadow and semblance? I will not dilate further on this subject. I defer it, intending to speak of it to you more at length another time, for I have yet to speak with you on this matter; and what I have now said is sufficient to let you see how much you sin alike against truth, and against discretion.

But it will perhaps be said that you at least do not sin against the last rule, which obliges us to desire the salvation of those whom we attack, and that you cannot be accused of this without violating the secret of your heart, which is known to God only. It is strange, fathers, that we, nevertheless, have the means of convicting you, even here, and that your hatred against your adversaries having carried you the length of wishing their eternal ruin, you have been blind enough to disclose this abominable wish; that so far from secretly forming wishes for their salvation, you have publicly made vows for their damnation; and after giving utterance to this miserable feeling in the town of Caen, to the scandal of the whole Church, you have since dared, in your printed works, to justify the diabolical act even at Paris. To such outrages on piety nothing can be added; such outrages as ridiculing and speaking unbecomingly of the most sacred things; uttering the falsest and vilest calumnies against virgins and priests; and, in fine, entertaining desires and putting up prayers for their damnation. I know not, fathers, how you avoid feeling confounded, and how you could even think of charging me with want of charity—me, who have spoken with so much truth and reserve—without calling to mind the fearful violations of charity which you yourselves commit by such deplorable outbreaks.

To conclude with another charge which you bring against me. Because, among the numerous maxims to which I refer, there are some which were objected to before, you complain *that I again say against you what had been said.* I answer, it is just because you have not profited by what was said that I again repeat it. For where is the fruit of the many written rebukes which you have received from learned doctors, and from the whole university? What have your fathers, Annat, Caussin, Pintereau, and Le Moine done, in the replies which they have made, but showered down insult on those who had given them salutary advice? Have you suppressed the books in which those wicked maxims are taught? Have you silenced the authors of them? Are you become more circumspect? Is it not since then that Escobar has been so often printed in France and in the Low Countries; while your fathers, Cellot, Bagot, Bauni, L'Amy, Le Moine, etc., cease not daily to publish the same things, and new ones, morever, as licentious as ever? Complain no longer, then, fathers, either that I have upbraided you for the maxims which you have not given up, or that I have objected to your new ones, and laughed at all. You have only to consider them, in order to behold your own confusion and my defence. Who can refrain from laughing at father Bauni's decision, regarding the man who sets fire to a granary; or that of father Cellot on restitution; the rule of Sanchez, in favour of sorcerers; the manner in which Hurtado avoids the sin of duelling, by walking in a field, and there waiting for a man; the contrivances of father Bauni to avoid usury; the mode of avoiding simony by a detour of intention and falsehood, by speaking at one time loud, at another low; and all the other opinions of your gravest doctors? Is more wanted, fathers, for my justification? and, as Tertullian says, is any thing more "due to the vanity and silliness of these opinions than laughter?" But, fathers, the corruption of manners which your maxims introduce must be treated differently, and we may well ask, with Tertullian again, "Whether should we ridicule their weakness or deplore their blindness?" *Rideam vanitatem, an exprobrem cœcitatem?* I believe, fathers, "we may laugh and weep in turn;" *hæc tolerabilius vel ridentur vel flentur,* says St. Augustine. Acknowledge, then, with Scripture, that "there is a time to laugh, and a time to weep." I wish, fathers, I may not experience in you the truth of a common proverb: "There are persons so unreasonable that there is no satisfaction in whatever way we deal with them, whether laughing or in anger."

LETTER TWELFTH.

TO THE REVEREND JESUIT FATHERS.

REFUTATION OF THE JESUIT QUIBBLES ON ALMS AND SIMONY.

9th September, 1656.

REVEREND FATHERS,—I was prepared to write you on the subject of the insulting epithets which you have so long applied to me in your writings, in which you call me *impious, buffoon, ignorant, farcer, impostor, calumniator, cheat, heretic, Calvinist in disguise, disciple of Du Moulin, possessed with a legion of devils,* and whatever else you please. I wish to let the world understand why you treat me in this fashion, for I would be sorry it should believe all this of me; and I had resolved to complain of your calumnies and impostures, when I saw your replies, in which you yourselves bring the same charge against myself; you have thereby obliged me to change my purpose, and yet I will still, in some measure, continue it, since I hope, while defending myself, to convict you of real impostures, in greater number than the false ones with which you charge me. Indeed, fathers, you are more suspected than I; for it is not probable, that single as I am, without power, and without human support, against so great a body, and sustained only by truth and sincerity, I have run the risk of losing every thing, by exposing myself to be convicted of imposture. In questions of fact like these, it is too easy to detect falsehood. I should not want people to accuse me, and justice would not be denied them. You, on the other hand, fathers, are not in those circumstances; and you may say against me whatever you please, while there is none to whom

I can complain. Such being the difference of our conditions, I must exercise no little self-restraint, though I were not inclined to it by other considerations. Meanwhile you treat me as a notorious impostor, and you thus force me to reply; but you know that this cannot be done without a new exposure, and even without going deeper into the points of your moral system; in this I doubt if you are good politicians. The war is carried on in your country, and at your expense; and though you have thought that by darkening the questions with scholastic terms, the answer would thereby become so long, so obscure, and so perplexing, that the relish for them would be lost, it will not perhaps be altogether so; for I will try to weary you as little as possible with this kind of writing. Your maxims have something so unaccountaby diverting, that every body is amused with them. Only remember that you yourselves oblige me to enter upon this explanation; and let us see which of us will make the best defence.

The first of your impostures is on "*Vasquez' opinions concerning alms.*" Allow me, then, to explain it precisely, that there may be no obscurity in our debate. It is very well known, fathers, that according to the mind of the Church, there are two precepts in regard to alms: the one, "to give of our superfluity in the ordinary necessities of the poor;" and the other, "to give even what is necessary for our station, when the necessity of the poor is extreme." So says Cajetan, after St. Thomas; and hence, in order to exhibit the spirit of Vasquez, touching alms, it is necessary to show how he has regulated what we ought to give, as well out of our superfluity as out of our necessary.

Alms from superfluity, which form the ordinary supply of the poor, are entirely abolished by this single maxim of El., c. 4, n. 14, which I have quoted in my Letters: "What men of the world reserve to keep up their own station and that of their kindred, is not called superfluity; and hence it will scarcely be found that there ever is any superfluity in men of the world, or even in kings." You see plainly, fathers, that by this definition, all who have ambition have no superfluity; and that thus almsgiving is annihilated, in regard to the greater part of mankind. But even those who should have superfluity are dispensed from giving it in common necessities, according to Vasquez, who is opposed to such as would oblige the rich to give. Here are his words, c. 1, n. 32: "Corduba teaches, that when we have superfluity, we are obliged to give to those who are in an ordinary necessity; at least, a part of it, so as to fulfil the precept in some degree; *but I don't think so; sed hoc non placet; for we have shown the contrary against Cajetan and Navarre.*" Thus, fathers, the obligation to give such alms is absolutely overthrown, according to the view which Vasquez takes.

As to the necessary which we are obliged to give in cases of extreme and pressing necessity, you will see by the conditions which he introduces in forming this obligation, that the wealthiest in Paris cannot be bound by it once in their lives. I will mention only two of them. The one is, "*we must know* that the poor person will not be relieved by any other; *hæc intelligo et cætera omnia, quando* scio *nullum alium opem laturum,*" c. 1, n. 28. What say you, fathers? Will it often happen that in Paris, where there are so many charitable persons, we can know that nobody will be found to assist a poor person, who is applying to us? And yet, if we have not this knowledge, we may send him off without relief, according to Vasquez. The other condition is, that the necessity of the poor applicant must be such, that "he is threatened with some mortal accident, or with the loss of his reputation," (n. 24, 26,) a case very far from common. But what shows its rarity still more is, that according to him, n. 45, the poor man who is in such a state as founds an obligation on us to give him alms, "may in conscience rob the rich man." And hence the case must be very extraordinary, unless he insist that it is ordinarily lawful to rob. Thus, after destroying the obligation to give alms of our superfluity, which is the chief source of charity, he obliges the rich to assist the poor out of their necessary only when he permits the poor to rob the rich. Such is the doctrine of Vasquez, to which you refer your readers for their edification.

I come now to your Impostures. You dilate at first on the obligation which Vasquez lays upon ecclesiastics to give alms;

but I have not spoken of this, and will speak when you please. There is no question about it here. As to the laity, of whom alone we speak, it seems as if you wished it to be understood that, in the passage which I have quoted, Vasquez only gives the view of Cajetan, and not his own. But as nothing is more false, and you have not said it distinctly, I am willing to believe, for your honour, that you did not mean to say it.

You afterwards complain loudly, that after having quoted this maxim of Vasquez, "Scarcely will it be found that men of the world, and even kings, ever have any superfluity," I have inferred that "the rich are scarcely obliged to give alms of their superfluity." But what do you mean, fathers? If it is true that the rich have seldom, if ever, any superfluity, is it not certain that they will seldom, if ever, be obliged to give alms of their superfluity? I would give you the argument in form, had not Vasquez, who esteems Diana so highly, that he calls him the "phœnix of minds," drawn the same inference from the same principle; for, after quoting Vasquez's maxim, he concludes, "that in the question, whether the rich are obliged to give alms of their superfluity, although the opinion which obliges them were true, it would never or seldom ever happen, that it was obligatory in practice." In all the discussion, I have only followed him word for word. What, then, is the meaning of this, fathers? When Diana quotes Vasquez's sentiments with eulogy, when he finds them probable, and very "convenient for the rich," as he says in the same place, he is neither calumniator nor forger, and you make no complaint of imposture; whereas, when I exhibit these same sentiments of Vasquez, but without treating him as a *phœnix*, I am an impostor, a forger, a corrupter of his maxims. Certainly, fathers, you have ground to fear that the different treatment you give those who differ not in their report, but only in the estimation in which they hold your doctrine, will discover the bottom of your heart, and make it apparent that your principal object is to maintain the credit of your Company. So long as your accommodating theology passes for wise condescension, you do not disavow those who publish it, but, on the contrary, laud them as contributing to your design. But when it is denounced as pernicious laxity, then the same interest of your Society leads you to disavow maxims which injure you in the world; and thus you acknowledge them, or renounce them, not according to truth, which never changes, but according to the diversities of time, as an ancient writer expressed it: "*Omnia pro tempore, nihil pro veritate.*" Take care, fathers; and that you may no longer charge me with drawing from Vasquez's principle an inference which he would have disavowed, know that he has drawn it himself, c. 1, n. 27, "Scarcely are we obliged to give alms when we are only obliged to give it of our superfluity, according to the opinion of Cajetan, and according to MINE; *et secundum nostram.*" Confess, then, fathers, that I have exactly followed his idea; and consider with what conscience you have dared to say, that "on going to the source it would be seen with astonishment, that he there teaches quite the contrary."

But the point on which you lay your principal stress is when you say, that if Vasquez does not oblige the rich to give alms of their superfluity, he in return obliges them to give alms of their necessary. But you have forgotten to specify the combination of conditions which he declares necessary to constitute this obligation; these, which I have stated, restrict it so much that they almost entirely annihilate it. Instead of thus candidly explaining his doctrine, you say, generally, that he obliges the rich to give even what is necessary to their station. This is saying too much, fathers; the rule of the Gospel does not go so far; it would be another error, though one which is far from being Vasquez's. To screen his laxity you attribute to him an excessive strictness, which would be reprehensible, and thereby deprive yourselves of all credit for being faithful reporters. But he does not deserve this reproach, since his doctrine is, as I have shown, that the rich are not obliged, either in justice or charity, to give of their superfluity, and still less of their necessary, in all the ordinary wants of the poor; and that they are only obliged to give of their necessary on emergencies so rare, that they almost never happen.

This is all you object to me, and, therefore, it only remains for me to show how false it is to pretend that Vasquez is stricter than Cajetan. This will be very easy, since the cardinal teaches that "we are bound in justice to give alms of our superfluity, even in the common necessities of the poor; because, according to the holy Fathers, the rich are only the stewards of their superfluity, to give it to whomsoever of the needy they may select." And thus, whereas Diana speaks of maxims "very convenient and very agreeable to the rich, and to their confessors," the cardinal, who has not like consolation, declares, De Eleem., c. 6, "that he has nothing to say to the rich, but these words of Jesus Christ: It is easier for a camel to go through the eye of a needle, than for a rich man to enter the kingdom of heaven: and to their confessors; If the blind lead the blind, they shall both fall into the ditch." So indispensable did he consider the obligation! This, accordingly, the saints and all the Fathers have laid down as an invariable truth. St. Thomas says, 2. 2, q. 118, art. 4, "There are two cases in which we are obliged to give alms as a just debt; *ex debito legali;* the one, when the poor are in danger; the other, when we possess superfluous goods." And, q. 87, a. 1, "The three-tenths which the Jews were to eat with the poor have been augmented under the new law; because, Jesus Christ requires us to give to the poor not only the tenth part, but all our superfluity." And yet Vasquez is unwilling that we should be obliged to give even a part of it; such is his complaisance to the rich and his hardness to the poor; such his opposition to those feelings of charity, which give a charm to the truth contained in the following words of St. Gregory; truth, however, which to the rich men of the world appears so rigid: "When we give to the poor what their necessity requires, we do not so much give what is ours, as restore what is their own: it is a debt of justice rather than a work of mercy."

In this fashion do the saints recommend the rich to share their worldly goods with the poor, if they would with the poor possess heavenly blessings. And, whereas, you labour to encourage men in ambition, owing to which they never have superfluity, and avarice, which refuses to give it when they have; the saints have laboured, on the contrary, to dispose men to give their superfluity, and to convince them that they will have much if they measure it not by cupidity which suffers no limits, but piety which is ingenious in retrenching, in order to have the means of diffusing itself in acts of charity. " We shall have much superfluity," says St. Augustine, " if we confine ourselves to what is necessary; but if we seek after vanity, nothing will suffice. Seek, brethren, as much as suffices for the work of God," in other words, for nature, " and not what suffices for your cupidity," which is the work of the devil; " and remember that the superfluity of the rich is the necessary of the poor."

I wish much, fathers, that what I say might not only have the effect of justifying myself (that were little), but also of making you feel and abhor what is corrupt in the maxims of your casuists, that we might thus be sincerely united in the holy rules of the Gospel, by which we are all to be judged.

As to the second point, which regards simony, before answering the charges which you bring against me, I will begin by explaining your doctrine on the subject. Finding yourselves embarrassed between the canons of the Church, which inflict fearful penalties on simonists, and the avarice of the many persons inclined to this infamous traffic, you have followed your ordinary method, which is to grant men what they desire, and give to God words and semblances. For what do simonists want, but just money, for bestowing their benefices? And it is this that you have exempted from simony. But, because the name of simony must remain, and there must be a subject to which it may be annexed, you have chosen for this an imaginary idea, which never enters the minds of simonists, and which would be of no use to them, namely, to value the money considered in itself as highly as the spiritual good considered in itself. For, who would think of comparing things so disproportioned, and so different in kind? And yet, provided this metaphysical comparison is not drawn, one may give his benefice to another, and receive money for it without simony, according to your authors.

It is thus you sport with religion, to favour the passions of men; and yet see, notwithstanding, with what gravity your Father Valentia deals out his dreams at the place quoted in my letters, tom. 3, disp. 16, p. 2044: "We may give a temporal for a spiritual in two ways: the one, while prizing the temporal more than the spiritual, and this would be simony; the other, while taking the temporal as the motive and end, which determines us to give the spiritual, without, however, prizing the temporal more than the spiritual, and then it is not simony. And the reason is, because simony consists in receiving a temporal as the exact price of a spiritual. Hence, if the temporal is asked, *si petatur temporale*, not as the price, but as the motive, which determines to bestow it, it is not at all simony, although the end and principal expectation be the possession of the temporal; *minime erit simonia, etiamsi temporale principaliter intendatur et expectetur.*" And has not your great Sanchez made a similar discovery, according to the report of Escobar, tr. 6, ex. 2, n. 40? Here are his words: "If a temporal good is given for a spiritual good, not as a *price*, but as a *motive*, determining the collator to bestow it, or as a grateful acknowledgment if it has already been received, is it simony? Sanchez affirms that it is not." Your Theses of Caen, of 1644, say, "A probable opinion taught by several Catholics is, that it is not simony to give a temporal good for a spiritual, when it is not given as the price." As to Tannerus, here is his doctrine, similar to that of Valentia, which will show that you are wrong to complain of my having said that it is not conformable to that of St. Thomas, since he himself admits this at the place quoted in my letter, t. 3, d. 5, p. 1519: "Properly and truly there is no simony unless in taking a temporal good as the price of a spiritual; but when it is taken as a motive disposing to give the spiritual, or as an acknowledgment for its having been given, it is not simony, at least in conscience." And, a little farther on: "The same thing must be said, even should the temporal be regarded as the spiritual motive, and be even preferred to the spiritual; although St. Thomas and others seem to say the contrary, inasmuch as they affirm that it is absolute simony to give a spiritual good for a temporal, when the temporal is the end.

Such, fathers, is your doctrine of simony, as taught by your best authors, who in this follow each other very exactly. It only remains for me, then, to reply to your impostures. You have said nothing of the opinion of Valentia, and thus his doctrine remains as before your reply. But you stop at that of Tannerus, and say that he has only decided that it was not simony by divine law; and you wish it to be believed that I have suppressed the words *divine law*. In this you are unreasonable, fathers, for the words *divine law* never were in this passage. You afterwards add that Tannerus declares it simony by *positive law*. You are mistaken, fathers; he has not said so generally, but in particular cases, *in casibus a jure expressis*, as he says at this place. In this he makes an exception to what he had established, generally, in this passage, namely, "that it is not simony in conscience," which implies that it is not simony by positive law, unless you would make Tannerus profane enough to maintain that simony by positive law is not simony in conscience. But you search about purposely for the words "divine law, positive law, natural law, external and internal tribunal, cases expressed in law, external presumption," and others little known, that you may make your escape under the cloud, and lead away the attention from your errors. Nevertheless, fathers, you shall not escape by these vain subtleties, for I will put questions to you so simple that they will not be subject to the *distinguo*.

I ask you, then, without speaking of *positive law*, or *presumption of external tribunal*, if a beneficed person will be a simonist, according to your authors, by giving a benefice of four thousand livres annually, and receiving ten thousand francs in cash, not as the price of the benefice, but as a motive determining him to give it. Answer me distinctly, fathers; what is the decision on this case according to your authors? Will not Tannerus say formally, that "it is not simony in conscience, since the temporal is not the price of the benefice, but only the motive which makes it to be given?" Will not Valentia, your Theses of Caen, Sanchez and Escobar, in like manner decide that "it is not simony," and for the same reason? Is more necessary to exempt this beneficiary from simony; and would you dare to treat him as a simonist in your confessionals, whatever your private opinion of him might be, since he would be entitled to shut your mouths by having acted on the opinion of so many grave doctors? Confess that, according to you, this beneficiary is exempt from simony; and now defend this doctrine if you can.

This, fathers, is the way to treat questions, in order to unravel them, instead of perplexing them either by scholastic terms, or by changing the state of the question, as you do in your last charge, and in this way, Tannerus, you say, declares at least that such an exchange is a great sin, and you reproach me with having maliciously suppressed the circumstance, which, as you pretend, *justifies him entirely*. But you are wrong, and in several respects. For, were what you say true, the question at the place I referred to was not whether there was sin, but only if there was simony. Now, these are two very distinct questions: sins, according to your maxims, only oblige to confession; simony obliges to restore; and there are persons to whom that would appear very different. For you have indeed found expedients to make confession mild; but you have not found means to render restitution agreeable. I have to tell you, moreover, that the case which Tannerus charges with sin is not simply that in which a spiritual good is given for a temporal, which is even its principal motive; but he adds, *where the temporal is prized more than the spiritual;* and this is the imaginary case of which we have spoken. And it does no harm to charge that with sin, since one would require to be very wicked, or very stupid, not to wish to avoid sin by means so easy as that of abstaining to compare the price of these two things, while the one is allowed to be given for the other. Besides, Valentia, at the place already quoted, examining whether there is sin in giving a spiritual good for a temporal, which is the principal motive, states the grounds of those who answer affirmatively, adding, "*Sed hoc non videtur mihi satis certum;* this does not seem to me quite certain."

Since that time, your father, Erade Bille, professor of cases of conscience, has decided that there is no sin in this; for probable opinions always go on ripening. This he declares in his writings of 1644, against which M. Du Pré doctor and professor at Caen, composed his fine printed address, which is very well known. For although this Father Erade Bille acknowledges that the doctrine of Valentia, followed by Father Milhard, and condemned in Sorbonne, is "contrary to the common sentiment suspected of simony in several respects, and punished by the law when the practice of it is discovered," he still hesitates not to say that it is a probable opinion, and consequently safe in conscience, and that there is neither simony nor sin in it. "It is," says he, "a probable opinion, and taught by many orthodox doctors, that there is no simony, and *no sin* in giving money, or another temporal thing, for a benefice, whether by way of gratitude, or as a motive, without which it would not be given, provided it is not given as a price equivalent to the benefice." This is all that can be desired. These maxims, as you see, fathers, make simony so rare, that they would have exculpated Simon Magus himself, who sought to purchase the Holy Ghost, in which he is the type of the purchasing simonist; and Gehazi, who received money for a miracle, and is therein the type of the selling simonist. For it cannot be doubted, that when Simon, in the Acts, *offered the apostles money* to obtain their power of working miracles, he made no use of the terms *buying*, or *selling*, or *price;* he did nothing more than offer money as a motive to make them give him this spiritual good. Being thus, according to your authors, exempt from simony, he would, if he had known your maxims, have been secure against the anathema of St. Peter. This ignorance, likewise, did great harm to Gehazi, when he was struck with leprosy by Elisha; for, having received money from the prince who had been miraculously cured, only as a grateful return, and not as a price equivalent to the divine virtue which had performed the miracle, he could have obliged Elisha to cure him under pain of mortal sin, since he would have acted with the sanction of so many grave doctors, and since, in like cases, your confessors are obliged to absolve their penitents, and to wash them from spiritual leprosy, of which corporeal is only a type.

In good sooth, fathers, it would be easy here to turn you into ridicule, and I know not why you lay yourselves open to it; for I would only have to state your other maxims, as that of Escobar, in the 'Practice of Simony according to the Society of Jesus,' n. 40: "Is it simony when two monks mutually stipulate in this way: Give me your vote for the office of Provincial, and I will give you mine for that of Prior? By no means." And this other, tr. 6, n. 14: "It is not simony to obtain a benefice by promising money when there is no intention actually to pay it; because it is only feigned simony, and is no more real than spurious gold is true gold." By this subtlety of conscience he has found means, and through the addition of knavery to simony, to secure benefices without money and without simony. But I have not leisure to say more, for it is now time to defend myself against your third calumny on the subject of bankruptcy.

Than this, fathers, nothing is more gross. You treat me as an impostor with reference to a sentiment of Lessius, which I did not quote for myself, but which is alleged by Escobar, in a passage from which I took it; and hence were it true that Lessius is not of the opinion which Escobar ascribes to him, what could be more unjust than to throw the blame upon me? When I quote Lessius and your other authors for myself, I am willing to answer for my accuracy; but as Escobar has collected the opinions of twenty-four of your doctors, I ask if I should be guarantee for more than I quote from him? and if I must, moreover, be responsible for the accuracy of his quotations in the passages which I have selected? That would not be reasonable; now that is the point considered here. In my letter I gave the following passage from Escobar, faithfully translated, and as to which, moreover, you have said nothing: "Can he who becomes bankrupt retain with a safe conscience as much of his means as may be necessary to live, with honour; *ne indecore vivat?* I answer, yes, with Lessius; *cum Lessio assero posse.*" Hereupon you tell me that Lessius is not of that opinion.

But think a little what you are undertaking; for if it really is the opinion of Lessius, you will be called impostors for asserting the contrary; and if it is not, Escobar will be the impostor; so that it is now absolutely certain that some member of the Society must be convicted of imposture. Consider a little how scandalous this will be! You want discernment to foresee the result of things. It seems to you that you have only to apply insulting epithets to persons, without thinking on whom they are to recoil. Why did you not acquaint Escobar with your difficulty before publishing it? He would have satisfied you. It is not so difficult to have news from Valladolid, where he is in perfect health, completing his great Moral Theology, in six volumes, on the first of which I will be able one day to say something to you. The ten first letters have been sent to him; you might also have sent him your objection, and I feel confident he would have given it a full answer, for he has, doubtless, seen the passage in Lessius from which he has taken the *ne indecore vivat*. Read carefully, fathers, and you will find it there, like me, lib. 2, c. 16, n. 45: "*Idem colligitur aperte ex juribus citatis, maxime quoad ea bona quæ post cessionem acquirit, de quibus is qui debitor est etiam ex delicto, potest retinere quantum necessarium est, ut pro sua conditione* NON INDECORE VIVAT. *Pctes, an leges id permittant de bonis, quæ tempore instantis cessionis habebat? Ita videtur colligi ex D.D.*"

I will not stop to show you that Lessius, in authorizing this maxim, defies the law which allows bankrupts mere livelihood only, and not the means of subsisting with honour. It it is enough to have justified Escobar from your charge; it is more than I was bound to do. But you, fathers, you do not what you are bound to do, namely, to answer the passage of Escobar, whose decisions are very convenient; because, from not being connected with any thing before or after, and being all contained in short articles, they are not subject to your distinctions. I have given you his passage entire, which permits "those who make cessio to retain part of their effects, though acquired unjustly, to enable their family to subsist with honour." On this I exclaimed in my letters, "How, fathers! by what strange charity will you have goods to belong to those who have improperly acquired them, rather than to lawful creditors?" This is what you have to answer; but it throws you into a sad perplexity, and you try to evade it by turning aside from the question, and quoting other passages of Lessius, with which we have nothing to do. I ask you, then, if this maxim of Escobar can be followed in conscience, by those who become bankrupt? Take care what you say. For if you answer, No, what will become of your doctor, and your doctrine of probability? and if you say Yes, I send you to the Parliament.

I leave you in this dilemma, fathers, for I have not room here to take up the next imposture on the passage of Lessius touching homicide. It will be my first, and the rest afterwards.

Meanwhile I say nothing of the advertisements filled with scandalous falshoods, with which you conclude every imposture. I will reply to all this in a letter, in which I hope to trace your calumnies to their source. I pity you, fathers, in having recourse to such remedies. The injurious things which you say to me will not clear up our differences, and the menaces which you hold out in so many modes will not prevent me from defending myself. You think you have force and impunity; but I think I have truth and innocence. All the efforts of violence cannot weaken the truth, and only serve to exalt it the more. All the light of truth cannot arrest violence, and only adds to its irritation. When force combats force, the stronger destroys the weaker; when discourse is opposed to discourse, that which is true and convincing confounds and dispels that which is only vanity and lies; but violence and truth cannot do any thing against each other. Let it not, however, be supposed from this that the things are equal; there is this extreme difference, that the course of violence is limited by the arrangement of Providence, who makes its effects conduce to the glory of the truth which it attacks; whereas truth subsists eternally, and ultimately triumphs over her enemies, because she is eternal and mighty as God himself.

LETTER THIRTEENTH.

TO THE REVEREND JESUIT FATHERS.

THE DOCTRINE OF LESSIUS ON HOMICIDE THE SAME AS THAT OF VICTORIA: HOW EASY IT IS TO PASS FROM SPECULATION TO PRACTICE: WHY THE JESUITS HAVE MADE USE OF THIS VAIN DISTINCTION, AND HOW LITTLE IT SERVES TO JUSTIFY THEM.

30th September, 1656.

REVEREND FATHERS,—I have just seen your last production, in which you continue your impostures as far as the twentieth, declaring that it finishes this sort of accusation which formed your first part, preparatory to the second, in which you are to adopt a new method of defence, by showing that many casuists besides yours are lax as well as you. Now, then, fathers, I see how many impostures I have to answer; and since the fourth, at which we left, is on the subject of homicide, it will be proper, while answering it, to dispose at the same time of the 11th, 13th, 14th, 15th, 16th, 17th, and 18th, which are upon the same subject.

In this letter, then, I will justify the fidelity of my quotations against the inaccuracies which you impute to them. But because you have dared to advance in your writings that the sentiments of your authors on murder are conformable to the decisions of the popes and the ecclesiastical laws, you will oblige me, in my following letter, to put down a statement so rash and so injurious to the Church. It is of importance to show that she is free from your corruptions, and thereby prevent heretics from availing themselves of your corruptions, to draw inferences dishonourable to her. Thus, seeing on one hand your pernicious maxims, and on the other the canons of the Church which have always condemned them, they will at once perceive both what they are to shun and what to follow.

Your fourth imposture is on a maxim respecting murder, which you pretend that I have falsely attributed to Lessius. It is as follows: "He who has received a blow, may at the very instant pursue his enemy, and even with the sword, not to take revenge, but to repair his honour. Here you say that this is the opinion of the casuist Victoria. That is not precisely the subject of dispute; for there is no contradiction in saying that it belongs both to Lessius and Victoria, since Lessius himself says that it belongs to Navarre and your father Henriquez, who teach that he who has received a blow, may, on the very instant, pursue his man, and give him as many strokes as he may judge necessary to repair his honour. The only question, then, is, whether Lessius agrees with these authors as his colleague does. And hence you add, that Lessius refers to this opinion only to refute it, and that thus I, by ascribing to him a sentiment which he adduces only to combat it, do the most cowardly and disgraceful act of which a writer can be guilty. Now, I maintain, fathers, that he adduces it only to follow it. It is a question of fact, which it will be very easy to decide. Let us see, then, how you prove your statement, and you will afterwards see how I prove mine.

To show that Lessius is not of this sentiment, you say that he condemns the practice of it. And to prove this, you refer to a passage, L. 2, c. 9, n. 82, in which he says, "I condemn it in practice." I readily admit that, if we turn to number 82 of Lessius, to which you refer for these words, we will find them. But what will be said, fathers, when it is seen, at the same time, that he there handles a very different question from that of which we are speaking, and that the opinion which he there says he condemns in practice, is not at all that of which he here treats, but one quite distinct. Yet, to be convinced of this, it is only necessary to open the book to which you refer. For the whole sequel of his discourse will be found to be to this effect.

He discusses the question, "Whether one may kill for a blow?" at number 79, and ends at number 80, without using throughout, a single word of disapprobation. This question concluded, he takes up a new one in article 81, namely, "Whether one may kill for evil speaking," and it is here, in number 82, he uses the words which you have quoted: "I condemn it in practice."

Is it not, then, shameful in you, fathers, to produce these words, for the purpose of making it believed that Lessius condemns the opinion, that one may kill for a blow? After producing this one solitary proof, you raise a shout of triumph, and say, "Several persons of distinction in Paris have been aware of this noted falsehood by reading Lessius, and have thereby learned what credit is due to this calumniator." What, fathers! is it thus you abuse the confidence which those persons of distinction place in you? To make them suppose that Lessius is not of a particular opinion, you open his book to them at a place where he condemns a different opinion. And as these persons have no suspicion of your good faith, and think not of examining whether, at that place, he treats of the question in dispute, you take advantage of their credulity. I feel confident, fathers, that to guarantee yourselves against the consequences of this disgraceful falsehood, you must have had recourse to your doctrine of equivocation; and, while reading the passage *aloud*, you said, *quite low*, that he was there treating of a different matter. But I know not if this reason, which indeed suffices to satisfy your conscience, will suffice to satisfy the just complaint which those people of distinction will make, when they find that you have hoaxed them in this way.

Take good care, then, fathers, to prevent them from seeing my letters, since this is the only means left you to preserve your credit some time longer. I do not treat yours in that way: I send them to all my friends; I wish all the world to see them. I believe we are both right; for, at last, after publishing this fourth imposture with so much *éclat*, behold your credit gone if it comes to be known that you have substituted one passage for another. It will readily be concluded that, if you had found what you wanted at the place where Lessius treats of the subject, you would not have gone to seek it elsewhere; and you have betaken yourselves to this shift, because you found nothing else to serve your purpose. You wished to show in Lessius, what you say in your imposture, p. 10, line 12, "that he does not grant that this opinion is probable in speculation," and Lessius says expressly in his conclusion, number 80, "This opinion of the lawfulness of killing for a blow received, is probable in speculation." Is not this, word for word, the reverse of your discourse? And now can one sufficiently admire your hardihood, in producing, in express terms, the opposite of a matter of fact; so that, while you infer that Lessius was not of this opinion, it is inferred very correctly, from the genuine passage, that he is of this opinion.

You wished, also, to make Lessius say that *he condemns it in practice.* And, as I have already said, there is not a single word of condemnation at that place, but he speaks thus, "It seems we should not easily allow it in practice: *In praxi non videtur facile permittenda.*" Fathers, is this the language of a man who condemns a maxim? Would you say that we must not *easily permit* the practice of adultery or incest? Should we not, on the contrary, conclude, that since Lessius says no more than that the practice of it ought not to be easily permitted, his opinion is, that it ought to be permitted sometimes, though rarely. And, as if he had wished to teach the whole world when it ought to be permitted, and to free injured parties from the scruples which might unseasonably disturb them, if they did not know on what occasions they might kill in practice, he has been careful to mark what they ought to avoid, in order to practise it conscientiously. Listen to him, fathers: "It seems it ought not to be easily permitted, *because* of the danger of acting herein from hatred or revenge, or with excess, or lest it should cause too many murders." Hence, it is clear that this murder will, according to Lessius, be quite lawful in practice, if we avoid these inconveniences; in other words, if we can act without hatred, without revenge, and in circumstances which do not lead to too many murders. Do you wish an example, fathers? Here is one of rather recent date. It is the blow of Compiegne. For you will admit that he who received it, proved himself, by his behaviour, master enough of the passions of hatred and revenge. All, then, that remained for him, was to avoid a too great number of murders; and you know, fathers, it is so rare for Jesuits to give blows to officers of the King's household, that there was no ground to fear that a murder on this occasion would have brought many others in its train. Hence, you cannot deny that this Jesuit was killable with a safe conscience, and that, on this occasion, the injured party might have practised upon him the doctrine of Lessius. And, perhaps, fathers, he would have done so, had he been taught in your school, and had he learned from Escobar, that "a man who has received a blow is reputed to be without honour until he has slain him who gave it." But you have ground to believe that the very opposite instructions, given him by a curate to whom you have not too great a liking, contributed not a little, on this occasion, to save the life of a Jesuit.

Speak no more, then, of those inconveniences which can be avoided on so many occasions, and but for which murder is lawful, according to Lessius, even in practice. This, indeed, is acknowledged by many of your authors, quoted by Escobar in the 'Practice of Homicide according to your Society.' "Is it lawful," he asks, "to kill him who has given a blow? Lessius says it is lawful in speculation, but that we must not counsel it in practice, *non consulendum in praxi*, because of the danger of hatred or murder, hurtful to the State, which might ensue. But others have judged that, on avoiding these inconveniences, it is lawful and sure in practice: *In praxi probabilem et tutam, judicarunt Henriquez, etc.* See how opinions gradually rise to the height of probability. For thither have you brought this one, by finally permitting it, without distinction of speculation or practice, in these terms: "It is allowable, when we have received a blow, forthwith to strike with the sword, not for revenge, but to preserve our honour." So taught your fathers at Caen, in 1644, in their public writings, which the University produced to Parliament, when it presented the third petition against your doctrine of homicide, as is seen at p. 339 of the volume which was then printed.

Observe, then, fathers, that your authors, of their own accord, destroy this vain distinction between speculation and practice, which the University had treated with ridicule, and the invention of which is one of the secrets of your policy, which it is right should be understood. For besides that the understanding of it is necessary for the 15th, 16th, 17th and 18th Impostures, it is always seasonable to give gradual developments of the principles of this mysterious policy.

When you undertook to decide cases of conscience in a favourable and accommodating manner, you found some in which religion alone was concerned, as questions of contrition, penitence, the love of God, and all those which only touch the interior of conscience. But you found others in which the State as well as religion has an interest, such as usury, bankruptcy, homicide, and the like. And it is a distressing thing to those who have a true love for the Church, to see that, on an infinity of occasions in which you had only religion to contend with, you have overturned its laws without reserve, without distinction, and without fear, as is seen in your very daring opinions against repentance and the love of God, because you know that this is not the place where God visibly exercises his justice; but in those in which the State is interested as well as religion, apprehension of the justice of men has made you divide your opinions, and form two questions on those subjects; the one, which you call *speculative*, in which, considering the crimes in themselves, without regarding the interest of the State, but only the law of God which forbids them, you have permitted them without hesitation, thus overthrowing the law of God which condemns them; the other, which you call *practical*, in which, considering the damage which the State would receive, and the presence of magistrates who maintain the public safety, you do not always approve in practice of those murders and crimes which you find permitted in speculation, that you may thus screen yourselves from animadversion by the judges. Thus, for example, on the question, whether it is lawful to kill for evil-speaking, your authors, Filiutius, tr. 29, c. 3, n. 52; Reginald, l. 21, c. 5, n. 63, and others answer, "This is lawful in speculation, *Ex probabili opinione licet*, but I do not approve of it in practice, because of the great number of murders which would take place, and do injury to the State, if all evil speakers were killed. Besides, any one killing for this cause, would be punished criminally." In this way it is, that your opinions begin to appear with this distinction, by means of which you only destroy religion, without directly offending the State. You thereby think yourselves secure; for you imagine that the credit which you have in the Church will save your attempts against the truth from being punished, and that the precautions which you give, against readily putting these permissions in practice, will screen you in regard to the magistrates, who not being judges of cases of conscience, have properly an interest only in outward practice. Thus, an opinion which would be condemned under the name of practice, is brought forward in safety under the name of speculation. But the foundation being secured, it is not difficult to rear up the rest of your maxims. There was an infinite distance between the divine prohibition to kill, and the speculative permission of it by your authors; but the distance is very small between this permission and practice. It only remains to show, that what is permitted speculatively, is also permitted practically. Reasons for this will not be wanting. You have found them in more difficult cases. Would you like to see, fathers, how it is accomplished? Follow this reasoning of Escobar, who has distinctly decided it in the first of the six volumes of his great Moral Theology, of which I have spoken to you, and in which he sees things very differently from what he did, when he made his collection of your four-and-twenty elders. At that time, he thought that there could be probable opinions in speculation, which were not safe in practice; but he has since ascertained the contrary, and very well proved it in the later work. Such is the growth, by mere lapse of time, of the doctrine of probability in general, as well as of each probable opinion in particular.

Listen, then, to him, in præloq., n. 15. "I do not see how it can be, that what appears lawful in speculation, should not be so in practice; since, what we may do in practice, depends on what we find permitted in speculation; and these things only differ from each other as the cause from the effect. For it is speculation that determines to action. *Hence it follows, that we may, with a safe conscience, follow in practice opinions, probable in speculation,* and even with more safety than those which have not been so well examined speculatively."

In truth, fathers, your Escobar reasons well enough sometimes. The union between speculation and practice is so close, that when the one has taken root, you have no difficulty in allowing the other to appear without disguise. This was seen in the permission to kill for a blow, which, from simple speculation, has been boldly carried by Lessius to a practice which *should not be* easily permitted; and thence by Escobar to an *easy practice;* whence your fathers of Caen have brought it to a *full permission,* without distinction of theory and practice, as you have already seen.

Thus you make your opinions grow by degrees. Did they appear all at once in their utmost excess, they would cause horror; but this slow and imperceptible progress gently habituates men to them, and takes off the scandal. By this means the permission to kill, a permission so abhorred by the State and by the Church, is first introduced into the Church, and thereafter from the Church into the State.

We have seen a similar success attend the opinion of killing for evil speaking. For, in the present day it has attained to a like permission without any distinction. I would not stop to give you the passages from your fathers, were it not to confound the assurance you have had to say twice, in your fifteenth Imposture, p. 26 and 30, "that there is not a Jesuit who makes it lawful to kill for evil speaking." When you say this, fathers, you ought to prevent me from seeing it, since it is so easy for me to answer. Not only have your fathers Reginald, Filiutius, etc., permitted it in speculation, as I have already said, while the principle of Escobar leads us surely from speculation to practice, but I have to tell you, moreover, that you have several authors who have permitted it in distinct terms; among others, Father Hereau, in his public lectures, for which the king caused his arrest in your house, because, in addition to several other errors, he had taught, that "when one disparages us before persons of distinction, after being warned to desist, it is lawful to kill him, not indeed, in public, for fear of scandal, but secretly; *sed clam.*"

I have already spoken to you of Father L'Amy, and you are not ignorant that his doctrine on this subject was censured in 1649, by the University of Louvain. Nevertheless, not two months ago, your father Des Bois maintained at Rouen the censured doctrine of Father L'Amy, and taught that "it is lawful to a monk to defend the honour which he has acquired by his virtue, EVEN BY KILLING him who attacks his reputation; *etiam cum morte invasoris.*" This caused such scandal in the town, that all the curates united in silencing him, and obliging him to retract his doctrine, by canonical proceedings. The process is at the Officiality.

What do you mean, then, fathers? How do you take it upon you, after this, to maintain that "no Jesuit thinks it lawful to kill for evil speaking?" And was more necessary to convict you, than the very opinions of your fathers which you quote, since they do not prohibit the killing speculatively, but only in practice, "because of the evil which would happen to the State." For I here ask you, whether any other point is debated betwen us than simply whether you have overthrown the law of God which forbids murder. The question is not, whether you have harmed the State, but whether you have harmed religion. Of what use, then, in this discussion, is it to show that you have spared the State, when you at the same time make it apparent that you have destroyed religion, by saying as you do, p. 28, l. 3, "that the meaning of Reginald, on the question of killing for evil speaking, is, that an individual is entitled to use this sort of defence, considering it simply in itself?" I need no more than this avowal for your confutation. "An individual," you say, "is entitled to use this defence;" in other words, to kill for evil speaking, "considering the thing in itself;" consequently, the law of God, which forbids to kill, is overthrown by this decision.

There is no use in saying afterwards, as you do, that "it is unlawful and criminal, even according to the law of God, by reason of the murders and disorder which it would cause in the State, because God obliges us to have respect to the welfare of the State." This is away from the question; for, fathers, there are two laws to be observed; the one which forbids to kill, and the other which forbids injury to the State. Reginald, perhaps, has not violated the law which forbids injury to the State, but he has certainly violated that which forbids to kill. Now, this is the only one which is here considered. Besides, your other authors, who have permitted these murders in practice, have overthrown both the one and the other. But let us get forward, fathers. We are well aware that you sometimes forbid injury to the State; and you say your design in this is to observe the law of God, which enjoins the maintenance of the State. That may be true, although it is not certain, since you might do the same thing, merely from fear of the judges. Let us, then, if you please, examine the principle from which this movement proceeds.

Is it not true, fathers, that if you really looked to God, and if the observance of his law was the first and leading object of your thoughts, this feeling would uniformly predominate in all your important decisions, and dispose you on all these occasions to espouse the interests of religion. But if it is seen, on the contrary, that you, on so many occasions, violate the most sacred injunctions which God has laid upon men whenever his law is the only obstacle, and that on the very occasions of which we speak you annihilate the law of God, which prohibits these actions as criminal in themselves, and show that your only ground for not approving them in practice is fear of the judges, do you not justify the belief that you pay no regard to God in this fear, and that, if you in appearance maintain his law in so far as regards the obligation not to injure the State, it is not for his law itself, but to serve your own ends, just as the least religious politicians have always done?

What, fathers! you will tell us that, if regard is had only to the law of God, which prohibits homicide, we may kill for evil speaking? And after having thus violated the eternal law of God, you think you can remove the scandal you have caused, and persuade us of your respect towards Him, by forbidding the practice of it from State considerations, and fear of the judges? Is not this, on the contrary, to cause new scandal? I do not mean scandal, because of the respect which you thereby testify for judges. It is not for that I reproach you, (and you make a ridiculous play upon it at p. 29.) I do not reproach you for fearing the judges, but for fearing only the judges. It is this I blame, because it is making God less the enemy of crime than men. Did you say that an evil speaker may be killed according to men, but not according to God, it would be less intolerable; but when you pretend that what is too criminal to be allowed by men, is innocent and righteous in the eyes of God, who is righteousness itself, what do you else but show to all the world that by this horrible subversion, so contrary to the spirit of the saints, you are bold against God, and cowardly towards men? Had you been sincere in wishing to condemn those murders, you would not have interfered with the order of God, which forbids them. And had you been daring enough to permit these murders at first, you would have openly permitted them, in defiance of the laws both of God and men. But as you wished to permit them insensibly, and steal by surprise on the magistrates, who watch over the public safety, you have resorted to the finesse of separating your maxims, and propounding on one hand "that it is lawful speculatively to kill for evil speaking," (for you are allowed to examine matters of speculation) and producing, on the other, this isolated maxim, " that what is lawful in speculation, is so, also, in practice." For what interest does the State seem to have in this general and metaphysical proposition? And thus these two unsuspected principles being received separately, the vigilance of the magistrate is lulled to sleep, and nothing more is required than to bring these maxims together, in order to obtain the conclusion at which you aim, namely, that it is lawful in practice to kill for simple slander.

For here, fathers, lies one of the craftiest artifices of your policy, namely, to give a separate place in your writings to the maxims which go together in your opinions. In this way you have separately established your doctrine of probability, which I have often explained. And the general principle being thus secured, you advance propositions separately, which, though possibly innocent in themselves, become horrible when joined to this pernicious principle. As an illustration, I will give the words which you use at p. 11 of your Imposture, and to which it is necessary for me to reply: "Several celebrated theologians are of opinion that we may kill for a blow received." It is quite certain, fathers, that if a person not holding the doctrine of probability had said so, there would be nothing to censure in it. In that case it would only be a simple statement, without any conclusion; but when you, fathers, and all who hold the dangerous doctrine, "that whatever celebrated authors approve is probable and safe in conscience," add to this, "that several celebrated authors are of opinion that one may kill for a blow received," what is this but to place a dagger in the hands of all Christians, to slay those who have offended them, by assuring them that they can do it with a safe conscience, because, in so doing they will follow the opinion of so many grave authors?

What horrible language is this, which, while it says that certain authors hold a damnable opinion, is, at the same time, a decision in favour of this damnable opinion, and authorises in conscience whatever it merely relates! This language of your school, fathers, is now understood; and it is astonishing how you can have the face to speak of it so openly, since it strips your sentiments of all disguise, and convicts you of holding it to be safe in conscience "to kill for a blow," the moment you tell us that this opinion is maintained by several celebrated authors.

You cannot defend yourselves from this, fathers, any more than avail yourselves of the passages of Vasquez and Suarez, with which you oppose me, and in which they condemn the murders which their colleagues approve. These testimonies, separated from the rest of your doctrine, might blind those who do not fully understand it. But it is necessary to bring your principles and your maxims together. You say, then, here, that Vasquez does not permit murder; but what say you on the other hand, fathers? " That the probability of a sentiment does not hinder the probability of its opposite." And, again, "that it is lawful to follow the opinion which is least probable and least safe, while discarding that which is most probable and most safe." What follows from all this taken together, but just that we have entire liberty of conscience to adopt any one of all these opposite opinions that we please? What, then, fathers, becomes of the benefit which you expected from these quotations? It disappears; since, for your condemnation, it is only necessary to bring together those maxims which you separate for your justification. Why produce passages from your authors which I have not quoted, to excuse those which I have quoted, since they have nothing in common? What right does it give you to call me *impostor?* Have I said that all your fathers are equally heterodox? Have I not shown, on the contrary, that your chief interest is to have them of all opinions, in order to supply all your wants? To those who would kill you will present Lessius, to those who would not kill you will produce Vasquez, in order that nobody may retire dissatisfied, and without having a grave author on his side. Lessius will speak as a heathen of homicide, and perhaps as a Christian of alms. Vasquez will speak as a heathen of alms, and as a Christian of homicide. But by means of the probability which Vasquez and Lessius maintain, and which makes all your opinions common, they will lend their sentiments to one another, and will be obliged to give absolution to those who have acted according to the opinions which each of them condemns. This variety, then, confounds you the more. Uniformity would be more tolerable, and there is nothing more contrary to the express order of St. Ignatius and your first generals, than this hotch potch of all sorts of opinions. I may perhaps some day speak of them to you, fathers, and it will cause surprise to see how far you have fallen away from the primitive spirit of your order, and how your own generals foresaw that the impurity of your doctrine in regard to morals, might be fatal not only to your Society, but to the whole Church.

I tell you meantime, that you cannot derive any advantage from the opinion of Vasquez. It would be strange if among so many Jesuits who have written, there should not be one or two who have said what all Christians confess. There is no honour in maintaining, according to the Gospel, that we cannot kill for a blow, but there is horrid disgrace in denying it. This is, therefore, so far from justifying you, that nothing goes farther to overwhelm you, than the fact, that having among you doctors who have told the truth, you have not remained in the truth, and have loved darkness rather than light. For you have learned from Vasquez, "that it is a heathen, and not a Christian opinion, to say that a blow with a fist may be returned by a blow from a stick; it is to overturn the Decalogue and the Gospel, to say that we can kill for a blow; and that the greatest villains among men acknowledge this." And yet, in opposition to these known truths, you have allowed Lessius, Escobar, and others, to decide that all the divine prohibitions against homicide do not hinder it from being lawful to kill for a blow. Of what use, then, is it now to produce this passage from Vasquez, against the sentiment of Lessius, unless it be to show that Lessius is a *Pagan* and a *villain*, according to Vasquez? And this is what I durst not say.. What inference can we draw, unless it be that Lessius overturns the Decalogue and the Gospel; that at the last day Vasquez will condemn Lessius on this point, as Lessius will condemn Vasquez on another; and that all your grave authors will rise up in judgment against each other, and mutually condemn each other, for their frightful excesses against the law of Jesus Christ.

Let us conclude, then, fathers, that since your probability renders the good sentiments of some of your authors useless to the Church, and useful only to your policy, their contrariety only serves to show the duplicity of your heart, which you have completely bared before us, in declaring on the one hand that Vasquez and Suarez are opposed to murder, and on the other, that several celebrated authors are in favour of murder; that you might thus offer two ways to men, thereby destroying the simplicity of the Spirit of God, who pronounces a woe on such as are double-minded, and choose for themselves double ways.

LETTER FOURTEENTH.

TO THE REVEREND JESUIT FATHERS.

THE MAXIMS OF THE JESUITS ON HOMICIDE REFUTED FROM THE FATHERS. ANSWER IN PASSING TO SOME OF THEIR CALUMNIES: THEIR DOCTRINE CONTRASTED WITH THE FORMS OBSERVED IN CRIMINAL TRIALS.

23rd October, 1656.

REVEREND FATHERS,—Had I only to answer the three remaining impostures on homicide, I should have no need of a long discourse. You will see them here refuted in a few words. But as I deem it far more important to give the world an abhorrence for your opinions on this subject, than to justify the fidelity of my quotations, I will be obliged to employ the greater part of this letter in the refutation of your maxims, to represent to you how widely you have wandered from the sentiments of the Church, and even of nature. The permissions to kill, which you give on so many occasions, make it apparent that, in this matter, you have to such a degree forgotten the law of God, and extinguished natural light, that you require to be brought back to the simplest principles of religion and common sense. For what is more natural than the sentiment, that "one individual has no right over the life of another?" "We are so taught this by ourselves," says St. Chrysostom, "that when God gave the commandment not to kill, he did not add, because homicide is an evil; because," says this Father, "the law presumes that we have already learned this truth from nature."

Accordingly, this commandment has been binding on men at all times. The Gospel confirmed that of the law, and the decalogue only renewed that which men had received from God before the law, in the person of Noah, from whom all men were to spring. For at this renewal of the world, God said to Noah, "Surely your blood of your lives will I require; at the hand of every beast will I require it, and at the hand of man. Whoso sheddeth man's blood, by man shall his blood be shed: for in the image of God made he man."

This general prohibition takes away from men all power over the life of men. And so completely has God reserved it to himself alone, that, according to Christian truth, opposed in this to the false maxims of Paganism, man has not even power over his own life. But, because it has pleased his providence to preserve human society, and punish the wicked who disturb it, he has himself established laws for depriving criminals of life; and thus, those deaths which would be punishable misdeeds without his order, become laudable punishments by his order, apart from which every thing is unjust. This has been admirably expounded by St. Augustine, in his City of God, b. i., c. 21. "God himself has somewhat modified this general prohibition to kill, both by the laws which he has established for executing criminals, and by the special orders which he has sometimes given to put individuals to death. In killing, in those cases, it is not man who kills, but God, of whom man is only the instrument, like a sword in the hand of him who uses it. But these cases excepted, whoso kills incurs the guilt of murder."

It is certain, then, fathers, that God alone has a right to take away life, and that, nevertheless, having established laws for adjudging criminals to die, he has made kings or republics the depositories of this power. This St. Paul teaches us, when speaking of the right which sovereigns have to put men to death, he makes it come down from heaven, saying, that "they bear not the sword in vain, because they are the ministers of God, to execute his vengeance on the guilty."

But as God gave them this right, so he obliges them to exercise it as he himself would do, that is, with justice, according to the words of St. Paul, in the same place, "Rulers are not a terror to good works, but to the evil.

Wilt thou, then, not be afraid of the power? do that which is good, and thou shalt have praise of the same: for he is the minister of God to thee for good." And this limitation, far from lowering their power, on the contrary, very highly exalts it; because it makes it like that of God, who is impotent to do evil and omnipotent to do good, and distinguishes it from that of devils, who are impotent for good, and have power only for evil. There is only this difference between God and rulers, that God being justice and wisdom itself, may put to death on the spot whom he pleases, and in what way he pleases. Besides being sovereign master of the life of men, it is certain that he never takes it from them without cause, or without cognizance, since he is as incapable of injustice as of error. But princes may not so act; because, while they are the ministers of God, they are still men, and not gods. Bad impressions might surprise them; false suspicions might sour them; passion might transport them; and it is this which has disposed them, of their own accord, to stoop to human means, and appoint judges in their States, to whom they have communicated this power, in order that the authority which God has given them may only be employed for the end for which they have received it.

Consider, then, fathers, that to be free from murder, it is necessary alike to act by the authority of God, and according to the justice of God; and that if these two conditions are not combined, there is sin either in killing with his authority, but without justice, or in killing with justice, but without his authority. From the necessity of this union, it follows, according to St. Augustine, that " he who without authority kills a criminal, becomes a criminal himself, chiefly on this ground, that he usurps an authority which God has not given him;" and on the contrary, judges who have this authority, are nevertheless murderers if they put an innocent man to death, against the laws which they ought to observe.

Such, fathers, are the principles of tranquillity and public safety, which have been received at all times and in all places, and on which all the legislators of the world, sacred and profane, have founded their laws; not even the heathens having ever made an exception to this rule, save when the loss of chastity or life could not otherwise be avoided, because they thought that *then*, as Cicero says, " the laws themselves seem to offer arms to those who are in such necessity."

But, apart from this occasion, of which I do not here speak, there never was a law which permitted individuals to kill, and which suffered it as you do, to ward off an insult, and to avoid the loss of honour or property, when life is not at the same time endangered. This, fathers, I maintain that the infidels themselves never did; on the contrary, they expressly forbade it. For the law of the twelve tables of Rome bore, that " it is not permitted to kill a robber in the day time, not defending himself with arms." This had already been prohibited in Exodus, xxii, and the law *Furem*, (*ad Leg. Cornel.*), which is taken from Ulpian, *forbids even the killing of robbers in the night time, who do not put our life in peril.* See this in *Cujas, de dig. justitia et jure*, l. 3.

Tell us, then, fathers, by what authority you permit, what laws, both divine and human, forbid, and what right Lessius has to say, l. 2, c. 9, n. 66–72: " Exodus forbids to kill robbers in the day time, not defending themselves by arms, and those who so kill are punished criminally. Nevertheless, they are not culpable in conscience, when they are not certain of being able to recover what is stolen, or are in doubt of it, as Sotus says, because we are not obliged to run the risk of any loss to save a robber. All this, moreover, is lawful even for ecclesiastics." What strange hardihood! The law of Moses punishes those who kill robbers when they do not attack our life, and the law of the Gospel, according to you, acquits them? What, fathers, did Jesus Christ come to destroy the law, and not to fulfil it? " The judges," says Lessius, "would punish those who should kill on this occasion, but they would not be culpable in conscience." Is the law of Jesus Christ, then, more cruel and less inimical to murder than that of the heathen, from whom judges have borrowed those civil laws which condemn it? Do Christians set more value on worldly goods, or less value on human life, than did idolaters and infidels? On what do you found, fathers? Not on any express law, either of God or man, but only on this strange reason: "The laws allow us to defend ourselves against robbers, and repel force by force. Now, defence being permitted, murder is also deemed permitted, since without it, defence would oft-times be impossible."

It is false, fathers, that defence being permitted, murder also is permitted. This cruel mode of defending is the source of all your errors, and is called by the Faculty of Louvain, *a murderous defence, defensio occisiva,* in their censure of the doctrine of father L'Amy on homicide. I maintain, then, that so great is the difference in the eye of the law, between killing and self-defence, that on the very occasions on which defence is permitted, murder is forbidden, provided life is not in danger. Listen to this, fathers, in Cujas, at the same place: "It is permitted to repel him who comes to seize upon our property, *but it is not permitted to kill him.*" And again, if any one comes to strike and not to kill us, it is indeed permitted to repel him, *but it is not permitted to kill him.*

Who, then, gave you power to say, as do Molina, Reginald, Filiutius, Escobar, Lessius, and others, "it is permitted to kill him who comes to strike us." And, again: "It is permitted to kill him who wishes to insult us, according to the opinion of all the casuists; *ex sententia omnium,*" as Lessius says, n. 74. By what authority do you, who are only individuals, give this power of killing to individuals, and to monks even? How dare you usurp this right of life and death, which belongs essentially to God only, and is the most glorious symbol of sovereign power? It was to this your answer was required; and you think you have satisfied it by simply saying in your thirteenth Imposture, "that the value for which Molina permits us to kill a robber, who is in flight without offering any violence, is not so small as I have said, and must be larger than six ducats." How weak this is, fathers! At what would you fix it? At fifteen or sixteen ducats? I will not reproach you less. At all events, you cannot say that it exceeds the value of a horse; for Lessius, l. 2, c. 9, n. 74, decides precisely, that "it is lawful to kill a thief who is running away with our horse." But I tell you, moreover, that according to Molina, this value is fixed at six ducats, as I have stated; and if you will not admit this, let us take an arbiter, whom you cannot refuse. I make choice, then, of your father Reginald, who, explaining this same passage of Molina, l. 21, n. 68, declares that Molina there fixes the value at which it is not permitted to kill at from three to five ducats. And thus, fathers, I shall not only have Molina, but also Reginald.

It will not be less easy for me to refute your fourteenth Imposture, concerning the permission " to kill a robber who would deprive us of a crown," according to Molina. This is so evident, that Escobar will testify it to you, tr. 1, ex. 7, n. 44, where he says " that Molina regularly fixes the value for which we may kill at a crown." Accordingly, in the fourteenth Imposture you merely charge me with having suppressed the last words of the passage, " that we must here observe the moderation of a just defence." Why, then, do you not also complain that Escobar has not given them? But how clumsy you are! You think we don't understand what is meant, according to you, by defending one's self. Do we not know that it is to use " a murderous defence?" You would wish it to be understood as if Molina meant that when life is put in peril by holding the crown, we may kill, because then it is in defence of our life. Were that the case, why should he say at the same place that herein " he is contrary to Carrerus and Bald," according to whom it is lawful to kill, in order to save our life? I declare to you, then, he simply means, that if our crown can be saved without killing the robber, we should not kill him; but if we can only save it by killing, even though we run no risk of our life, as when the robber has no arms, we may lawfully take them, and kill him, to save our crown; and in so doing we do not, according to him, exceed the moderation of a just defence. To show you this, allow him to explain himself, tom. 4, tr. 3, d. 11, n. 5, " we fail not in the moderation of a just defence although we take arms against those who have none, or take better than theirs. I know that some take an opposite view, but I approve not of their opinion, even in the external tribunal."

Accordingly, fathers, it is evident that your authors make it lawful to kill in defence of property and honour where life is in no danger. On the same principle they authorize duelling, as I have shown by numerous passages, to which you have given no answer. In your papers you only attack a single passage of your father Layman, who permits it, "when otherwise there would be a risk of losing fortune or honour;" and you say that I have suppressed the additional words, that "that case is rare." I wonder at you, fathers! Pleasing impostures these you charge me with! It is the question, then, is it, Whether that case is rare? The question is, Whether or not duelling is there permitted? These are two and separate questions. Layman, in his capacity of casuist, has to decide whether duelling is permitted, and he declares that it is. We will easily judge without him, whether the case is rare, and will declare to him that it is a very ordinary case. If you like better to believe your good friend, Diana, he will tell you that it is very common, p. 5, tr. 14, misc. 2, resol. 99. But whether it be rare or not, and whether in this Layman follows Navarre, as you are so anxious to make out, is it not abominable in him to consent to the opinion, that to preserve a false honour it is permitted in conscience to accept a duel, against the edicts of all Christian States, and against all the canons of the Church; while you cannot produce, in support of all these diabolical maxims, either laws or canons, the authority of Scripture or Fathers, or the example of any saint, but only the impious syllogism: "Honour is dearer than life; but it is lawful to kill in defence of life; therefore it is lawful to kill in defence of honour"? What, fathers! because the corruption of men makes them love this false honour more than the life which God has given them to serve him, they shall be permitted to kill in order to preserve it? The very circumstance of loving that honour more than life is itself a fearful evil; and yet this vicious attachment, which is capable of polluting the holiest actions, if it is made their end, will be capable of justifying the most criminal actions, *because* it is made their end!

What perversion, fathers! And who sees not to what excess it may lead? For it is visible that it goes the length of killing for the most trivial things, when it is made a point of honour to preserve them; I say, even to *kill for an apple!* You would complain of me, fathers, and say that I draw malicious inferences from your doctrine, were I not supported by the authority of the grave Lessius, who thus speaks, n. 68: "It is not lawful to kill to preserve a thing of little value, as a crown or *an apple; aut pro pomo;* unless in a case where it were disgraceful to lose it; for then one might take it back again, and even kill, if necessary, to recover it; *et si opus est, occidere;* because this is not so much to defend property as honour." That is precise, fathers; and to finish your doctrine with a maxim which comprehends all the others, listen to this one from your father Hereau, who had taken it from Lessius: "The right of self-defence extends to all that is necessary to defend us from all injury."

What strange consequences are contained in this inhuman principle! and how strong the obligation to oppose it, which lies upon all men, and especially all men in authority! To this they are bound, not only by the public interest, but by their own; since your casuists, quoted in my letters, extend the permission to kill even to them. And thus the factious, who fear the punishment of their attempts, which they never think unjust, easily persuading themselves that they are put down by violence, will, at the same time, think "that the right of self-defence extends to all that is necessary to keep them from injury." They will no longer have to vanquish remorse of conscience, which arrests the greater part of crimes in their birth; their only thought will be how to surmount the obstacles from without.

I will not speak of them here, fathers, any more than of other murders you have permitted, which are still more abominable, and more important to States than all these, and of which Lessius treats so openly in Doubts 4th and 10th, as well as many others of your authors. It were to be wished that those horrible maxims had never come out of hell; and that the devil, the first author of them, had never found men so devoted to his orders as to publish them among Christians.

From all I have hitherto said, it is easy to judge how contrary the laxity of your opinions is to the strictness of civil and even heathen laws. What, then, will it be when we contrast them with ecclesiastical laws, which should be incomparably more holy, since the Church alone knows and possesses true holiness! Accordingly, this chaste spouse of the Son of God, who, in imitation of her husband, well knows how to shed her blood for others, but not to shed that of others for herself, regards murder with very special abhorrence, an abhorrence proportioned to the special light which God has communicated to her. She considers men not only as men, but as images of the God whom she adores. She has for each of them a holy respect, which makes them all venerable in her eyes, as ransomed by an infinite price, to become temples of the living God. And thus she regards the death of a man who is slain without the order of her God, as not only a murder, but an act of sacrilege, which deprives her of one of her members, since whether he be or be not a believer, she always considers him as either actually one of her children, or as capable of being one.

These, fathers, are the holy grounds which, ever since God became man for the salvation of men, have made their condition of so much importance to the Church, that she has always punished homicide, which destroys them, as one of the greatest crimes which can be committed against God. I will mention some of these examples, though not under the idea that all these severe rules prescribed should still be observed, (I know that the Church may vary this external discipline,) but to show what is her immutable mind on this subject; for the penances which she ordains for murder may differ according to diversity of times, but no change of time can ever change her abhorrence for murder.

For a long time the Church would not, till death, be reconciled to persons guilty of wilful murder; such as those forms of it which you permit. The celebrated Council of Ancyra subjects them to penance during their whole life; and the Church has since deemed it sufficient indulgence to reduce the period to a great number of years. Still more to deter Christians from wilful murder, she has very severely punished even those which had happened through imprudence, as may be seen in St. Basil, St. Gregory of Nyssen, the decrees of Pope Zachariah, and Alexander II. The canons reported by Isaac, bishop of Langres, t. 2, 13, imposed seven years of penance for killing in self-defence. And we see that St. Hildebert, bishop of Mans, replied to Yves of Chartres, "that he had done rightly in interdicting a priest for life, who had, in self-defence, killed a robber with a stone."

No longer then, have the effroutery to say that your decisions are conformable to the spirit and the canons of the Church. We defy you to show one which allows us to kill to defend our property merely, for I am not speaking of the occasions on which we should also have to defend our life, *se suaque liberando*. That there is none, is confessed by your own authors, among others, your father L'Ami, tom. 5, disp. 26, n. 136, "There is not," says he, "any law, human or divine, that expressly permits us to kill a robber who does not defend himself:" And yet this is what you expressly permit. We defy you to show one which permits to kill for honour, for a blow, for insult, and evil-speaking. We defy you to show one which permits to kill witnesses, judges, and magistrates for any injustice apprehended from them. The spirit of the Church is altogether a stranger to those seditious maxims which open the door to those commotions to which nations are so naturally disposed. She has always taught her children not to render evil for evil, to give place unto wrath; not to resent violence, to render to all their due, honour, tribute, submission, obedience to magistrates and superiors, even those of them who are unjust, because we ought always to respect in them the power of God, who has placed them over us It prohibits them still more strongly than civil laws, from taking justice into their own hands: it is in her spirit that Christian monarchs do not so even in crimes of high treason, but hand over the criminals to judges, that they may be punished according to the laws and the rules of justice; a procedure so different from yours, that the contrast will put you to the blush. Since the subject suggests it, I pray you to follow this comparison between the mode in which we may kill our enemies according to you, and that in which judges put criminals to death.

All the world knows, fathers, that private individuals are never allowed to demand the death of any one, and that although a man should have ruined us, maimed us, burned our house, slain our parent, and would fain moreover assassinate ourselves, and destroy our reputation, no court of justice would listen to any demand we might make for his death. Hence it was necessary to establish public officers, who demand it on the part of the king, or rather on the part of God. In your opinion, fathers, is it from grimace and pretence, that Christian judges have established this regulation? Have they not done it in order to adapt civil laws to those of the Gospel, lest the external practice of justice might be contrary to the inward sentiments which Christians ought to have? It is plain how strongly these initiatory steps of justice confutes you; the sequel will crush you.

Suppose then, fathers, that these public officers demand the death of him who has committed all these crimes, what will be done thereupon? Will the dagger be forthwith plunged into his bosom? No, fathers: the life of man is too important; it is treated with more respect; the laws have not placed it at the disposal of all classes of persons, but only at the disposal of judges of proved integrity and ability? And do you think that one only is sufficient to condemn a man to death? Seven at least are necessary, fathers. It is necessary that, of these seven, there be not one whom the criminal has offended, lest passion might influence or corrupt his judgment. And you know, fathers, how, in order that their intellect may be clear, it is still the practice to devote the morning to these duties. Such are the anxious provisions to prepare them for this great act, in which they stand in the place of God, whose ministers they are, in order that they may condemn those only whom he condemns.

And this is the reason why, in order to act as faithful stewards of this divine power in taking away the lives of men, they must, in judging, proceed on the depositions of witnesses, and according to all the other forms which are prescribed: after all this, they must decide conscientiously in terms of law, and judge none worthy of death save those whom the laws condemn to die. And then, fathers, if the order of God obliges them to give up the bodies of these wretched beings to punishment, the same order of God obliges them to take care of their guilty souls; and it is just because they are guilty that they are obliged to take care of them, so that they are not sent to execution till means have been given them to provide for their conscience. All this is very pure and very innocent; and yet, so much does the Church abhor blood, that those who have taken part in a sentence of death, though accompanied with all the circumstances of religion, she judges incapable of ministering at her altars; from this it is easy to conceive what idea the Church has of homicide.

Such, fathers, is the manner in which, in the order of justice, the lives of men are disposed of; let us now see how you dispose of them. In your new laws there is only one judge, and this judge the very person who is offended. He is at once judge, party, and executioner. He passes sentence and executes it on the spot; and, without respect to either the body or the soul, he kills and damns him for whom Jesus Christ died; and all this to avoid a blow, or a calumny, or an outrageous word, or other similar offences, for which a judge, with lawful authority, would be criminal in passing sentence of death on those who had committed them, because the laws are very far from so condemning them. And, in fine, to crown these excesses, there is no sin or irregularity in killing in this manner, without authority, and against the laws, be the killer a monk, or even a priest. Where are we, fathers? Are those who speak in this way monks and priests? Are they Christians? Are they Turks? Are they men? Are they devils? And are these *mysteries revealed by the Lamb to those of his Society*, or abominations suggested by the dragon to his followers?

In short, fathers, for whom do you wish to be taken? for children of the Gospel, or for enemies of the Gospel? It must be the one or the other, for there is no middle party. He who is not with Jesus Christ is against him; these two classes include all men. According to St. Augustine, there are two nations and two worlds spread over the whole earth: the world of the children of God, forming a body of which Christ is head and king; and the world, inimical to God, of which the devil is head and king. Hence, Jesus Christ is called the prince and God of the world, because he has subjects and worshippers every where; and the devil is also called in Scripture the prince and god of this world, because he every where has supporters, and slaves. Jesus Christ has introduced into the Church, which is his empire, the laws which please his eternal wisdom; and the devil has introduced into the world, which is his kingdom, the laws which he wished there to establish. Jesus Christ has made it honourable to suffer; the devil, not to suffer. Jesus Christ has told those who receive a blow on the one cheek, to turn the other; and the devil has told those to whom a blow is offered, to kill those who would so injure them. Jesus Christ declares those happy who share his ignominy, and the devil declares those miserable who are in ignominy. Jesus Christ says, " Woe to you when men shall speak well of you;" and the devil says, Woe to those of whom the world speaks not with esteem.

See, now, then, fathers, to which of those two kingdoms you belong. You have heard the language of the city of peace, which is called the mystical Jerusalem; and you have heard the language of the city of confusion, which Scripture calls " spiritual Sodom." Which of these two languages do you understand? Which of them do you speak? According to St. Paul, those who are Christ's have the same sentiments as Christ; and those who are children of the devil, *ex patre diabolo*, who has been a murderer from the beginning of the world, do, as our Saviour says, follow the maxims of the devil. Let us listen, then, to the language of your school, and interrogate your authors. When a blow is given us, ought we to bear it rather than kill him who gives it? or is it lawful to kill in order to avoid the affront? " It is lawful," say Lessius, Molina, Escobar,

Reginald, Filiutius, Baldellus, and other Jesuits, "it is lawful to kill him who would give us a blow." Is that the language of Jesus Christ? Answer once more, would a man be without honour if he suffered a blow without killing him who gave it? "Is it not true," says Escobar, "that so long as the man lives who has given us a blow, we remain without honour?" Yes, fathers, *without that honour* which the devil has transfused with his proud spirit into that of his proud children. This honour has always been the idol of men possessed by the spirit of the world. To preserve this honour, of which the devil is the true dispenser, men make a sacrifice to him of their lives, by the rage for duelling to which they abandon themselves; of their honour, by the ignominious punishments to which they become obnoxious; and of their salvation, by the peril of damnation which they incur, even sepulture being denied to them by the ecclesiastical canons. But we should praise God for having illumined the mind of the king with a purer light than that of your theology. His stern edicts on this subject have not made duelling a crime; they only punish the crime inseparable from duelling. By the fear of his strict justice, he has arrested those who were not arrested by the fear of divine justice; and his piety has made him aware that the honour of Christians consists in the observance of the commands of God and the rules of Christianity, and not in that phantom of honour, which, vain though it be, you hold forth as a legitimate excuse for murder. Thus your murderous decisions are now the aversion of the whole world, and your wiser course would be to change your sentiments, if not from a principle of religion, at least on grounds of policy. By a voluntary condemnation of these inhuman opinions, fathers, prevent the bad effects which might result from them, and for which you would be responsible; and in order to conceive a greater abhorrence of homicide, remember that the first crime of fallen man was a murder in the person of the first saint; his greatest crime, a murder in the person of the chief of all the saints; and, that murder is the only crime which destroys at once the State, the Church, nature and piety.

I have just seen the reply of your apologist to my Thirteenth Letter. But if he has no better answer to this one, which meets the most of his difficulties, he will not deserve a reply. I am sorry to see him hourly breaking away from his subject to vent calumnies and insults against the living and the dead. But, to gain credit for the memorandums with which you furnish him, you should not make him publicly disavow a fact so public as the blow of Compiegne. It is certain, fathers, from the acknowledgment of the injured party, that he was struck on the cheek by the hand of a Jesuit, and all that your friends have been able to do, is to make it doubtful whether it was with the palm or with the back of the hand, and raise the question, whether a stroke on the cheek with the back of the hand be or be not a blow. I know not to whom it belongs to decide, but in the mean time, I will believe that it is at all events a *probable* blow. This saves my conscience.

LETTER FIFTEENTH.

TO THE REVEREND JESUIT FATHERS.

THE JESUITS ERASE CALUMNY FROM THE LIST OF SINS, AND MAKE NO SCRUPLE OF USING IT TO CRY DOWN THEIR ENEMIES.

25th November, 1656.

REVEREND FATHERS,—Since your impostures increase every day, and you employ them in cruelly outraging the feelings of all persons of piety who are opposed to your errors, I feel obliged, on their behalf, and that of the Church, to unfold a mystery in your conduct, which I promised long ago, in order that men may be able to ascertain from your own maxims what faith they ought to put in your accusations and insults.

I am aware that those who do not fully know you, have difficulty in making up their minds on this subject, because they feel themselves under the necessity of either believing the incredible crimes of which you accuse your enemies, or of holding you as impostors, which also seems to them incredible. What! they ask, if these things were not true, would monks publish them; would they renounce their conscience and damn themselves, by their calumnies? Such is their mode of reasoning; and thus the visible proofs by which your falsehoods are overthrown, running counter to the opinion which they have of your sincerity, their mind remains suspended between the evidence of the truth, which they cannot deny, and the duty of charity, which they are apprehensive of violating. Hence, as the only thing which hinders them from rejecting your calumnies is the good opinion they have of you, the moment they come to understand that you have not that idea of calumny which they imagine you have, there cannot be a doubt that the weight of truth will forthwith determine them no longer to believe your impostures. This, then, fathers, will be the subject of this letter.

I will not only show that your writings are full of calumny; I will go farther. One may utter falsehoods, believing them to be truths, but the character of liar includes an intention to lie. I will show, then, fathers, that your intention is to lie and calumniate; and that knowingly and with design you charge your enemies with crimes of which you know that they are innocent, because you think you can do it without falling from a state of grace. Though you know this point of your morality as well as I do, I will, nevertheless, tell it you, in order that there may be no doubt of it when it is seen that I address myself to you, and maintain it to yourselves, while you cannot have the assurance to deny it, without confirming my charge by the very disavowal; for the doctrine is so common in your schools, that you have maintained it not only in your books, but in your public theses (the last degree of hardihood); among others, in your Theses of Louvain of 1645, in these terms: "It is only a venial sin to calumniate and bring false accusations to destroy the credit of those who speak ill of us; *Quidni non nisi veniale sit, detrahentis autoritatem magnam, tibi noxium, falso crimine elidere?*" This doctrine is so universal among you, that any one who dares to assail it, is treated as ignorant and presumptuous.

This was recently experienced by Father Quiroga, a German Capuchin, when he sought to oppose it. Your Father Dicastillus took him up at once, and speaks of the dispute in these terms, *de Just.*, l. 2, tr. 2, disp. 12, n. 404: "A certain grave monk, cowled and barefooted, *cucullatus gymnopoda*, whom I name not, had the temerity to cry down this opinion among women and ignorant persons, and to say that it was pernicious and scandalous, contrary to good morals, the peace of States and society; and, in fine, contrary not only to all orthodox doctors, but to all who can be orthodox; but I have maintained against him, as I still maintain, that calumny, when used against a calumniator, though it be a falsehood, is, nevertheless, not a mortal sin, nor contrary either to justice or charity; and to prove it I referred him *en masse* to our fathers, and entire universities consisting of them, all of whom I consulted; among others the reverend father John Gans, confessor to the emperor; the reverend father Daniel Bastele, confessor to archduke Leopold; father Henri, who was tutor to these two princes; all the public and ordinary professors of the university of Vienna" (wholly composed of Jesuits); "all the professors of the university of Gratz"(wholly of Jesuits); "all the professors of the university of Prague" (where the Jesuits are masters); "from all of whom I hold approvals of my opinion, written and signed with their own hands; besides, also, having with me father De Pennalossa, a Jesuit, preacher to the emperor and king of Spain; Father Pillicerolli, Jesuit; and many others, who had judged this opinion probable, before our dispute." You see plainly, that there are few opinions which you have taken so much pains to establish, as there were few of which you stood so much in need. Hence you have so fully sanctioned it that your casuists use it as an indubitable principle. "It is certain," says Caramuel, n. 1151, "that it is a probable opinion that there is no mortal sin in calumniating falsely to save one's reputation. For it is maintained by more than twenty grave doctors, by Gaspar Hurtado and Dicastillus, Jesuits, etc., so that, if this doctrine were not probable, there would not be one probable in all theology."

Abominable theology! a theology so corrupt in all its heads, that if according to its maxims it were not probable and safe in conscience to calumniate without sin, in order to preserve reputation, scarcely one of its decisions would be sure! How very probable, fathers, that those who hold this principle do sometimes put in practice! The corrupt will of man so impetuously inclines him to it, as makes it impossible not to believe that when the obstacle of conscience is removed it will diffuse itself with all its natural vehemence. Would you have an illustration? Caramuel will give it at the same place. He says, "This maxim of Father Dicastillus, Jesuit, respecting calumny, having been taught by a German countess, to the emperor's daughters, their belief that at the most they only sinned venially by calumnies, gave rise to such a number in a few days, and to so many false reports, that the whole court was set in a blaze and filled with dismay. For it is easy to imagine how soon they became adepts in the art of using them; so that to appease the disturbance it became necessary to send for a good Capuchin, of exemplary life, named Father Quiroga," (it was for this Father Dicastillus quarrelled with him so much,) " who assured them that this maxim was very pernicious, especially among women, and took particular care to get the empress to abolish the use of it entirely." We cannot be surprised at the bad effects caused by this doctrine; on the contrary, it would be wonderful if it did not produce this licence. It is always easy for self-love to persuade us that we are attacked unjustly; to persuade you, especially, fathers, who are so blinded by vanity, that in all your writings you would have it believed that to injure the honour of your Company is to injure the honour of the Church. And thus, fathers, it might well seem strange, if you did not put the maxim in practice. We must not say, as do those who know you not, How should these worthy fathers wish to calumniate their enemies, since they could not do it without the loss of their salvation? On the contrary, we must say, How should these worthy fathers be willing to lose the opportunity of crying down their enemies, since they can do it without hazarding their salvation? Let no one, then, be astonished at seeing the Jesuits calumniators; they are so with a safe conscience, and nothing can keep them from it, since from the credit they have in the world they can calumniate without fear of punishment from man, and from the power they have assumed in cases of conscience, they have established maxims to enable them to do it without fear of punishment from God.

Such, fathers, is the source from which all those black impostures spring; such the cause which led your Father Brisacier to circulate so many as to draw upon himself the censure of the late archbishop of Paris; such the inducement to your Father D'Anjou to declaim publicly in the pulpit of the church of St. Benedict at Paris, 8th March, 1655, against persons of rank who received alms for the poor of

Picardy and Champagne, to which they had themselves so liberally contributed, and to utter the horrid lie which might have dried up the source of this charity, had any credit been given to your impostures, "that he had certain information that those persons had misapplied the money to employ it against the Church and the State," which obliged the curate of the parish, who is a doctor of Sorbonne, to mount the pulpit next day, and denounce these calumnies. From this same principle your father Crasset preached so many falsehoods in Orleans, that it became necessary for the bishop of Orleans to interdict him, as a public impostor, by his injunction of 9th September last, in which he declares that "he prohibits friar John Crasset, priest of the Company of Jesus, from preaching in his diocese, and all his people from hearing him, under pain of mortal disobedience; in respect he has learned that the said Crasset had delivered a discourse from the pulpit filled with falsehoods and calumnies against the clergy of this town, falsely and maliciously charging them with holding the heretical and impious propositions, that the commandments of God are impossible; that inward grace is never resisted; that Jesus Christ died not for all men; and other similar propositions, condemned by Innocent X;" for this is your ordinary slander, and the first charge you bring against all whom you are anxious to discredit. And although it is as impossible for you to prove this of any of these persons, as for your father Crasset to prove it of the clergy of Orleans, your conscience, nevertheless, remains at rest, "because you believe that this manner of calumniating those who attack you is so certainly permitted" that you fear not to declare it publicly, and in the face of a whole town.

We have a notable proof of this in the quarrel which you had with M. Puys, curate of St. Nisier at Lyons; and as this story gives a perfect manifestation of your spirit, I will state the principal circumstances. You know, fathers, that in 1649, M. Puys translated into French an excellent work of a Capuchin friar, 'on the Duty of Christians to their Parish, and against those who dissuade them from it,' without using any invective, and without naming any monk, or any particular Order. Your fathers, nevertheless, took it to themselves, and without any respect for an aged pastor, judge in the Primacy of France, and respected by the whole town, your father Albi wrote a furious book against him, which you yourselves retailed in your own church on Assumption-day, in which he charged him with several things, and among others, "with having made himself scandalous by his gallantry, with being suspected of impiety, with being a heretic, deserving of excommunication; and, in short, fit to be burned." M. Puys replied, and Father Albi, in a second writing, reiterated his charge. Is it not certain, then, fathers, either that you were slanderers, or that you believed all this of the worthy priest, and behoved to see him clear of his errors before you could deem him worthy of your friendship? Listen then, to what passed at the reconciliation, which took place in presence of the first persons in the town, whose names are given below,[1] as they appear in the minute which was drawn up, 25th September, 1650. In presence of all these persons, M. Puys did nothing more than declare " that what he had written was not addressed to the Jesuit fathers; that he had spoken in general of those who alienate the faithful from their parishes, without intending thereby to attack the Society, which, on the contrary, he esteemed and loved." By these simple words he got quit of his apostacy, gallantry, and excommunication, without retractation and without absolution; and Father Albi thereafter said to him as follows: "Sir, the belief I had that you were attacking the Company to which I have the honour to belong, made me take up my pen in reply; and I thought the manner in which I used it *was permitted me;* but being better informed as to your intention, I here declare that *there is no longer any thing* to prevent me from regarding you as a man of talent, very enlightened, profoundly learned, and *orthodox,* of *irreprehensible* morals; and, in one word,

[1] M. De Ville, Vicar-General of the Cardinal of Lyons; M. Scarron, Canon and Curate of St. Paul; M. Margat, Chanter; Messrs. Bouvand, Seve, Aubert, and Dervieu, Canons of St. Nisier; M. du Gué, President of the Treasurers of France; M. Groslier, Dean of Guild; M. de Fléchère, President and Lieutenant-General; Messrs. de Boissat, De S. Romain, and De Bartoly, gentlemen; M. Bourgeois, First King's Advocate to the Treasury Board; Messrs. Cotton, father and son; M. Boniel; who all signed the original declaration, with M. Puys and Father Alby.

worthy pastor of your Church. This declaration I gladly make, and I beg these gentlemen to remember it."

They have remembered it, fathers, and the reconciliation has caused more scandal than the quarrel. For who would not wonder at this language of father Albi? He does not say he comes to retract, because he has been informed of a change in the manners and doctrine of M. Puys, but only that, "knowing it was not his intention to attack your Company, there is nothing to prevent his regarding him as orthodox." He did not believe, then, in fact, that he was heretical? And yet, after having accused him against his conviction, he does not declare himself in the wrong; on the contrary, he dares to say that "the manner in which he acted was lawful."

Of what are you thinking, when you testify thus publicly that you measure the faith and virtue of men only by the feelings with which they regard your Society? How were you not apprehensive of making yourselves pass, on your own confession, for impostors and calumniators? What, fathers! the same individual, without undergoing any change, will, according as you believe that he honours or attacks your company, be "pious" or "impious," "unblameable" or "excommunicated," "fit pastor of a church," or "fit to be burned," in fine, "Catholic or heretic." In your language then, to attack your Society and be heretical is the same thing. That is a droll heresy, fathers. And thus, when we see in your writings so many orthodox persons called heretics, the whole meaning is, that *you think they attack you.* It is good, fathers, to understand this strange language, according to which there cannot be a doubt that I am a great heretic. Accordingly, it is in this sense that you so often give me the name. You cut me off from the Church, only because you think my Letters do you harm; and thus, all that remains to make me orthodox, is either to approve of the corruptions of your morality, which I could not do without renouncing every pious sentiment, or to persuade you that in this I am only seeking your true welfare, a persuasion which you must be very far returned from your errors to recognize. So that I am strangely involved in heresy, since the purity of my faith being of no use to recall me from this species of error, I cannot get quit of it, except by either betraying my own conscience, or by reforming yours. Till then I shall always be a wicked man and an impostor; and however faithful I may have been in quoting your authors, you will go about crying, "He must be a limb of Satan, to impute to us things of which there is not a mark or vestige in our books;" and in this you will only act agreeably to your maxim and your ordinary practice, so extensive is the privilege which you have of lying. Allow me to give you an instance, which I purposely select, as at the same time furnishing an answer to your ninth imposture, which, like the others, deserves only a passing refutation.

Ten or twelve years ago you were reproached with this maxim of Father Bauny, "that it is lawful to seek directly, *primo et per se*, a proximate cause of sin, for the spiritual or temporal good of ourselves or our neighbour," tr. 4, q. 14, of which he adduces in illustration, that "it is lawful to enter notorious houses with the view of converting abandoned women, though it is probable we will sin there, from having already often experienced that we are wont to allow ourselves to be carried into sin by the caresses of these women." What was the answer to this by your father Caussin, in 1644, in his 'Apology for the Company of Jesus,' p. 128: "Show the place in father Bauni, read the page, the margin, the advertisement, the appendix, every thing else, even the whole book, and you will not find a single trace of such a sentence, which could only come into the mind of a man extremely devoid of conscience, and must apparently have been suggested by the instrumentality of the devil." And your father Pintereau says in the same style, part 1, p. 24, "A man must be devoid of conscience to teach such a detestable doctrine, but he must be worse than a devil to ascribe it to father Bauni. Reader, there is not a mark or vestige of it throughout his book." Who would not believe that people who speak in this tone had ground to complain, and that Father Bauni had, in fact, been taxed unjustly? Have you affirmed any thing against me in stronger terms?

And how could one venture to suppose that a passage could be in the exact words, at the very place from which it is quoted, when it is said that "there is not a mark or vestige of it throughout the book?"

In truth, fathers, that is the method of making yourselves believed until you are answered; but it is also the method of making you never more believed, after you have been answered. For so certain is it you lied at that time, that you have no difficulty, in the present day, in admitting in your Answers, that this maxim is in father Bauni, at the very place which had been quoted; and what is wonderful, whereas it was "detestable" twelve years ago, it is now so innocent that, in your ninth Impostures, p. 10, you accuse me of "ignorance and malice, in quarrelling father Bauni for an opinion which is not rejected in the school. What an advantage it is, fathers, to have to do with people who deal in the *pro* and the *con!* I need none but yourselves to confute you. For I have only to show two things: the one, that this maxim is worthless; the other, that it is father Bauni's; and I will prove both by your own confession. In 1644 you acknowledge that it is "detestable," and in 1656 you confess that is in father Bauni. This double acknowledgment, fathers, sufficiently justifies me; but it does more; it discloses the spirit of your policy. For, tell me, pray, what is the end which you propose in your writings? Is it to speak with sincerity? No, fathers, since your answers destroy each other. Is it to follow sound doctrine? Just as little, since you authorise a maxim which, according to yourselves, is detestable. Be it considered, however, that when you said the maxim was "detestable," you at the same time denied it to be in father Bauni, thus making him innocent; and when you confess that it is his, you at the same time maintain its soundness, thus still making him innocent. So that the innocence of this father, being the only thing common to your two answers, it is plain that it is the only thing you seek, and that your only object is the defence of your fathers, by saying of the same maxim, that it is in your books, and that it is not; that it is good, and that it is bad;

not according to truth, which never changes, but according to your interest, which changes every hour. What might I not say to you here, for you see plainly how conclusive it is? Nothing, however, is more common with you. To omit an infinite number of examples, I believe you will be contented with one more.

You were reproached at divers times with another proposition of the same father Bauni, tr. 4, q. 22, p. 100: "We should neither refuse nor delay giving absolution to those who are habitual sinners against the law of God, of nature, and the Church, although we see no prospect of amendment: *etsi emendationis futuræ spes nulla appareat.*" Here, fathers, I pray you to tell me which of the two answered best, according to your taste, your father Pintereau or your father Brisacier, who defend father Bauni in your two modes: the one, by condemning the proposition, but denying it to be father Bauni's, and the other by admitting it to be his, but at the same time justifying it? Listen, then, to what they say: here is father Pintereau, p. 18: "What is meant by overleaping the bounds of all modesty and exceeding all impudence, if it is not to impose such a damnable doctrine on father Bauni, as a thing averred by him? Judge, reader, of this unworthy calumny: see with whom the Jesuits have to do, and whether the author of so black an imposture ought not henceforth to pass for the interpreter of the father of lies." Here, now, is your father Brisacier, 4 p., p. 21: "In fact, father Bauni says what you relate:" this is giving the lie direct to father Pintereau: "but," he adds, in justification of father Bauni, "do you who censure it wait when a penitent is at your feet, till his guardian angel pledges all the rights he has to heaven for his security: wait till God the Father swears by his head, that David lied when he said by the Holy Spirit that all men are liars, deceitful, and frail; and till this penitent be no longer lying, frail, fickle and sinful, like others, and you will not apply the blood of Christ to any one."

What think you, fathers, of these extravagant and impious expressions, that if it were necessary to wait "till there was some hope of amendment in sinners" before absolving them, it would be necessary to wait " till God should swear by his head" that they would never more fall. What, fathers! is there no difference between hope and certainty? How injurious to the grace of Jesus Christ, to say that it is so little possible for Christians ever to get quit of sins against the law of God, of nature, and the Church, that it could not be hoped for " unless the Holy Spirit had lied!" So that, according to you, were absolution not given to those of whom " we have no hope of amendment," the blood of Jesus Christ would remain useless, and " we should never apply it to any one." To what state, fathers, are you reduced by your excessive desire to preserve the honour of your authors, since you find only two ways of justifying them, imposture or impiety; so that your most innocent mode of defence, is boldly to deny facts that are clear as day.

Hence it is that you so often use it. Still, this is not your only shift. You forge writings to render your enemies odious, as the ' Letter of a Minister to M. Arnauld,' which you retailed over Paris, to make it believed that the work on ' Frequent Communion,' approved by so many bishops and so many doctors, but which, in truth, was somewhat opposed to you, had been composed on a secret understanding with the ministers of Charenton. At other times, you attribute to your opponents, writings full of impiety, as the ' Circular Letter of the Jansenists,' the impertinent style of which makes the cheat too gross, and too clearly exposes the ridiculous malice of your father Meynier, who dares to employ it, p. 28, in support of his blackest impostures. You sometimes quote books which never existed, as the ' Constitutions of the Holy Sacrament,' from which you give passages which you fabricate at pleasure, and make the hair of the simple stand on end, who know not your effrontery in inventing and publishing lies; for there is no species of calumny which you have not put in practice. Never could the maxim which excuses it be in better hands.

But these expedients are too easily defeated, and therefore you have others of a more subtle nature, in which you give no particulars, that you may thus leave nothing to your opponents to fasten upon in reply; as when father Brisacier says, "that his enemies commit abominable crimes, but he is unwilling to state them." Does it not look as if a charge so indefinite could not be convicted of imposture? A man of ability has nevertheless found out the secret; and he is again, fathers, a Capuchin. You are at present unfortunate in Capuchins; and I foresee that some other time you will very likely be so in Benedictines. This Capuchin is father Valerien, of the house of the Counts of Magnis. You will learn by the following short story, how he replied to your calumnies: He had happily succeeded in the conversion of Prince Ernest, Landgrave of Hesse-Rheinsfelt. But your fathers being somewhat annoyed at seeing a sovereign prince converted without their being called in, forthwith composed a book against him (for you are every where persecutors of the good), in which, falsifying one of his sentences, they charge him with *heretical* doctrine. They also circulated a letter against him, in which they said to him, "O! what things we could disclose," without saying what, "at which you would be very sorry! For, if you do not put matters to rights, we will be obliged to give notice to the Pope and Cardinals." There is some adroitness in this, and I have no doubt that you speak of me in the same way; but see what kind of answer he gives in his book printed at Prague, last year, p. 112, etc. "What shall I make of these vague and indefinite slanders? How shall I rebut charges which are not explained? Here, nevertheless, is the method. I declare, loudly and publicly, to those who menace me, that they are notorious impostors, and very practised and very impudent liars, if they do not discover these crimes to all the world. Come forward then, accusers, and publish these things upon the housetops, instead of whispering them in the ear, and from so whispering, lying with assurance. There are some who imagine that these disputes are scandalous. It is true, it is a horrid scandal to impute to me such a crime as heresy, and make me suspected of many other crimes. But I only meet this scandal by maintaining my innocence."

In good sooth, fathers, you are here rather roughly

handled; and never was defence more complete. For even the least semblance of crime must have been wanting, since you have not replied to his challenge. You sometimes meet with troublesome rencounters; but it does not make you any wiser. For some time after, you again attacked him in the same way, on another subject, and he again defended himself in these terms, p. 151: "This kind of men, who are making themselves insupportable to all Christendom, aspire, under the pretext of good works, to grandeur and domination; perverting to their own ends almost all laws, divine, human, positive, and natural. Either by their doctrine, or by fear, or by hope, they attract all the grandees of the earth, whose authority they abuse, for the accomplishment of their detestable intrigues. But their attempts, criminal though they be, are neither punished nor arrested: on the contrary, they are rewarded; and they commit them with as much boldness as if they were doing God a service. All the world acknowledges this, and all the world speaks of it with execration. But few are capable of opposing this mighty tyranny. This, however, I have done. I have stopped their impudence, and by the same means will stop it again. I declare, then, that they have lied most impudently, *mentiris impudentissime.* If their charges against me are true, let them prove them, or let them stand convicted of a lie fraught with impudence. Their procedure hereupon will show who is right. I pray all the world to attend to it, and observe, in the meanwhile, that this kind of men, who never put up with the smallest injury they can repel, make a pretence of submitting very patiently to those from which they cannot defend themselves, and give the cloak of a false virtue to their mere impotence. My object in cutting thus sharply was to make the dullest among them aware, that if they are silent, their silence will be the effect, not of meeknsss, but of a troubled conscience."

These are his words, fathers, and he ends thus: "Those people, whose fabrications are universally known, are so obviously unjust, and from impunity so insolent, that I must have renounced Jesus Christ and his Church, if I did not detest their conduct, and publicly denounce it, as well to justify myself as to prevent the simple from being led astray."

Reverend fathers, there is now no room to draw back. You must pass for convicted calumniators, and recur to your maxim, that this sort of calumny is not a crime. The Capuchin has found out the secret of shutting your mouths; and this is the course that must be taken every time you accuse people without proof. It is necessary only to reply to each of you, with the Capuchin father, *Mentiris impudentissime.* For what other answer could be given, for example, when your father Brisacier says, that those against whom he writes are "gates of hell; pontiffs of the devil: people fallen from faith, hope, and charity; who build the treasury of Antichrist. This," he adds, "I say not by way of insult, but through force of truth?" Must a man seriously go about to prove that he is not "a gate of hell," and that he is not building the treasury of Antichrist?

In the same way, what answer must I give to all the vague language of this sort which is in your books and advertisements, concerning my letters; for example, that "we apply the doctrine of restitution, by reducing creditors to poverty; that we have offered bags of money to learned monks, who have refused them; that we give benefices to procure the circulation of heresies against the faith; that we have pensioners among the most illustrious ecclesiastics, and in sovereign courts; that I, also, am a pensioner of Port-Royal; and that I composed romances before my letters," I, who have never read one, and don't even know the names of those which your apologist has made. What is to be said to all this, but just *mentiris impudentissime*, if you do not specify all those persons, their words, the time, the place? For you must be silent, or state and prove all the circumstances, as I do, when I tell the stories of father Albi and John of Alba. Otherwise, you will only injure yourselves. Your fables might, perhaps, have been of service, before your principles were known; but now that all is discovered, should you think of whispering " that a man of honour, who wishes his name to be concealed, has told you dreadful things of those people," you will forthwith be reminded of the *Men-*

tiris impudentissime, of the worthy Capuchin father. You have too long been deceiving the world, and abusing the credit which was given to your impostures. It is time to restore the reputation of the many whom you have calumniated. For what innocence can be so generally acknowledged as not to sustain some injury from the bold impostures of a Company diffused over the whole earth, and who, under a religious dress, hide souls so irreligious, that they commit such sins as calumny, not against their maxims, but in accordance with their maxims? I shall not be blamed, therefore, for having destroyed the faith which might have been placed in you; since it is far more just to preserve to the many persons whom you have decried the reputation for piety, which they deserve not to lose, than to leave you a reputation for sincerity which you deserve not to possess. As the one could not be done without the other, you see how important it was to let men understand who you are. This I have begun to do here; but it will take a long time to finish. It shall be seen, however, fathers, and all your policy will not save you from detection; since any efforts which you might make to prevent it would only serve to convince the least discerning that you are afraid, and that your conscience upbraiding you with what I had to say, you have left no means untried to prevent me from saying it.

LETTER SIXTEENTH.

TO THE REVEREND JESUIT FATHERS.

HORRIBLE CALUMNIES OF THE JESUITS AGAINST PIOUS ECCLESIASTICS AND HOLY NUNS.

4th December, 1656.

REVEREND FATHERS,—Here is the sequel of your calumnies. I will first reply to those contained in your advertisements; but as all your other books are equally filled with them, they will furnish me with matter enough to discourse to you on this subject so long as I shall deem it necessary. I will tell you, then, in one word, in regard to the fabrications which you have scattered up and down through all your writings against M. d'Ypres, that you maliciously pervert a few ambiguous words in one of his letters, which, admitting of a good meaning, ought to be interpreted favourably, according to the spirit of the Church, and cannot be interpreted otherwise, except according to the spirit of your Society. For why will you insist that in saying to his friend, "Don't give yourself so much trouble about your nephew, I will furnish him with what is necessary from the money in my hands," his meaning was, that he took this money not intending to return it; and not that he merely advanced it to be repaid? But must you not be very imprudent, to have yourselves furnished proof of your falsehood from the other letters of M. d'Ypres, which you have printed, and which clearly show that the sums were in fact mere *advances*, which he was to replace. This appears from the one of 30th July, 1619, which you give, to your own confutation, in these terms: "Be not anxious about the *advances;* he shall want nothing while he is here;" and from that of 6th

January, 1620, when he says, "You are in too great haste; and though it were necessary to render an account, the little credit I have here would enable me to find the money wanted."

You are impostors, then, fathers, as well on this subject as in your ridiculous tale of the trunk of St. Merri. For what advantage can you derive from the accusation which one of your good friends reared up against this ecclesiastic, whom you would fain tear to pieces? Must we infer that a man is guilty, because he is accused? No, fathers; persons of piety, like him, will always be liable to be accused, so long as the world contains calumniators like you. It is not, then, by the accusation that we must judge, but by the decision. Now the decision, which was given 23rd February, 1656, fully acquits him; and, moreover, the party who had rashly involved himself in this proceeding was disavowed by his colleagues, and forced to retract. As to what you say in the same place of the "famous director, who became rich in a moment, to the extent of nine hundred thousand livres," it is enough to refer you to the curates of St. Roch and St. Paul, who will attest to all Paris his perfect disinterestedness in this affair, and your inexcusable malice in this imposture.

But enough for these vain falsehoods; they are only first attempts by your novices, and not the master-strokes of your great adepts. I come to these, then, fathers, and begin with one of the blackest calumnies ever conjured up by your spirit. I speak of the intolerable audacity with which you have dared to charge holy nuns, and their directors, with "not believing in the mystery of transubstantiation, and the real presence of Jesus Christ in the Eucharist." Here, fathers, is an imposture worthy of you; here a crime which God alone is capable of punishing, as you alone are capable of committing. One would require to be as humble as these calumniated sufferers, to bear it with patience; and to be as wicked as the wicked calumniators, to believe it. I do not, therefore, undertake to justify them; they are not suspected. If they needed defenders, they would have better than I. What I shall say here will be, not to demonstrate their innocence, but to demonstrate your malice. My only wish is to make you abhor yourselves, and let all the world understand, that after this there is nothing of which you are not capable.

You will not fail, nevertheless, to say that I am of Port-Royal; for it is the first thing you say to every one who combats your excesses, as if Port-Royal only contained persons zealous enough to defend the purity of Christian morality against you. I am aware, fathers, of the merit of those pious men who live there in solitary retirement, and how much the Church is indebted to their instructive and solid writings. I know how pious and enlightened they are. For, although I have never had any connection with them, as you wish to be believed, although you know not who I am, I nevertheless, am acquainted with some of them, and I honour the virtue of all. But God has not confined exclusively to their body the number of those whom he is pleased to oppose to your disorders. With his aid, fathers, I hope to make you sensible of this; and if he gives grace to support me in the purpose which he inspires, the purpose to employ in his service whatever I have received of him, I will speak to you in such a way as will perhaps make you regret that you have not to do with an inmate of Port-Royal. And in testimony of this, fathers, while those whom you outrage by this notorious calumny, content themselves with offering up prayers to God for your pardon, I feel obliged, I, who suffer not by the injustice, to put you to the blush in the presence of the whole Church, that I may thereby produce in you that salutary shame of which Scripture speaks, and which is almost the only remedy of a hardened impenitence like yours: "Fill their faces with shame, and they will seek thy name, O Lord!"

This insolence, from which even the holiest places are not safe, must be arrested. For who will be secure after a calumny of this nature? What, fathers! for you to advertise in Paris that scandalous book, with the name of your Father Meinier at the head of it, and under this infamous title of 'Port-Royal and Geneva at one as to the holy Sacrament of the Altar,' in which you charge this apostacy not only on the Abbé of St. Cyran, and M. Arnauld, but also on his sister, Mother Agnes, and all the nuns of this monastery, of whom you say, p. 96, "that their faith, respecting the Eucharist, is as suspicious as that of M. Arnauld," which you maintain, p. 4, to be "in effect Calvinist!" I here appeal to the whole world, and ask if there are any persons in the Church against whom you can bring so abominable charges with less probability? For, tell me, fathers, if those nuns and their directors had "an understanding with Geneva against the holy Sacrament of the Altar," (the very idea is horrible,) why should they have selected as the principal object of their piety this Sacrament, which they must hold in abomination? Why should they have joined to their rule the institution of the holy Sacrament? Why should they have taken the habit of the holy Sacrament, the name of Daughters of the holy Sacrament, and called their church the Church of the holy Sacrament? Why should they have asked and obtained from Rome a confirmation of this institution, and permission every Thursday to use the office of the holy Sacrament, in which the faith of the Church is so perfectly expressed, if they had conspired with Geneva to destroy the faith of the Church? Why should they have obliged themselves by a special devotion, also approved by the Pope, to have nuns continually night and day in presence of this holy victim, that by their perpetual adoration towards this perpetual sacrifice, they might make reparation for the impious heresy which seeks to annihilate it? Tell me, then, fathers, if you can, why, of all the mysteries of our religion, they should have omitted those which they believe, to select one which they do not believe? And why should they have dedicated themselves so fully and entirely to this mystery of our faith, if they, like heretics, held it to be the mystery of iniquity? What answer, fathers, will you give to these clear evidences; not of words, but of actions; and not of some particular action, but of the whole course of a life entirely consecrated to the adoration of Jesus Christ, as he sits upon our altars? What answer will you give to what you call the books of Port-Royal, in every page of which you find the very terms which the Fathers and Councils have used, in order to define the essence of this mystery? It is ridiculous, yet horrible, to see you, throughout your whole libel, giving such answers as the following: M. Arnauld indeed talks of "transubstantiation," but he perhaps means a "significative transubstantiation." He indeed declares his belief in "the real presence;" but how do we know that he does not mean "a true and real figure?" Where are we, fathers, and whom will you not make a Calvinist at your pleasure, if licence is given you to corrupt the most canonical and sacred expressions, by the malicious subtleties of your new equivocations? For who has ever used other terms than these, especially in plain pious treatises, in which no controversy is discussed? And yet the love and respect which they have for this holy mystery has made all their writings so full of it, that I defy you, fathers, with all your cunning, to find in them either the least appearance of ambiguity, or the least accordance with the sentiments of Geneva.

Every body knows, fathers, that the heresy of Geneva essentially consists, as you yourselves state, in holding that Jesus Christ is not contained in the Sacrament; that he cannot possibly be in several places; that he is truly only in heaven, where only he ought to be worshipped, and not upon the altar; that the substance of the bread remains; that the body of Jesus Christ does not pass into the mouth, or into the stomach; that he is eaten only by faith, and that thus the wicked do not eat him; and that the mass is not a sacrifice but an abomination. Listen, then, fathers, to the kind of "understanding which the books of Port-Royal have with Geneva." To your confusion we there read that "the flesh and blood of Jesus Christ are contained under the species of bread and wine," (second letter of M. Arnauld, p. 259;) that "the Holy of Holies is present in the sanctuary, and should there be adored," (ibid, p. 243;) that Jesus Christ "dwells in sinners who communicate by the real and true presence of his body in their stomach, though not by the presence of his Spirit in their heart;" Freq. Com., 3rd part, c. 16, that "the dead ashes of the bodies of the saints derive their principal dignity from this seed of life which remains to them from contact with the immortal and vivifying flesh of JesusChrist;" (1st p., c. 10:) that "it is not by natural power, but by the omnipotence of God, to which nothing is impossible, that the body of Jesus Christ is contained under the host, and under the minutest part of each host;" ('Theol. Fam., lec. 15,') that "the divine word is present to produce the effect which the words of consecration express;" (ibid.) that "Jesus Christ, who is humbled and laid upon the altar, is at the same time exalted in glory;" that "he is by himself, and by his ordinary power, in different places at the same time; in the midst of the Church triumphant, and in the midst of the Church militant and sojourning," (De la Suspension, rais. 21:) That "the sacramental species remain suspended, and subsists extraordinarily, without being supported by any subject; and that the body of Jesus Christ is thus suspended under the species;" that "it depends not on them, as substances depend on accidents;" (ibid. 23;) that "the substance of bread is changed by leaving the accidents immutable;" ('Heures dans la prose du saint Sacrement;') that "Jesus Christ reposes in the eucharist with the same glory that he has in heaven;" ('Lettres de M. de S. Cyran,' tr. 1, let. 93;) that "his glorious humanity resides in the tabernacles of the Church, under the species of bread, which visibly conceal him; and that knowing how gross we are, he thus conducts us to the adoration of his divinity, present in all places, by that of his humanity, present in a particular place;" (ibid.) "that we receive the body of Jesus on the tongue, and that he sanctifies it by his divine contact;" (letter 32;) that "he enters the mouth of the priest;" (letter 72;) that "although Jesus Christ has made himself accessible in the holy Sacrament, by means of his love and mercy, he, nevertheless, preserves his inaccessibility as an inseparable condition of his divine nature; for although the body alone and the blood alone are there, by virtue of the words, *vi verborum*, as the school speaks, this does not prevent his whole divinity as well as his whole humanity, from being there, by a necessary conjunction;" ('Defense du Chaplet du S. Sacrement,' p. 217.) And, in fine, "that the eucharist is at once sacrament and sacrifice;" (Theol. Fam., lec. 15;) and that "although this sacrifice is a a commemoration of that of the cross, there is, however, this difference, that that of the mass is offered for the Church alone, and for the faithful, who are in her communion; whereas, that of the cross has been offered for all the world, as Scripture speaks," (ibid., p. 153.)

Enough here, fathers, to show that perhaps there never was greater impudence than yours. But I mean, moreover, to make you pronounce your own sentence. For what do you require in order to take away all semblance of fraternising with Geneva? "Had M. Arnauld," says your father Meinier, p. 83, "said that, in this adorable mystery there is no substance of bread under the species, but only the flesh and blood of Jesus Christ, I would have confessed that he had entirely declared against Geneva." Confess it, then, impostors, and give him public reparation. How often have you seen this in the passages which I have just quoted? But, moreover, the Familiar Theology of M. de S. Cyran being approved by M. Arnauld, contains the sentiments of both. Read, then, the whole of lesson 15th, and especially the second article, and you will find the words which you require, expressed even more formally than you yourselves express them: "Is there bread in the host and wine in the cup?" No; for the whole substance of bread and wine is taken away, to make way for that of the body and blood of Jesus Christ, which remain there alone, covered by the qualities and species of bread and wine."

Well, fathers, will you still say that Port-Royal teaches nothing which "Geneva does not receive?" and that M. Arnauld has said nothing in his second letter which "might not have been said by a minister of Charenton? Make Mestrezat, then, speak as M. Arnauld speaks, in this letter, p. 237, etc. Make him say, "It is an infamous lie to accuse him of denying transubstantiation; that the foundation of his treatise is the truth of the real presence of the Son of God as opposed to the heresy of the Calvinists; that he considers himself happy in being in a place where the Holy of Holies is continually adored in the sanctuary." This is much more contrary to the belief of the Calvinists than even the real presence is; since as Cardinal Richelieu says in his controversies, p. 536, "the new ministers of France having united with the Lutherans, who believe the real presence of Jesus Christ in the eucharist, have declared that they remain separated from the Church in regard to this mystery, only because of the adoration which Catholics pay to the eucharist." Make

Geneva sign all the passages which I have quoted from the works of Port Royal, and not only the passages but the entire treatises respecting this mystery, as the book on Frequent Communion, Explanation of the Ceremonies of the Mass, the Reasons of the Suspension of the Holy Sacrament, the translation of the Hymns in the Hours of Port Royal, etc., and, in fine, procure the establishment etc., at Charenton of this holy institution for incessantly adoring Jesus Christ contained in the Eucharist, as is done at Port-Royal, and it will be the most signal service you can render to the Church, since then Port-Royal will not *have an understanding with Geneva*, but Geneva an understanding with Port-Royal and the whole Church.

In truth, fathers, you could not have chosen your ground worse than to accuse Port Royal of not believing the Eucharist; but I wish to show what induced you. You know that I somewhat understand your policy. You have strictly followed it on this occasion. Had the Abbé de St. Cyran and M. Arnauld only spoken of what ought to be believed concerning this mystery, and not of what should be done in preparing for it, they would have been the best Catholics in the world, and no ambiguity would have been found in their terms of *real presence* and *transubstantiation*. But because all who combat your corruptions must be heretical, and on the very point for which they combat them, must not M. Arnauld be so after having written a book expressly against your profanations of this sacrament? What, fathers, shall he have said with impunity, "that the body of Jesus Christ should not be given to those who are ever relapsing into the same sins, and in whom we see no hope of amendment, and that they should for a time be kept away from the altar to purify themselves by a sincere repentance, so as afterwards to approach it with benefit"? Do not suffer them to speak thus, fathers; if you do, you will not have so many frequenters of your confessionals; for your father Brisacier says, that if "you followed this method, you would not apply the blood of Jesus Christ to any one." It is far better for you to follow the practice of your Society, which your father Mascarenhas, in a book approved by your doctors and even by your reverend father General, describes as follows: "All sorts of persons, and even priests, may receive the body of Jesus Christ the same day they have defiled themselves by abominable sins: so far from there being any irreverence in these communions, it is on the contrary laudable to use them in this manner. Confessors ought not to dissuade them, but ought on the contrary to counsel those who have just committed these crimes, to communicate at the instant; because although the Church has forbidden it, the prohibition is rendered obsolete by the universal practice of the whole earth."

See, fathers, what it is to have Jesuits over the whole earth. Such is the universal practice which you have introduced, and which you wish to maintain. It matters not though the tables of Jesus Christ should be filled with abomination, provided your churches are full of people. See then, that those who oppose this are made heretical on the holy Sacrament. It must be done, cost what it may; but how will you be able to do it after the many invincible evidences they have given of their faith? Are you not afraid I will state your four great proofs of their heresy? Well may you, fathers; but I ought not to spare you the shame. Now then, for the first of them.

"M. de St. Cyran," says father Meinier, "in consoling a friend for the death of his mother, tom. 1, Lett. 14, says, that the most pleasing sacrifice which can be offered to God on this occasion, is patience; therefore he is Calvinist." This is very subtle, fathers; and I know not if any one sees the ground of it; let us then learn it from himself. "Because," says this great controversialist, "he does not believe in the sacrifice of the Mass, for it is the most pleasing of all to God." Let them now say that the Jesuits cannot argue. So skilful are they, that they will make any one they please, and even the Holy Scriptures, to be heretical. For would it not be heresy to say as Ecclesiasticus does, "There is nothing worse than the love of money: *Nihil est iniquius quam amare pecuniam*," as if adultery, murder, and idolatry were not greater crimes? And is there a man who does not, every hour, say similar things; for example, that the sacrifice of a broken and contrite heart is the most pleasing in the sight of God; because by this language we merely mean to compare some internal virtues with others, and not with the sacrifice of the Mass, which is of a different order altogether, and infinitely more exalted? Are you not, then, ridiculous, fathers! and must I, to complete your confusion, give you the terms of this very letter, in which M. de St. Cyran speaks of the sacrifice of the Mass, as "the most excellent of all," saying, "offer to God daily, and in all places, the sacrifice of the body of his Son, who has not found *a more excellent means* than this of honouring his Father"? And again, "Jesus Christ has obliged us, when dying, to take his sacrificed body, that we may thereby render the sacrifice of our own body more agreeable to God; and to unite himself to us when we die, in order to strengthen us by sanctifying, by his presence, the last sacrifice we make to God, of our life and our body." Conceal all this, fathers, and cease not to say that he dissuaded from communicating at death, as you do, p. 33, and that he did not believe the sacrifice of the Mass. Nothing is too hardy for calumniators by profession.

Your second proof gives strong evidence of this. To make a Calvinist of the late M. de St. Cyran, to whom you ascribe the authorship of *Petrus Aurelius*, you bring forward a passage in which Aurelius explains, p. 89, in what manner the Church conducts herself towards priests, and even bishops whom she means to depose or degrade. "The Church," says he, "not being able to divest them of the gift of ordination, because it is ineffaceable, does what in her lies: she erases from her memory the character which she cannot erase from the souls of those who have received it: she considers them as if they were no longer priests or bishops, so that, according to the ordinary language of the Church, we may say they are so no longer, although they always are so in respect of character, *ob indelebilitatem characteris.*" You see, fathers, that this author, who was approved by three general assemblies of the Clergy of France, says clearly, that "the character of the priesthood is ineffaceable." Here, therefore, you have uttered a notable calumny; in other words, according to you, committed a petty venial sin. For this book had injured you, by refuting the heresies of your colleagues in England, respecting Episcopal authority. But here is a remarkable extravagance: having falsely supposed that M. de St. Cyran holds the character to be effaceable, you conclude that he does not believe the real presence of Jesus Christ in the Eucharist.

Do not expect me to answer this, fathers. If you have not common sense, I cannot give it to you. All who have, will, without my aid, laugh enough at you, as well as at your third proof, which you found upon these words of the Frequent Communion, 3rd p. ch. 11, "that God in the Eucharist gives us the *same meat* as he gives to the saints in heaven, with only this difference, that here he removes the sensible sight and taste, reserving both for heaven." Indeed, fathers, these words so simply express the sense of the Church, that, at this moment, I forget what means you take to pervert them. For I see nothing in them but what the Council of Trent teaches, sess. 13, c. 8; that there is no difference between Jesus Christ in the Eucharist, and Jesus Christ in heaven, except that here he is veiled, and there, not. M. Arnauld says not that there is no other difference in the manner of receiving Jesus Christ, but only that there is no other in Jesus Christ who is received. And yet you insist, against all reason, on making him say in this passage, that Christ is not eaten with the mouth here any more than in heaven: and hence you infer his heresy.

I pity you, fathers. Must further explanation be given you? Why do you confound this divine nourishment with the manner of receiving it? There is, as I have just said, only a single difference between this nourishment on earth and in heaven, namely, that here it is hidden under veils, which deprive us of the sight and sensible taste of it; but there are several differences between the manner of receiving it here and there, the principal of which is, as M. Arnauld says, part 3, ch. 16, "here it enters the mouth and stomach both of the good and bad, which is not the case in heaven."

If you are ignorant of the cause of this difference, I will

tell you, fathers; that the reason why God has established these different modes of receiving the same meat, is the difference which subsists between the state of Christians in this life, and that of the blessed in heaven. The state of Christians, says Cardinal Perron, after the Fathers, holds a middle place between the state of the blessed and the state of the Jews. The blessed possess Jesus Christ really, without figure and without veil. The Jews possessed Jesus Christ only by figures and veils, as were the manna and paschal lamb. And Christians possess Jesus Christ in the Eucharist, truly and really, but still covered with veils. "God," says St. Eucherius, "has made three tabernacles: the synagogue, which had only shadows, without reality; the Church, which has reality and shadows; and heaven, where there are no shadows but reality only." We should change the state in which we are, (which is the state of faith, and which St. Paul contrasts as well with the law as with clear vision,) did we possess figures only, without Jesus Christ; because the peculiarity of the law is to have only the shadow of things, and not the substance; and we should also change it, did we possess them visibly, because faith, as the same apostle says, respects not things which are seen. And thus the Eucharist is perfectly adapted to our state of faith, because it contains Jesus Christ truly, though under a veil. So that this state would be destroyed, were not Jesus Christ really under the species of bread and wine, as heretics pretend; and it would also be destroyed if we received him uncovered, as in heaven, since this would be to confound our state, either with the state of Judaism or that of glory.

Behold, fathers, the mysterious and divine ground of this most divine mystery. It is this which makes us abhor the Calvinists, as reducing us to the condition of the Jews, and makes us aspire to the glory of the blessed, when we shall have the full and eternal fruition of Jesus Christ. Hence you see that there are several differences between the manner in which he communicates himself to Christians and to the blessed; among others, that here we receive him with the mouth, not so in heaven; but they all depend merely on the difference between the state in which we are, and that in which they are. And this, fathers, is what M. Arnauld expresses so clearly in these terms: "There cannot be any other difference between the purity of those who receive Jesus Christ in the Eucharist, and that of the blessed, than there is between faith and the clear vision of God, on which alone depends the different modes in which we eat on earth and in heaven." Your duty, with regard to these words, fathers, was to have revered their holy truth, instead of corrupting them, for the purpose of rearing up a heresy, which they do not, and never can contain, namely, that we eat Jesus Christ only by faith, and not by the mouth, as they are maliciously expounded by your fathers, Annat and Meynier, so as to form the head of their accusation.

Here, then, you are sadly at a loss for proof, fathers; and this is the reason why you have had recourse to a new artifice, namely, to falsify the Council of Trent, in order to make out that M. Arnauld is not conformable to it; so numerous are the means you have to make people heretical. This is done by father Meynier in fifty places of his book, and eight or ten times in the single page 54; where he pretends that, in order to speak orthodoxly, it is not enough to say, "I believe Jesus Christ is present really in the Eucharist," but that it is necessary to say, "I believe, *with the Council*, that he is present with a true *local presence*, or locally. And on this he quotes the Council, sess. 13, can. 3, can. 4, can. 6. Who would not believe, on seeing the words "local presence," quoted from three canons of a universal council, that they are there in reality? This might have served your purpose before my Fifteenth Letter; but people are no longer taken in by it. They go and look at the Council, and find you impostors. For these terms, "local presence, locally, locality," never were there. And I declare to you, moreover, fathers, that they are not in any other part of this Council, nor in any other preceding Council, nor in any Father of the Church. Here, therefore, fathers, I beg you to say, if you mean to bring a suspicion of Calvinism on all who have not used this term. If so, the Council of Trent is suspected, and all the holy Fathers without exception. Have you no other way of rendering M. Arnauld heretical, without offending so many persons who never did you harm; among others, St. Thomas, who is one of the greatest defenders of the Eucharist; and who, so far from using that term, has expressly rejected it, 3 p. qu. 76, a. 5, where he says: *Nullo modo corpus Christi est in hoc sacramento localiter.* Who are you, then, fathers, that of your own authority impose new terms, which you ordain us to use for the proper expression of our faith, as if the profession of faith prepared by the Popes, on the order of the Council, where this term is not to be found, were defective, and left in the creed of the faithful, an ambiguity which you alone have discovered? What presumption, to prescribe these terms even to doctors! What falsehood, to palm them upon general Councils! And what ignorance, not to know the difficulties which the most enlightened saints have had to admit them! Blush, fathers, at "your ignorant impostures;" as Scripture says to impostors ignorant like you: *De mendacio ineruditionis tuae confundere.*

No longer, then, attempt to play the master. You have neither character nor ability for it. But if you would advance your propositions more modestly, one might listen to them. For although the term "local presence" was rejected by St. Thomas, as you have seen, because the body of Christ is not in the Eucharist, with the ordinary dimensions of bodies in their place: nevertheless, the term has been received by some new authors on controversy, because they simply mean by it, that the body of Jesus Christ is truly under the species; and as these are in a particular place, the body of Christ is also there. In this sense, M. Arnauld will have no difficulty in admitting it, M. de St. Cyran and he having so often declared that Jesus Christ in the Eucharist, is truly in a particular place, and miraculously in several places at once. Thus, all your refinements tumble to the ground, and you have not been able to give the least semblance to an accusation which ought not to have been advanced without invincible proof.

But of what use is it, fathers, to oppose their innocence to your calumnies? You do not attribute heresy to them in the belief that they are heretical, but in the belief that they do you harm. This, according to your theology, is enough to calumniate them without criminality; and you may say mass without confession or repentance, at the very time you are charging priests who say it every day with believing it to be pure idolatry; sacrilege so dreadful, that you yourselves hung your own father Jarrige in effigy for having said it " at a time when he was in terms with Geneva."

I am astonished, then, not at your charging them so unscrupulously with great and spurious crimes, but at your imprudence in charging them with crimes which are so very improbable. For you indeed dispose of sins at your pleasure; but do you think you can in the same way dispose of men's belief? Truly, fathers, were it the only alternative, that either you or they must be suspected of Calvinism, I should consider you in a bad plight. While their language is as orthodox as yours, their conduct confirms their faith, and yours belies it. For if you believe, as well as they, that the bread is really changed into the body of Jesus Christ, why do you not, like them, require that the hard and stony heart of those whom you counsel to approach, should be truly changed into a heart of flesh? If you believe that Jesus Christ is there in a state of death, that those approaching may thereby learn to die to the world, to sin, and to themselves, why do you induce any to approach, while their criminal passions are altogether unmortified? And how do you deem those worthy to eat the bread of heaven who would not be worthy to eat earthly bread?

O great worshippers of this sacred mystery! worshippers who manifest their zeal by persecuting those who honour it by many holy communions, and flattering those who dishonour it by so many sacrilegious communions! How becoming in those defenders of this pure and adorable sacrifice, to surround the table of the Lord with hardened sinners, who have just sallied forth from their places of infamy; and to place amidst them a priest, whom even his confessor sends from his unchastity to the altar, there to act as the representative of Jesus Christ, presenting this holy victim to the God of holiness, and putting it, with his polluted hands, into their polluted mouths! Is it not most seemly in those who thus act "over all the earth," according to maxims approved by their own General, to charge the author of 'Frequent Communion,' and the Daughters of the Holy Sacrament, with not believing the holy sacrament?

Even this does not suffice. To satisfy their passion they must at last accuse them of having renounced Jesus Christ and their baptism. These, fathers, are not the blustering tales you generally tell; they are the fatal excesses by which you have filled up the measure of your calumnies. This notable falsehood would not have been in fit hands, had it been allowed to remain in the hands of your good friend, Filleau, to whom you suggested it: your Society has openly taken it upon itself; and your father Meynier has just maintained "as a certain truth," that Port-Royal has for thirty-five years formed a secret cabal, of which M. de St. Cyran and M. d'Ypres have been the heads, "for the purpose of overthrowing the mystery of the incarnation, making the Gospel pass for an apocryphal history, exterminating the Christian religion, and rearing Deism upon the ruins of Christianity." Is this all, fathers? Will you be satisfied if all this is believed of those whom you hate? Will your animosity be at last satiated, when you have produced a feeling of abhorrence against them, not only among those who are in the Church, because of their being on terms with Geneva, as you accuse them, but also among all those who believe in Jesus Christ, though out of the Church, because of the *Deism* which you impute to them?

But how do you expect to persuade us on your word alone, without the least appearance of proof, and in the face of the strongest imaginable contradictions, that priests who preach only the grace of Jesus Christ, the purity of the Gospel, and the obligations of baptism, have renounced their baptism, the Gospel, and Jesus Christ? Who will believe it, fathers? Do you believe it yourselves, wretches that you are? And to what extremes are you reduced, since you are under the necessity of either proving that they do not believe in Jesus Christ, or of passing for the most abandoned calumniators that ever existed? Prove it, then, fathers. Name "this ecclesiastic of merit," who you say was present at the assembly of Bourg-Fontaine in 1621, and disclosed to your father Filleau the design which was there formed to destroy the Christian religion. Name the six persons who you say formed this conspiracy. Name him who is designated by the letters A. A., which you say, p. 15, " means not Antony Arnauld," because he has convinced you he was then only nine years of age, but another who you say "is still in life, and too good a friend of M. Arnauld, to be unknown to him." You know him, then, fathers; and consequently, unless you are yourselves without religion, you are obliged to denounce the impious man to the king and the parliament, that he may be punished as he deserves. You must speak out, fathers; you must name him, or submit to the ignominy of being henceforth regarded as liars, unfit even to be believed. This, as the worthy father Valerien has taught us, is the way to "curb" and push such impostors. Your silence will amount to a full and complete proof of your diabolical calumny. The most blinded of your friends will be compelled to confess that "it will be the effect not of your virtue, but of your impotence," and to wonder how you have been so wicked as to extend the charge even to the nuns of Port-Royal, and to say as you do, p, 14, that "the Secret Chaplet of the Holy Sacrament," framed by one of them, was the first fruit of this conspiracy against Jesus Christ; and in p. 95, that "they have been taught all the detestable maxims of that writing," which is, according to you, a lesson in *Deism*. Your impostures, in regard to this writing, have already been completely ruined by the defence of the censure which the late Archbishop of Paris pronounced on your father Brisacier. You have no answer to give, and yet you cease not to act more shamefully than ever, by attributing the worst of impieties to virgins whose piety is known to all. Cruel and cowardly persecutors! Cannot even the most retired cloisters be asylums against your calumnies? While these holy virgins day and night worship Jesus Christ in the holy sacrament, according to their institution, you cease not day and night to publish that they do not believe him to be either in the Eucharist, or even on the right hand of his Father; and you publicly cut them off from the Church, while they are in secret praying for you, and for the whole Church. You calumniate those who have no ears to hear, no mouth to answer you. But Jesus Christ, in whom they are hid, to appear one day along with him, hears you, and answers for them. This day is heard that holy and dreadful voice which at once fills nature with dismay, and consoles the Church. And I fear, fathers, that those who harden their hearts, and obstinately refuse to hear him when he speaks as God, will be forced to listen in terror, when he shall speak to them as Judge. For, in fine, fathers, what account will you be able to give of all these calumnies, when he will examine them, not on the fancies of your fathers Dicastillus, Gans, and Pennalossa, who excuse them, but on the rules of eternal truth, and the holy ordinance of his Church, which, far from excusing this crime, so abhors it that she has punished it as severely as wilful murder? For calumniators, as well as murderers, were debarred from the holy communion until death by the first and second Councils of Arles. The Council of Lateran adjudged those convicted of it to be unfit for the priesthood, though they had reformed. The popes have even threatened the calumniators of bishops, priests, or deacons, with exclusion from the communion till death. And the authors of a libellous writing, who cannot prove what they have advanced, are condemned by Pope Adrian *to be whipped;* reverend fathers, *flagellentur!* So far has the Church been from countenancing the errors of your Society, a Society so corrupt as to excuse the heinous sin of slander, that it may itself be able to commit it with more freedom.

Certainly, fathers, you might thus be capable of doing a world of mischief had not God permitted that you should yourselves furnish the antidote, and render all your impostures unavailing. For it is only necessary to publish the strange maxim which exempts them from sin in order to deprive you of all credit. Calumny is unavailing, if it is not combined with a great reputation for candour. An evil speaker cannot succeed if he is not thought to abhor evil speaking as a crime of which he is incapable. And thus, fathers, your own principle betrays you; you have established it to secure your conscience; for your wish was to slander without being damned, and to belong to *those pious and holy calumniators* of whom St. Athanasius speaks. You have, accordingly, to save yourselves from hell, adopted a maxim which saves you from it on the faith of your doctors, but a maxim, which, guaranteeing you from the evils which you dread in the other life, deprives you of the advantage which you hoped to gain by it in the present life; so that, while thinking to avoid the punishment of evil speaking you have lost the benefit of it: so self-contradictory is evil, and so much does it embarass and destroy itself by its innate malice.

You would calumniate more successfully by professing to hold with St. Paul, that evil-speakers, *maledici,* are unworthy to see God. In that case, your slanders would, at least, be more readily believed, although you would thereby pronounce your own condemnation. But in saying, as you do, that calumny against your enemies is not a sin, you cause your calumnies to be disbelieved, and you damn yourselves, notwithstanding. For it is certain, fathers, that your grave authors cannot annihilate the justice of God, and that you cannot give a surer proof of not being in the truth than by having recourse to falsehood. If the truth was for you, it would combat for you, it would vanquish for you; and whatever enemies you might have, the truth would, according to the promise, *make you free.* You have recourse to falsehood merely to maintain the errors with which you flatter the sinners of the world, and to prop up the calumnies with which you oppress the pious who oppose them. Truth being contrary to your ends, you have found it necessary to put your confidence in lies, as a prophet expresses it. You have said: "The evils which afflict men will not befal us, for we have hoped in falsehood, and falsehood will protect us." But what says the prophet? "Inasmuch as you have put your trust in calumny and tumult, *sperastis in calumnia et in tumultu,* your iniquity will be imputed to you, and your overthrow will be like that of a lofty wall which tumbles down unexpectedly, and like an earthen vessel which is broken and dashed in pieces by a blow so mighty and so complete, that not a fragment shall remain fit for drawing a little water, or carrying a little fire;" "because," as says another prophet, "you have afflicted the heart of the just, whom I have not afflicted, and you have flattered and confirmed the malice of the wicked. I will therefore withdraw my people from your hands, and will cause it to be known that I am their Lord and yours."

Yes, fathers, it is to be hoped that if you do not change your spirit, God will deprive you of the charge of those whom you have so long deceived, by either leaving these disorders uncorrected through your misconduct, or by poisoning them with your slanders. He will give some of them to understand that the false rules of your casuists cannot shelter them from his anger, and he will inspire others with a just dread of destroying themselves by listening to you and giving credit to your impostures, as you will destroy yourselves by inventing and circulating them. For be not deceived, God is not mocked; no man can with impunity violate the command which he has given in the Gospel, not to condemn our neighbour without being well assured of his guilt. And thus, whatever profession of piety may be made by those who lend a willing ear to your falsehoods, and under whatever pretext of devotion they may do so, they have reason to apprehend that they will be excluded from the kingdom of God for this single sin, for having imputed such heinous crimes as heresy and schism to catholic priests and holy nuns, without other proof than your gross impostures. "The devil," says the bishop of Geneva, "is on the tongue of the evil speaker, and in the ear of him who listens to him." And "evil speaking," says St. Bernard, "is a poison which extinguishes charity in both. So that a single calumny may be mortal to an infinite number of souls, not only killing those who publish, but also those who do not reject it."

Reverend fathers, my Letters were not wont to follow so close, or to be so much extended. The little time I have had is the cause of both. I have made this one longer, only because I have not had leisure to make it shorter. The reason which obliges me to hasten is better known to yourselves than to me. Your answers were succeeding badly; you have done right to change your plan, but I know not if you have taken the right one, and if people will not say that you were afraid of the Benedictines.

I have just learned that he who was universally regarded as the author of your Apologies, disavows them, and is sorry that they should be attributed to him. He is right; and I was wrong in suspecting him: for however strongly assured of the fact, I should have considered that he has too much judgment to believe your impostures, and too much honour to publish them without believing them. Few persons in the world are capable of the excesses which are proper to you, and which too well mark your character, so that I cannot be excused for not having recognised you. Common report misled me. But this excuse, which would be too good for you is not sufficient for me, who profess not to say any thing without certain proof, and have not, with this exception. I repent of it, I retract it, and I wish that you may profit by my example.

LETTER SEVENTEENTH.

TO THE REVEREND FATHER ANNAT, JESUIT.

PROOF ON REMOVING AN AMBIGUITY IN THE MEANING OF JANSENIUS, THAT THERE IS NO HERESY IN THE CHURCH: BY THE UNANIMOUS CONSENT OF ALL THEOLOGIANS, AND ESPECIALLY OF THE JESUITS, THE AUTHORITY OF POPES AND ŒCUMENICAL COUNCILS NOT INFALLIBLE IN QUESTIONS OF FACT.

23rd January, 1657.

REVEREND FATHER,—Your procedure made me suppose you desirous that we should remain at rest on both sides; and I was disposed to do so: but you have since, within a short time, produced so many writings as makes it very apparent that peace is far from being secure, when it depends on the silence of the Jesuits. I know not if the rupture will be much to your advantage; but, for my part, I am not sorry at the opportunity it gives me of refuting that ordinary charge of heresy with which you fill all your books.

It is time to put a stop, once for all, to your effrontery, in treating me as a heretic; an effrontery which increases every day. You do it in the book which you have just published, in a way which cannot be tolerated, and which would bring me under suspicion were I not to answer a charge of this nature as it deserves. I despised this insulting charge in the writings of your colleagues, as well as an infinite number of other charges, in which they deal on all occasions. To them my fifteenth letter was a sufficient reply; but you now speak in another style. You seriously make it the leading point of your defence; it is almost the only one which you employ. For you say, that "as a complete reply to my fifteen letters, it is sufficient to say fifteen times that I am a heretic; and that being declared such, I am unworthy of belief." In fine, you put my apostacy as no longer a question; you presuppose it is a sure principle on which you build boldly. You are thus, father, quite serious in treating me as a heretic; quite seriously, also, am I going to reply.

You know well, father, from the serious nature of this accusation, that it is intolerable presumption to advance it if you have not the means of proving it. I ask you, then, what proofs you have: When was I seen at Charenton? When did I fail at mass, or in the duties which Christians owe to their parish? When did I do an act in union with heretics, or in schism from the Church? What Council have I contradicted? What papal constitution have I violated? You must answer, father, or . . . You perfectly understand me. And what is your answer? I pray all the world to attend to it. You assume, first, that "he who writes the letters is of Port-Royal." Next, you say "that Port-Royal is declared heretical;" and thence you infer that "he who writes the letters is declared heretical." It is not on me, then, father, that the chief weight of your accusation falls, but on Port-Royal, and you charge me only because you suppose I belong to it. I shall thus have no great difficulty in defending myself, since I have only to say that I do not belong to it; and to refer you to my letters, in which I have said "I am single;" and in express terms "that I am not of Port-Royal," as I said in the sixteenth letter, which is earlier in date than your book.

Prove, then, in some other way, that I am heretical, or it will be universally understood that you cannot. Prove by my writings that I do not receive the Constitution. They are not very numerous: you have only sixteen letters to examine, and in these I defy you, you and the whole world, to produce the least evidence of this. But I will show you plainly the contrary. For example, when I said, Letter Fourteenth, that "by killing our brethren in mortal sin, agreeably to your maxims, we damn those for whom Jesus Christ has died," have I not distinctly admitted that Jesus Christ died for those so damned, and consequently, that it is not true "he died only for the elect;" the point condemned in the fifteenth proposition. It is certain, then, father, that I have said nothing in support of those impious propositions, which I detest with all my heart. Even should the Port-Royal hold them, I declare to you, that you cannot from this infer any thing against me, because, thank God, I have no tie upon earth but the Catholic Apostolic Roman Church, in which I mean to live and die; and in communion with the Pope, its sovereign head, out of which Church I am persuaded there is no salvation.

What will you make of a person who speaks in this manner, and on what side will you attack me, since neither my language nor my writings give any pretext for your charges of heresy; and I am secured against your menaces by the obscurity in which I live? You feel struck by an invisible hand, which makes your corruption visible to the whole earth; and you try, in vain, to attack me in the person of those with whom you think me united. I am not afraid of you, either for myself or any other, not being attached to any community, or to any individual whatever. All the influence you may have, is useless as regards me. I hope nothing from the world; I apprehend nothing; I wish nothing: by the grace of God, I have no need either of the property or the patronage of any one. Thus, father, I escape all your machinations. You cannot reach me in any direction which you may try. You may reach Port-Royal, but not me. People have indeed been dislodged from Sorbonne; but that does not dislodge me from my home. You may prepare violent measures against priests and doctors; but none against me, who am in none of these capacities. And thus, perhaps, you never had to do with any one who was so completely beyond your reach, and so proper to combat your errors; being free, without engagement, without attachment, without tie, without relation, without business; while I am sufficiently acquainted with your maxims, and firmly resolved to assail them, so far as I think God approves; no earthly consideration being capable either to arrest or retard my pursuit.

Of what use, then, is it, father, seeing you can do nothing against me, to publish so many calumnies against persons who are not meddling with our quarrel, as all your fathers do? You shall not escape by these evasions. You shall feel the force of the truth which I oppose to you. I tell you that you annihilate Christian morality, by separating it from the love of God, from which you give a dispensation; and you speak to me of the death of father Mester, whom I never saw in my life. I tell you that your authors give permission to kill for an apple, if it is disgraceful to lose it; and you tell me that "a trunk has been opened at St. Merri!" What, again, do you mean by daily taking me to task on the book of 'Holy Virginity,' composed by a father of the Oratory whom I never saw any more than his book? I wonder, father, at your thus considering all who are opposed to you, as a single individual. Your hatred embraces them all at once; and packs them, as it were, into one body of reprobates, each of whom, you insist, shall answer for all the rest.

There is a wide difference between the Jesuits and those who combat them. You truly compose one body, united under a single head; and your rules, as I have shown, forbid any thing of yours to be printed without the sanction of your superiors, who thus become responsible for the errors of all individuals, and *cannot excuse themselves by saying that they have not observed the errors taught, because they ought to observe them*, as is said in your regulations, and the letters of your generals Aquaviva, Vitelleschi, etc. Rightly, then, are you charged with the errors of your brethren, when these exist in works approved by your superiors, and by the theologians of your Company. But, with regard to me, father, the process must be different. I have not subscribed the treatise of 'Holy Virginity.' All the trunks in Paris might be opened without making me less orthodox. In short, I declare to you publicly and distinctly, that nobody is responsible for my Letters, but myself; and that I am responsible for nothing but my Letters.

Here, father, I might rest without speaking of the other persons whom you treat as heretics, in order to include me in the charge. But as I am the occasion, I feel in a manner obliged to use it, in order to draw three advantages from it. One, of some importance, is to display the innocence of the many persons calumniated. Another, very suitable to my subject is, to give constant proof of the artifices of your policy in this accusation. But the third, on which I set the highest value, is that I will thereby acquaint all the world with the falsehood of the scandalous report which you are disseminating in all quarters, that "the Church is divided by a new heresy." And as you impose upon a vast number of persons, by making them believe that the points about which you try to raise so great a storm are essential to faith, I deem it of the utmost importance to destroy those false impressions, and to explain precisely wherein they consist; so as to show that, in point of fact, there are no heretics in the Church.

For is it not true that were the question asked, Wherein consists the heresy of those whom you call Jansenists? you would forthwith answer, that it consists in their saying, "that the commandments of God are impossible; that grace cannot be resisted, and that we are not free to do good and evil; that Jesus Christ died not for all men, but only for the predestinate; and in fine, in their maintaining the five propositions condemned by the Pope." Do you not give out that it is for this cause you persecute your opponents? Is not this what you say in your books, in your discourses, in your catechisms, as you did last Christmas at St. Louis, asking one of your little shepherdesses, "For whom did Jesus Christ come, my girl?" "For all men, father." "What, my girl, then you are not one of those new heretics, who say that he came only for the predestinate?" The children believe you on this, and many others besides, for you entertain them with the same fables in your sermons as did your father Crasset at Orleans, when he was interdicted. And I confess that at one time I also believed you myself; you had given me the same idea of all those persons; so that when you were pressing them on those propositions, I carefully attended to what their answer might be, and was very much disposed never to see them again, had they not declared that they renounced them as visibly impious. But this they did very distinctly. For M. de Sainte Beuve, king's professor at Sorbonne, censured these five propositions in his published writings long before the pope, and those doctors printed several works, among others, that of *Victorious Grace*, which they produced at the same time, in which they reject those propositions as both heretical and novel. For they say in the preface, "that they are heretical and Lutheran propositions, fabricated and forged at pleasure, and not found either in Jansenius or his defenders." These are their terms. They complain of being charged with holding them, and on this account apply to you the words of St. Prosperus, the first disciple of St. Augustine their master, to whom the Semi-Pelagians of France imputed similar sentiments, to throw obloquy upon him: "There are persons," says the saint, "who have such a blind passion for decrying us, that they have taken to a course which ruins their own reputation. For they have purposely fabricated certain impious and blasphemous propositions, which they circulate in all quarters, to make it believed that we hold them in the sense expressed in their writings; but from this reply will be seen both our innocence and the malice of those who impute to us impieties of which they are the sole inventors.

Indeed, father, when I heard them speak in this way before the Constitution, when I afterwards saw that they received it with all possible respect, that they offered to subscribe it, and that all this had been declared by M. Arnauld in his second Letter more strongly than I am able to express, I should have thought it a sin to doubt their faith; and in fact, those who had been inclined to refuse absolution to their adherents before M. Arnauld's Letter, have since declared, that after he had so distinctly condemned the errors imputed to him, there was no ground for cutting off either him or his friends from the Church. But you have not acted so. It was on this I began to suspect that you were actuated by passion.

You had threatened that you would compel them to sign the Constitution, when you thought they would refuse; but when you saw them inclined of their own accord, you spoke no more of it. But although it seems that after this you ought to have been satisfied with their conduct, you still continued to treat them as heretics, "because" as you expressed it, "their heart belied their hand, and they were outwardly orthodox, but inwardly heretical, as you yourself have said in your reply to certain demands, pp. 27, 47.

How strange this procedure appeared to me, father! For of whom may not as much be said? And what disturbance might not be produced by this pretext? "If we refuse," says St. Gregory, "to believe the Confession of Faith, by those who make it agreeably to the sentiments of the Church, we bring the faith of all the orthodox into doubt." I feared, then, father, that *your purpose was to make those persons heretical without being so*, as the same pope says on a similar dispute in his day: "Because," says he, "it is not opposing heresies, but making a heresy, to refuse to believe those who testify by their confession that they are in the true faith: *hoc non est haeresim purgare, sed facere.* But, indeed, I knew that there was truly no heretic in the Church, when I saw them so completely exculpated from all those heresies, that, instead of continuing to accuse them of any error in faith, you were reduced to the necessity of confining your charge to questions of fact concerning Jansenius, which could not be matter of heresy; for you insisted on compelling them to admit, that "these propositions are in Jansenius, word for word, all of them, and in exact terms," as you yourselves expressed it, *Singulares, individuæ, totidem verbis apud Jansenium contentæ*, in your 'Cavilli,' p. 39.

From that time your dispute began to be a matter of indifference to me. When I thought you were disputing as to the truth or falsehood of the propositions, I listened to you with attention, for faith was concerned; but when I saw that the whole subject of your dispute was, whether or not they were "word for word" in Jansenius, as religion was no longer interested, neither did I feel interested. Not that there was not a very strong probability of the truth of your assertion; for when you said that expressions were in an author, "word for word," the very nature of the thing seemed to leave no room for mistake. Accordingly, I am not astonished at the many persons, both in

France and at Rome, who believed in a statement so unsuspicious, that Jansenius had, in fact, taught these propositions. I was, of course, not a little surprised to learn that this point of fact, which you had set forth as so certain and important, was false; and that, though defied to quote the pages of Jansenius, in which you had found these propositions " word for word," you have never been able to do it.

I give this full statement, because it seems to me that it fully discloses the spirit of your Society in all this business; and people will be surprised to see that, notwithstanding all I have just said, you have not ceased to publish that they are heretics, but have only changed their heresy to suit the times. For the moment they cleared themselves of one heresy, your fathers supplied its place by another, in order that they might never be without one. Thus, in 1653, their heresy was on the merits of the propositions; afterwards, it was the "word for word." Since then, you placed it in their heart. But, in the present day, nothing of all this is spoken of; you only insist, that they must be heretics if they do not, by subscription, declare that "the meaning of the doctrine of Jansenius is contained in that of those five propositions."

Such is the subject of your present dispute. It is not enough for you that they condemn the five propositions, and, moreover, every thing in Jansenius which might be conformable to it, and contrary to St. Augustine. For they do all this. So that there is no question, for example, "whether Jesus Christ died only for the predestinate, (they condemn this as well as you,) but whether or not Jansenius thought so. And on this I declare to you more strongly than before, that your dispute concerns me little, as it little concerns the Church. For though I am not a doctor any more than yourself, father, I nevertheless see that there is here no point of faith, the only question being the meaning of Jansenius. If they believed his doctrine conformable to the proper and literal sense of these propositions, they would condemn it; and they refuse to do so, only because they believe it to be very different. Hence, though they should understand it wrong, this would not make them heretical; since they only understand it in an orthodox sense.

To illustrate this by an example, I will take the difference of sentiment between St. Basil and St. Athanasius, concerning the writings of St. Dionysius, of Alexandria, in which St. Basil, thinking he had detected the views of Arius against the equality of the Father and the Son, condemned them as heretical; while St. Athanasius, on the contrary, thinking he found the true sense of the Church, maintained them as orthodox. Think you, father, that St. Basil, who held these writings to be Arian, would have been entitled to treat Athanasius as a heretic because he defended them? What ground would there have been, since it was not Arianism that he defended, but the true doctrine which he thought they contained? Had these two saints agreed as to the true meaning of these writings, or had they both recognised this heresy, then, doubtless, St. Athanasius could not have approved them without heresy; but as they differed as to the meaning, St. Athanasius was orthodox in maintaining them, even though he should have understood them ill; since it would only have been an error of fact, and the only part of the doctrine defended by him was the orthodox faith which he supposed them to contain.

I say the same to you, father: if you were considering the meaning of Jansenius, and your opponents were agreed with you, that he held, for example, that grace *is irresistible*, those refusing to condemn him would be heretical; but when you are disputing as to his meaning, and they believe his doctrine to be, that grace *may be resisted*, you have no ground for treating them as heretics, whatever heresy you may attribute to him; since they condemn the meaning which you suppose in him, and you dare not condemn the meaning which they suppose. If you would convict them, show that the meaning which they attribute to Jansenius is heretical; for in that case, they too will be heretical. But how could you do so, since it is evident, on your own confession, that the meaning they assign to him is not condemned.

To show you this clearly, I will assume the principle which you yourselves admit, namely, "that the doctrine of effectual grace has not been condemned; and that the Pope has not touched it by his Constitution." And, in fact, when he was pleased to give sentence on the five propositions, the point of effectual grace was reserved from all censure. This is perfectly apparent, from the opinion of the counsellors to whom the Pope remitted the examination of them. I have these opinions in my possession, as well as several persons in Paris; among others, the bishop of Montpellier, who brought them from Rome. It appears they were divided in opinion; the Master of the Sacred Palace, the Commissary of the Holy Office, the General of the Augustinians, and others, holding that these propositions might be understood in the sense of effectual grace, were of opinion that they ought not to be censured; whereas, the others, while agreeing that they ought not to be condemned if that had been their meaning, thought they ought to be censured, because, as they declared, the natural and proper meaning was very different. It was for this the Pope condemned them, and all submitted to his decision.

It is certain, then, father, that effectual grace has not been condemned. Indeed, it is so powerfully maintained by St. Augustine, by St. Thomas and his whole school, by so many popes and councils, and by all tradition, that it would be impiety to tax it with heresy. Now, all those whom you treat as heretics, declare that they find nothing else in Jansenius than this doctrine of grace. Accordingly, this was all they maintained at Rome. You yourself have admitted this, *Cavilli*, p. 35, when you declare that, "in pleading before the Pope, they did not say a word on the propositions, *ne verbum quidem*, and that they employed the whole time in speaking of effectual grace." Hence, whether they are mistaken in this supposition or not, it is at least beyond a doubt, that the meaning which they suppose is not heretical; and, consequently, that they are not heretical. For, to say the thing in two words, either Jansenius merely taught effectual grace, and in that case he is free from error; or he taught something different, and in that case he has no defenders. The whole question, then, is, whether Jansenius, in fact, taught any thing else than effectual grace. And if this question is decided in the affirmative, you will have the honour of having understood him best; but they will not have the unhappiness of having erred in the faith.

Let us, therefore, father, thank God that there is indeed no heresy in the Church, since the whole subject under discussion is matter of fact, which cannot form a heresy; for the Church decides points of faith with divine authority, and cuts off from her body all who refuse to receive them; but she does not act so in regard to matters of fact. The reason is, that our salvation is annexed to the faith which has been revealed to us, and is preserved in the Church by tradition, but depends not on other particular facts which God has not revealed. Thus, we are obliged to believe that the commandments of God are not impossible; but we are not obliged to know what Jansenius has taught on this subject. This is the reason why God guides his Church in the determination of points of faith, by the assistance of his Spirit, which cannot err; whereas, in matters of fact, he leaves her to act by sense and reason, the natural judges of fact. For God only could instruct the Church in faith; whereas, one has only to read Jansenius to know whether certain propositions are in his book. Hence, it is heresy to resist decisions in faith, because it is to oppose our own spirit to the Spirit of God. But it is not heresy, although it may be presumption, not to believe certain particular facts; because this is only to oppose reason, which may be clear, to an authority which, though great, is not infallible.

This all theologians acknowledge, as appears by the following maxim of Cardinal Bellarmine, of your Society: " General and lawful councils cannot err in defining dogmas of faith; but they may err in questions of fact." And elsewhere: " The pope, as pope, and even at the head of a general council, may err in particular controversies of fact, which depend principally on the information and testimony of men." And Cardinal Baronius, likewise: " It is necessary to submit implicitly to the decisions of councils in points of faith;

but, in regard to what concerns individuals and their writings, the censures which have been made are not found to have been regarded so strictly, because there is nobody who may not happen to be deceived." For this reason, also, the Archbishop of Toulouse has drawn this rule from the letters of the two great popes, St. Leon and Pelagius II.: "That the proper object of councils is faith; and that any point decided there which is not of faith, may be reviewed and examined anew; whereas, what has been decided in matter of faith, must no longer be examined; because, as Tertullian says, the rule of faith is alone immoveable, irretractable."

Hence, while lawful general councils have never been opposed to each other in points of faith, " because," as the Archbishop of Toulouse says, " it is not even permitted to examine anew what has already been decided in matter of faith," the councils have sometimes been seen opposed on points of fact, when the meaning of an author was in question, " because," as he says again, after the popes whom he quotes, " every thing decided in councils, except faith, may be reviewed and examined anew." Thus the fourth and fifth Councils appear contrary to each other in the interpretation of the same authors; and the same thing happened between two popes in regard to a proposition of certain monks of Scythia. For, after Pope Hormisdas had condemned it, understanding it in a bad sense, Pope John II., his successor, examining it anew, and understanding it in a good sense, approved it, and declared it orthodox. Would you say from this that one of these popes was heretical? And must it not, then, be admitted, that provided we condemn the heretical sense which a pope may have supposed in a writing, we are not heretical for not condemning this writing, while taking it in a sense which it is certain the pope has not condemned, since otherwise one of the two popes would have fallen into error.

I wished, father, to accustom you to these contrarieties, which happen among the orthodox, on questions of fact regarding the meaning of an author, by showing you one father of the Church against another, and a pope against a pope, and a council against a council, to lead you on to other instances of a like opposition, but more disproportioned. For in these you will see councils and popes on the one side, and Jesuits on the other, opposing their decisions touching the sense of an author, without your accusing your brethren, I say not of heresy, but not even of presumption.

You know well, father, that the writings of Origen were condemned by different councils and different popes, and even by the fifth general council, as containing heresies, among others that " of the reconciliation of devils at the day of judgment." Think you from this, that it is absolutely necessary, in order to be orthodox, to confess that Origen in fact held these errors, and that it is not sufficient to condemn them without attributing them to him? Were it so, what would become of your father Halloix, who maintained the purity of Origen's faith, as well as of several other Catholics, who undertook the same thing, as Pico de la Miranda, and Genebrard, doctor of Sorbonne? Is it not also certain, that the same fifth general Council condemned the writings of Theodoret against St. Cyril, " as impious, contrary to the true faith, and containing the Nestorian heresy;" and yet Father Sirmond, Jesuit, has not hesitated to defend him, and to say in his life of this father, " that these very writings are free of the Nestorian heresy."

You see, then, father, that when the Church condemns writings, it supposes an error which it condemns. It thus becomes a point of faith that this error is condemned; but it is not a point of faith that these writings do in fact contain the error which the Church supposes. I hold this to be sufficiently proved; and therefore I will finish these illustrations with that of Pope Honorius, whose history is well known. We know, that at the beginning of the seventh century, the Church being troubled by the heresy of the Monothelites, this pope, to terminate the dispute, made a decree which seemed to favour these heretics, so that several were scandalised at it. The thing, however, passed over with little noise, under his pontificate; but fifty years after, the Church being assembled in the sixth general Council, in which Pope Agatho presided by his legates, this decree was submitted to it; and after being read and examined, was condemned, as containing the heresy of the Monothelites, and burned in this character in presence of the whole council, with the other writings of those heretics. And this decision was received by the whole Church with such respect and unanimity, that it was afterwards confirmed by two other general councils, and even by popes Leo II. and Adrian II., who lived two centuries after, nobody having disturbed this universal and peaceful consent during seven or eight centuries. Notwithstanding some authors in those later times, among others Cardinal Bellarmine, did not think they made themselves heretical by maintaining against all these popes and councils, that the writings of Honorius are free from the error which they declared to be in them, " because," says he, " general councils being capable of error in matters of fact, we may say in all confidence that the sixth council was mistaken in that fact, and, not having rightly understood the meaning of the letters of Honorius, did wrong in classing this pope with heretics."

Observe, then, carefully, father, that it is not heretical to say that Pope Honorius was not so, although several popes and councils declared it even after examination. Now I come to our question; and I allow you to make your case as strong as you can. What will you say, father, in order to make your opponents heretical? "That Pope Innocent X. has declared that the error of the five propositions is in Jansenius?" I allow you to do all this. What is your inference? "That it is heresy not to acknowledge that the error of the five propositions is in Jansenius?" How seems it, father? Is not this a question of fact of the same nature as those above? The pope has declared that the error of the five propositions is in Jansenius just as his predecessors had declared that the error of the Nestorians and Monothelites was in the writings of Theodoret and Honorius. On this your fathers have written that they indeed condemn those heresies, but they are not agreed that those authors hold them; just as your opponents in the present day say that they condemn the five propositions, but are not agreed that Jansenius taught them. In truth, father, the cases are very similar; and if there is any difference, it is easy to see how much it is in favour of the present question, from a comparison of several special circumstances which are self-evident, and which I do not stay to mention. How comes it, then, father, that in the same situation your fathers are orthodox, and your opponents heretical? And by what strange exception do you deprive them of a liberty which you give to all the rest of the faithful?

What will you say to this, father? That the pope has confirmed his Constitution by a brief? I will answer, that two general councils and two popes have confirmed the condemnation of the letters of Honorius. But what do you mean to found upon the words of this brief, by which the pope declares " that he condemns the doctrine of Jansenius in the five propositions?" What does this add to the constitution? and what follows from it? Just that as the sixth council condemned the doctrine of Honorius, believing it to be the same as that of the Monothelites, in the same way the pope has said that he condemns the doctrine of Jansenius in the five propositions, because he supposed it was the same as the five propositions. And how could he but believe it? Your Society publishes nothing else; and you, yourself, father, who have said that they are in it " word for word," were at Rome at the time of the censure; for I meet you at every turn. Could he distrust the sincerity or competency of so many grave monks? And how could he but believe that the doctrine of Jansenius was the same as that of the five propositions, assured as he was by you that they were " word for word" in that author? It is obvious, then, father, that if it turns out that Jansenius did not hold them, it will be necessary to say, not as your fathers did in their cases, that the pope was deceived in the point of fact, which it is always grievous to publish, but that you deceived the pope; a circumstance which does not occasion much scandal, now that you are so well known.

Thus, fathers, this whole matter is very far from being fit to form a heresy; but as you wish to make one, cost what it may, you have tried to turn aside the question of fact, and convert it into a point of faith, and the way in which you do it is this: " The pope," you say, " declares that he has condemned the doctrine of Jansenius in those five propositions, therefore it is of faith that the doctrine of Jansenius regarding these five propositions is heretical, be it what it may." Here, father, is a very curious point of faith, namely, that a doctrine is heretical, be it what it may. What! if according to Jansenius "we can resist internal grace," and if, according to him it is false to say that Jesus Christ "died only for the predestinate," will this also be condemned because it is his doctrine? Will it be true in the Constitution of the pope, "that we are free to do good and evil," and will it be false in Jansenius? And by what fatuity will he be so unfortunate, that truth becomes, in his book, heresy? Must it not then be confessed that he is heretical only provided he is conformable to these condemned errors, since the Constitution of the pope is the rule to which we must apply Jansenius, to judge what he is according to the relation in which he stands to it. Thus the question, whether or not "his doctrine is heretical, must be solved by the question of fact "whether or not it is conformable to the natural sense of these propositions; it being impossible not to be heretical, if it is conformable to them, and not to be orthodox if it is contrary to them. For in fine, seeing that according to the pope and the bishops, "the propositions are condemned in their proper and natural sense," it is impossible they can be condemned in the sense of Jansenius, unless it be true that the sense of Jansenius is the proper and natural sense of these propositions; which is a point of fact.

The question then always turns on this point of fact, out of which it is impossible to take it, so as to convert it into a point of doctrine. It cannot, therefore, be made matter of heresy, though you might indeed make it a pretext for persecution, were there not ground to hope that none will be found to enter so keenly into your interests, as to adopt such unjust procedure, and insist, at your suggestion, on a compulsory subscription, "condemning the propositions in the sense of Jansenius," without explaining what the sense of Jansenius is. Few people are disposed to sign a confession of faith in blank. But this were to sign one in blank which might afterwards be filled up in whatever way you please, since you would be free to give any interpretation you chose to this sense of Jansenius, which had not been explained. Let us have the explanation first, otherwise you will give us another case of proximate power; *abstrahendo ab omni sensu.* You know that that does not succeed in the world. There ambiguity is hated, especially in matters of faith, as to which it is but just, at least, to understand what it is that is condemned. And how could doctors, who are persuaded that Jansenius has no other meaning than that of effectual grace, consent to declare that they condemn his doctrine without explaining it; since with the belief which they have, and in which they are not corrected, this were nothing else than to condemn effectual grace, which cannot be condemned without criminality? Would it not, then, be strange tyranny, to place them under the unhappy necessity of either incurring guilt before God, by signing this condemnation against their conscience, or of being treated as heretics for refusing to do so?

But all this is managed with mystery. All your steps are politic. I must explain why you do not explain the sense of Jansenius. I write only to disclose your designs, and by disclosing, frustrate them. I must, then, inform those who know it not, that your principal object in this dispute being to exalt the sufficient grace of your Molina, you cannot do this without overthrowing effectual grace, which is directly opposed to it. But as you see this now sanctioned at Rome, and among all the learned of the Church, not being able to combat it in itself, you have fallen on the device of attacking it in disguise, under the name of the doctrine of Jansenius, without explaining it; and in order to succeed, you have given out that his doctrine is not that of effectual grace, with the view of making it believed that the one may be condemned without the other. Hence your effort in the present day to produce this persuasion in those who have no acquaintance with the author. This you yourself attempt, father, in your Cavilli, p. 23, by the following subtle argument: "The pope has condemned the doctrine of Jansenius. Now, the pope has not condemned the doctrine of effectual grace: therefore, the doctrine of effectual grace is different from that of Jansenius." Were this proof conclusive, we might in the same way show that Honorius and all his supporters are heretics. Thus the sixth council condemned the doctrine of Honorius; now the council did not condemn the doctrine of the Church; therefore, the doctrine of Honorius is different from that of the Church; therefore, all who defend him are heretics. It is plain that your argument is good for nothing; since the pope has only condemned the doctrine of the five propositions, which he was given to understand was that of Jansenius.

But no matter; for you have no wish to use this reasoning for any length of time. Feeble as it is, it will last long enough to serve your purpose. The only necessity for it is to induce those who are unwilling to condemn effectual grace to condemn Jansenius without scruple. This done, your argument will soon be forgotten, and the signatures remaining as perpetual evidence of the condemnation of Jansenius, you will take the opportunity to make a direct attack upon effectual grace by another argument far more solid than the other, which you will put into shape in due time, thus: "The doctrine of Jansenius has been condemned by the universal signatures of the whole Church. But this doctrine is manifestly that of effectual grace," (you will prove this very easily,) "therefore the doctrine of effectual grace is condemned even by the confession of its defenders."

This is the reason why you propose to get this condemnation of a doctrine signed without explaining it. This is the advantage which you mean to derive from these subscriptions. But if your opponents resist, you lay another trap for their refusal. Having dexterously joined the question of doctrine to that of faith, without allowing them to separate them, or to sign the one without the other, as they will not be able to subscribe both together, you will go and publish every where that they have refused both. And thus, though they in fact only refuse to acknowledge that Jansenius held these propositions which they condemn, a refusal which cannot form a heresy, you will say boldly that they have refused to condemn the propositions in themselves, and that therein lies their heresy.

Such is the benefit which you would gain by their refusal, and which would not be less useful to you than that which you would gain from their consent. So that if the signatures are insisted on, they will fall equally into your snare, whether they sign or do not sign, and you will have your account one way or other; such has been your dexterity in putting things into a state which will always be advantageous to you, whatever direction they may take.

How well I know you, father! and how grieved I am to see that God abandons you so far, as to give you complete success in your unhappy course! Your success is deserving of pity, and can only be envied by those who know not wherein true success consists. It is an act of charity to thwart you in the object at which you aim by all this conduct; since you found it upon a lie, and labour to give currency to one of two falsehoods: either that the Church has condemned effectual grace, or that its defenders hold the five errors which have been condemned.

It is necessary, therefore, to let all the world know, both that by your own confession effectual grace is not condemned, and that no one maintains those errors; thus making them aware that those who would refuse the subscription which you would exact from them, refuse it only because of the question of fact; while being ready to sign that of faith, they cannot be heretical in their refusal; since, though it is indeed a point of faith to admit that the propositions are heretical, it will never be a point of faith to admit that they were held by Jansenius. They are free from error; and that is enough. Perhaps they interpret Jansenius too favourably; but perhaps you do not interpret him favourably enough. I do not enter into this. I know at least, that according to your maxims, you think you can without sin proclaim him a heretic against your own knowledge; whereas, according to theirs, they could not, without sin, say that he is orthodox, if they were not persuaded of it. They are thus more sincere than you, father; they have examined Jansenius more carefully than you; they are not less intelligent than you; they are, therefore, not less credible than you. But come of this point of fact what may, they are certainly orthodox; since, in order to be so, it is not necessary to say that another is not so; and in regard to heresy, it is enough, without charging another, to discharge one's self.

LETTER EIGHTEENTH.

TO THE REVEREND FATHER ANNAT, JESUIT.

PROVED STILL MORE INVINCIBLY BY FATHER ANNAT'S REPLY, THAT THERE IS NO HERESY IN THE C URCH: EVERY BODY CONDEMNS THE DOCTRINE WHICH THE JESUITS ASCRIBE TO JANSENIUS, AND THUS THE VIEWS OF ALL THE FAITHFUL ON THE MERITS OF THE FIVE PROPOSITIONS ARE THE SAME: DIFFERENCE BETWEEN DISPUTES AS TO DOCTRINE, AND AS TO FACT: IN QUESTIONS OF FACT MORE WEIGHT DUE TO WHAT IS SEEN THAN TO ANY HUMAN AUTHORITY.

24th March, 1657.

Reverend Father,—You have long been labouring to detect some heresy in your opponents; but I am confident you will at last confess that perhaps nothing is so difficult as to make those heretical who are not, and who do their utmost to avoid being so. In my last letter I have shown how many heresies, one after another, you have ascribed to them, from inability to find one which you could maintain for any length of time, so that nothing was left for you but to accuse them of refusing to condemn the sense of Jansenius, which you insisted on their condemning without explanation. You must, indeed, have wanted heresies to charge them with, when you were reduced to this. For who ever heard till now, of a heresy which cannot be expressed? Accordingly, they have easily answered you by representing, that if Jansenius has no errors, it is not just to condemn him; and that if he has, you ought to declare them, in order that they may at least know what it is that is condemned. This, nevertheless, you have never chosen to do; but you have endeavoured to strengthen your case by decrees which make nothing for you, since they do not in any way explain the sense of Jansenius, which is said to have been condemned in those five propositions. Now, that was not the way to terminate your dispute. Did you both agree as to the true meaning of Jansenius, and were you no longer at variance as to whether or not this meaning is heretical, these judgments declaring it to be heretical would touch the true question. But the great question in dispute being,

What is this meaning of Jansenius? some saying that they only see the meaning of St. Augustine and St. Thomas, and others that they see one which is heretical, but which they do not explain, it is clear that a Constitution which does not say a word concerning this difference, and which only condemns the sense of Jansenius generally, without explaining it, decides nothing in this dispute.

Hence it has been said to you a hundred times, that your disagreement being as to the fact, you will never terminate it, except by declaring what you understand to be the meaning of Jansenius. But as you have always obstinately refused this, I have at length brought the matter to its true bearing in my last letter, in which I have shown that it was not without a secret purpose you had laboured to obtain the condemnation of this sense, without explaining it; and that your design is to make this indefinite condemnation one day tell against the doctrine of effectual grace, by showing that it is nothing but the doctrine of Jansenius, a point which will not be difficult for you to establish. This has put you under the necessity of replying. For had you, after this, still persisted in not explaining the meaning, the least enlightened would have seen that effectual grace was really aimed at; a fact which must have turned to your utter confusion, from the veneration which the Church has for this holy doctrine.

You have, therefore, been obliged to declare yourself; and this you have done in answering my letter, in which I had represented to you, "that if Jansenius had, with reference to these five propositions, any other meaning than that of effectual grace, he had no defenders; and if he had no other meaning than that of effectual grace, he had no errors." You have not been able to deny this, father; but you draw a distinction in this manner, p. 21: "It is not a sufficient justification of Jansenius to say that he only holds effectual grace, because it can be held in two ways; the one heretical, in accordance with Calvin, which consists in saying that the will moved by grace has no power to resist it; the other, orthodox, in accordance with the Thomists and Sorbonnists, and founded on principles established by councils, namely, that effectual grace by itself governs the will, but in such a way that there is always a power of resisting.

All this is granted, father: you end with saying, that

"Jansenius would be orthodox if he defended effectual grace according to the Thomists, but that he is heretical because he is contrary to the Thomists, and conformable to Calvin, who denies the power of resisting grace." I do not here, father, examine the point of fact, whether Jansenius is indeed conformable to Calvin. It is enough for me that you pretend it, and that you now inform us that, by the meaning of Jansenius, you understand nothing else than the meaning of Calvin. Was this, then, father, all that you meant to say? Was it only the error of Calvin that you wished to be condemned, under the name of the meaning of Jansenius? Why did you not declare it sooner? You would have spared a world of trouble; for without bulls or briefs, every one would have condemned this error along with you. How necessary this explanation was, and how many difficulties it removes! We did not know, father, what error the popes and bishops meant to condemn under the name of the sense of Jansenius. The whole Church was in extreme perplexity, and no one would explain it. You now do so, father; you, whom all your party considers as the head and prime mover of all its counsels, and who know the secret of all this proceeding. You have told us, then, that this sense of Jansenius is nothing else than the sense of Calvin, condemned by the Council. This solves a vast number of doubts. We now know that the heresy which they designed to condemn, under the term " sense of Jansenius," is nothing else than the sense of Calvin; and hence we yield obedience to their decrees, when we condemn with them the sense of Calvin, which they meant to condemn. We are no longer astonished at seeing popes and bishops so zealous against the sense of Jansenius. How could they be otherwise, father, while giving credit to those who publicly say, that this sense is the same as that of Calvin?

I declare to you, then, father, that you have no longer any thing to reprove in your opponents, because they assuredly detest what you detest. I am only astonished to see that you were ignorant of this, and have so little knowledge of their sentiments on this subject, which they have so often declared in their works. I am confident, that if you were better informed, you would regret your not having made yourself acquainted, in a spirit of peace, with this pure and Christian doctrine, which passion makes you combat without knowing it. You would see, father, that not only do they hold that we effectually resist that feeble grace which is termed exciting and inefficacious, by not doing the good which it suggests, but that they are also as firm in asserting, against Calvin, the power which the will has to resist even effectual and victorious grace, as in defending against Molina the power of this grace over the will; as jealous of the one of these truths as of the other. They only know too well that man, by his own nature, has always the power of sinning and resisting grace; and that, since his fall, he bears about with him a miserable load of concupiscence, which infinitely augments this power; but that, nevertheless, when God is pleased to touch him in mercy, he makes him do what he wills, and in the way he wills; though this infallibility of the divine operation does not in any way destroy man's natural liberty, in consequence of the secret and wonderful manner in which God produces the change, as is admirably explained by St. Augustine; a manner which dissipates all the imaginary contradictions which the enemies of effectual grace fancy to exist between the sovereign power of grace over free will, and the power of free will to resist grace. For, according to this great saint, whom the popes and the Church have made the rule in this matter, God changes the heart of man by a mild celestial influence which he diffuses through it, which, overcoming the delight of the flesh, has this effect, namely, that man, feeling on the one hand his mortality and nothingness, and discovering on the other the greatness and eternity of God, becomes disgusted with the pleasures of sin, which separate him from incorruptible good. Finding his greatest joy in the God of his delight, he infallibly turns towards him of his own accord, by a movement full of freedom, full of love, so that it would be a pain and a punishment to be separated from him. Not that he is not always liable to become estranged, or that he might not effectually estrange himself, did he will it; but how should he will it, since the will always inclines to what pleases it most, and nothing then pleases it so much as this only good, which comprehends in itself all other good?

"*Quod enim amplius nos delectat, secundum id operemur, necesse est*, as St. Augustine says.

It is thus that God disposes of the free will of man, without laying necessity upon it; and that free will, which always may resist grace, but does not always choose to do so, inclines to God as freely as infallibly, when he is pleased to attract it by his mild but effectual inspiration.

These, father, are the divine principles of St. Augustine and St. Thomas, according to which it is true that *we are able to resist grace*, contrary to the opinion of Calvin; and that nevertheless, as Pope Clement VIII. says, in his writing addressed to the congregation *de Auxiliis*, "God forms within us the movement of our will, and disposes efficaciously of our heart, by the empire which his supreme majesty has over the wills of men, as well as over the rest of the creatures who are in heaven, according to St. Augustine."

According to these principles, moreover, we act of ourselves, and thus have merits which are truly ours, contrary to Calvin's heresy; and yet God, being the first beginning of our actions, and "working in us what is well pleasing to him," according to St. Paul, "our merits are," as the Council of Trent says, "gifts of God."

This overthrows the impiety of Luther, condemned by the same council, that "we do not co-operate in our salvation in any way, any more than inanimate things;" and this moreover overthrows the impiety of the school of Molina, who refuses to admit that it is the power of grace itself which causes us to co-operate with it in the work of our salvation, and by so refusing destroys the principle established by St. Paul, "that it is God who worketh in us, both to will and to do."

By this means, in fine, are reconciled all those passages of Scripture which seem most opposed to each other: "Turn unto the Lord: O Lord, turn us to thyself. Put away your iniquities from you: It is God who taketh away the iniquities of his people. Bring forth fruits meet for repentance: Lord thou hast made in us all our works. Make you a new heart and a new spirit: I will give you a new spirit, and create in you a new heart."

The only means of reconciling these apparent contradictions, which ascribe our good actions sometimes to God, and sometimes to ourselves, is to acknowledge with St. Augustine that "our actions are our own, because of the free will which produces them; and are also God's, because of his grace which makes our free will produce them," and because, as he elsewhere says, "God makes us do what he pleases, by making us will what we might be able not to will:" *a Deo factum est ut vellent quod et nolle potuissent.*

Thus, father, your opponents are perfectly at one with the new Thomists, since the Thomists like them hold both the power of resisting grace, and the infallibility of the effect of grace, which they profess to maintain so strongly, according to the capital maxim of their doctrine, which Alvarez, one of the most distinguished among them, repeats so often in his work, and expresses, (Disp. 72, n. 4,) in these terms: "When effectual grace moves free will, it consents infallibly, because the effect of grace is to cause that though it has the power of not consenting, it nevertheless does in fact consent," of which he assigns the reason from his master, St. Thomas: "That the will of God cannot fail to be accomplished; and thus when he wills that man consent to grace, he consents infallibly, and even necessarily, not from an absolute necessity, but a necessity of infallibility." Here grace does not interfere with "the power which we have to resist if we will it," since it only makes us unwilling to resist, as your father Peter acknowledges in these terms, tom. 1, p. 602: "The grace of Jesus Christ makes us persevere in piety infallibly, though not of necessity, for we are able as the Council says, not to consent if we will; but this same grace causes that we do not so will."

This, father, is the uniform doctrine of St. Augustine, and St. Prosperus, of the Fathers who succeeded them, of Councils, of St. Thomas, and all the Thomists in general. It is also that of your opponents, although you thought not; it is that, in fine, which you yourself have just approved in these terms: "The doctrine of effectual grace, which recognizes our power of resisting it, is orthodox, founded on Councils, and maintained by the Thomists and Sorbonnists." Tell the truth, father; had you known that your opponents really hold this doctrine, perhaps the interest of your Company would have prevented you from giving it this public approval; but having imagined that they were opposed to it, this same interest of your Company has led you to sanction sentiments which you believed contrary to theirs; and from this mistake, while wishing to ruin their principles, you have yourselves completely established them; so that in the present day, by a kind of miracle, we see the defenders of effectual grace justified by the defenders of Molina; so admirably does the providence of God make all things contribute to the honour of his truth.

Let all the world, then, learn from your own declaration, that this doctrine of effectual grace, necessary to all actions of piety, a doctrine which is dear to the Church, and was purchased by the Saviour's blood, is so uniformly Catholic, that there is not a Catholic, even among the Jesuits themselves, who does not recognize it as orthodox. At the same time it will be known by your own confession, that there is not the least suspicion of error in those whom you have so often accused of it; for when you imputed hidden errors, without choosing to disclose them, it was as difficult for them to defend, as it was easy for you to accuse in this manner. But now, since you have made the declaration, that the error which obliges you to combat them is that of Calvin, which you thought they held, every man sees clearly that they are free from all error, seeing they are so strongly opposed to the only error which you impute to them, and protest by their discourses, their books, and every thing which they can produce in evidence of their sentiments, that they condemn this heresy with all their hearts, and in the same way as do the Thomists, whom you recognise without difficulty to be orthodox, and who were never suspected of not being so.

What, then, will you now say against them, fathers? That although they adopt not Calvin's meaning, they are nevertheless heretical, because they will not acknowledge that the meaning of Jansenius is the same as that of Calvin? Will you venture to say that that is matter of heresy? Is it not a pure question of fact, which cannot form a heresy? It would indeed be one, to say that we have not power to resist effectual grace; but is it one to doubt whether Jansenius maintains this? Is it a revealed truth? Is it an article of faith which must be believed under pain of damnation? Is it not, in spite of you, a point of fact, on account of which it would be ridiculous to pretend that there are heretics in the Church?

No longer, then, give them that name, father, but some other, corresponding to the nature of your difference. Say that they are ignorant and stupid, and misunderstand Jansenius; such charges will be suitable to your dispute; but to call them heretics is out of the question. This, however, being the only injurious charge from which I wish to defend them, I will not give myself much trouble to show that they properly understand Jansenius. I will only say this, father, that, judging by your own rule, it is difficult not to hold him orthodox: for here are the tests by which you propose to try him.

Your words are: "To determine whether Jansenius is free from challenge, it is necessary to determine whether he defends effectual grace after the manner of Calvin, who denies that we have power to resist it; for then he would be heretical; or, after the manner of the Thomists, who admit it, for then he would be orthodox." See, then, father, whether he holds that we have power to resist, when he says in whole treatises, and among others, tr. 3, l. 8, c. 20, "That we have always the power of resisting grace according to the Council; that *free will may always act and not act*, will and not will, consent and not consent, do good and evil; that man in this life has always these two liberties, which you charge with contradiction." See, likewise, if he is not opposed to the error of Calvin, as you yourself represent it, when he shows throughout the whole of the 21st chap. that "the Church has condemned this heretic, who maintains that effectual grace does not act upon free will in the manner in which it has been so long believed in the Church, namely, by leaving it the power of consenting or not consenting; whereas, according to St. Augustine and the Council, we have always the power, if we choose, of not consenting; and, according to St. Prosper, God gives even his elect the will to persevere, but without depriving them of power to will the contrary." Judge, in fine, if he is not at one with the Thomists, when he declares, c. 4, that all that the Thomists have written to reconcile the efficacy of grace with the power of resisting it, is so conformable to his view, that it is necessary only to consult their books, in order to learn his sentiments: *Quod ipsi dixerunt, dictum puta.*

In this way he speaks on all these heads; and I presume

that he believes in the power of resisting grace, that he is contrary to Calvin and conformable to the Thomists, because he says it; and therefore is, according to you, orthodox. But if you have some other way of getting at the meaning of an author than by his expressions, and if, without quoting from him, you insist, in the face of all his expressions, that he denies the power of resisting, and favours Calvin against the Thomists, fear not, father, that I accuse you of heresy for that; I will only say that you seem to misunderstand Jansenius; but that shall not prevent us from being children of the same Church.

How comes it then, father, that in this misunderstanding you act so much under the influence of passion, and treat as your worst enemies, and as the most dangerous heretics, those whom you cannot charge with any error, or with any thing but not understanding Jansenius as you do? For on what do you dispute, except the meaning of this author? You insist on their condemning him, and they ask you what you mean by it; you say you mean the heresy of Calvin, they answer they condemn it; and hence, if you cling not to syllables, but to the thing which they signify, you ought to be satisfied. If they refuse to say that they condemn the meaning of Jansenius, it is because they believe it to be that of St. Thomas. Thus the term used between you is very ambiguous; in your mouth it signifies the meaning of Calvin, in theirs the meaning of St. Thomas; so that the different ideas which you attach to the same term is the cause of all your divisions. Were I umpire, I would interdict both from using the word Jansenius; and thus, both only expressing what is meant by it, it would be seen that all you ask is the condemnation of Calvin's meaning, which they are willing to give, and that all they ask is the defence of the meaning of St. Augustine and St. Thomas, as to which you are agreed.

I declare to you, then, father, that for my part I will always regard them as orthodox, whether they condemn Jansenius if they find errors in him, or refuse to condemn him when they only find what you yourself declare to be orthodox; and I will say to them, as St. Jerome said to John, bishop of Jerusalem, when accused of holding eight propositions of Origen: "Either condemn Origen, if you acknowledge that he held these errors, or deny that he held them: *Aut nega hoc dixisse eum qui arguitur; aut, si locutus est talia, eum damna qui dixerit.*"

Such, father, is the way in which those act who aim at errors only, and not at persons; whereas, you who aim at persons more than errors, count it as nothing to condemn errors, without condemning the persons to whom you are pleased to ascribe them.

How violent your procedure, father, but how incapable of succeeding! I have told you elsewhere, and I repeat it: violence and truth can do nothing against each other. Never were your accusations more outrageous, and never was the innocence of your opponents better known; never was effectual grace more artfully attacked, and never was it seen so firmly established. You employ your utmost efforts to persuade us that your disputes are on points of faith; and never was it better known that your whole dispute is only on a point of fact. In fine, you leave no means untried to convince us that this point of fact is true, and never were men more disposed to doubt its truth. The reason, father, is obvious. You do not take the natural way of establishing a fact, namely, convincing the senses, by taking up the book and pointing out the words which you allege to be in it. You go about searching for means so foreign to this simple course, that the most stupid are necessarily struck by it. Why do you not take the same method which I observed in my Letters, when, in order to disclose the many bad maxims of your authors, I faithfully mentioned the places from which they are taken. It was thus the curates of Paris acted, and it never fails to convince. But what would you have said, what would have been thought, if, when they charged you, for example, with the proposition of father L'Amy, that "a monk may kill him who threatens to propagate calumnies against him or his community, if he cannot otherwise prevent them," they had not quoted the place which contains it in express terms? if, notwithstanding of any demand that might have been made, they had always refused to show it, and instead of this, had gone to Rome to obtain a Bull which should enjoin all the world to acknowledge it? Would it not have been at once concluded that they had taken the Pope by surprise, and that they never would have resorted to this extraordinary means, but from want of the natural means which, when statements of fact are made, lie within the reach of all who make them? Thus, they have simply intimated that father L'Amy teaches this doctrine in tom. 5, disp. 36, n. 118, page 544, edition of Douay; and thus all who desired to see it have found it, and no body has been able to entertain a doubt. This is a very easy and a very prompt method of disposing of questions of fact, when one is in the right.

How comes it, then, father, that you do not act in this way? You have said in your Cavilli, that "the five propositions are in Jansenius, word for word, entire and in express terms," *iisdem verbis.* Others say no. In this case, what ought to be done but just to quote the page, if you have really seen them, or to confess that you were mistaken? You do neither; but, instead of this, while seeing plainly that all the passages of Jansenius which you occasionally alleged as a blind, are not the "condemned individual and special propositions," which you had undertaken to point out in his book, you merely present us with Constitutions which declare that the propositions are extracted from his book, but make no reference to the place.

I know, father, the respect which Christians owe to the Holy See, and your opponents give sufficient proof of their firm determination never to fail in it. But do not imagine they would have failed, had they represented to the Pope, with all the submission which children owe to their father, and members to their head, that he may have been surprised on this point of fact; that he has not submitted it to examination since his pontificate, and that the only point submitted to examination by his predecessor, Innocent X., was whether the propositions were heretical, not whether they were in Jansenius. That hence the Commissary of the Sacred Office, one of the principal examinators, observed, "that they could not be censured in the sense of any author: *Non sunt qualificabiles in sensu proferentis:* because they had been brought forward to be examined in themselves, and without considering to what author they might belong: *In abstracto, et ut præscindunt ab omni proferente,*" as is seen in their opinions recently printed: that more than sixty doctors, and a great number of able and pious persons besides, have read the book carefully, without ever seeing the propositions, while they found others contrary: that those who had given this impression to the Pope might well have abused the confidence which he had in them, interested as they are to discredit this author, who has convicted Molina of more than fifty errors: that this is rendered more credible by a maxim which they hold, and regard as one of the best ascertained in their theology, namely, that "they can, without sin, calumniate those by whom they think themselves unjustly attacked:" and that thus their testimony being so suspicious, while that of the other party is of so much weight, there is some ground to supplicate his Holiness, with all possible humility, to submit this fact to examination, in presence of doctors from both sides, in order to come to a formal and regular decision. "Let fit judges be assembled," said St. Basil on a similar occasion; "let each there be free; let my writings be examined; let it be seen if there are errors in faith; let the objections and the answers be read, in order that judgment may be given after examination, and in proper form; and not defamation without examination."

Think not, father, of charging those who should act in this manner with want of submission to the Holy See. The popes are far from treating Christians with that tyranny which some would exercise in their name. "The Church," says Pope St. Gregory, in Job, lib. 8, c. 1, "which has been trained in the school of humility, commands not with authority, but by reason persuades what she teaches her children, whom she believes entangled in some error; *Recta quæ errantibus dicit, non quasi ex auctoritate præcipit, sed ex ratione persuadet.*" And so far from deeming it dishonour to correct a judgment in which they might have been surprised, they, on the contrary, glory in it, as St. Bernard testifies, Ep., 180: "The Apostolic See," says he, "has this to recommend it, that it does not pique itself upon honour, and is readily disposed to revoke what may have been drawn from it by surprise; accordingly it is very just that none should profit by injustice, and especially before the Holy See."

Such, father, are the true sentiments with which popes ought to be inspired; since all theologians agree that they may be surprised, and that their sovereign capacity, so far from insuring them against it, on the contrary exposes them the more, because of the great number of cases which distract them. Hence St. Gregory says to some persons who were astonished that another pope had allowed himself to be deceived, "Why do you wonder," says he, (l. 1, in Dial.) "that we are deceived, we who are only men? Have you not seen how David, a king who possessed the spirit of prophecy, by giving credit to the imposture of Ziba, gave an unjust sentence against the son of Jonathan? Who, then, will think it strange that impostors sometimes surprise us, us who are not prophets? The load of business oppresses us, and our spirit being distracted by so many things, applies less to each in particular, and is more easily deceived in any one." In truth, father, I believe the popes know better than you, whether or not they can be surprised. They themselves declare that the popes and the greatest kings are more exposed to be deceived than persons with less important occupations. We must believe them. It is easy to imagine that they may happen to be surprised. St. Bernard, in the letter which he wrote to Innocent II., describes it in this way: "It is nothing strange or new for the mind of man to deceive, or be deceived. Monks have gone to you in a spirit of falsehood and deception; they have spoken to you against a bishop, whom they hate, and whose life was exemplary. These persons bite like dogs, and would fain make good pass for evil. Meanwhile, most holy father, you become enraged against your son. Why have you given cause of joy to his enemies? Believe not every spirit; but try the spirits, whether they be of God. I hope that when you come to know the truth, all that has been founded on a false report will be dissipated. I pray the Spirit of truth to give you grace to separate light from darkness, and to reprove evil in favour of good." You thus see, father, that the exalted station of the popes does not exempt them from surprise, and that it only serves to make the surprise more dangerous and more important. So St. Bernard represents it to pope Eugene, de Consid., lib. 2., c. ult.: "There is another defect so general, that I have not seen one of the great who avoids it. It is, holy father, the excessive credulity from which so many disorders arise. For from this come violen persecutions against the innocent, unjust prejudices against the absent, and fearful anger, for mere nothings; *pro nihilo.* Here, holy father, is a universal evil, from which, if you are exempt, I will say that you are the only one among all your fellows who have this advantage."

I presume, father, this begins to persuade you that the popes are liable to be surprised. But to make it perfectly clear to you, I will only put you in mind of instances which you yourself give in your book, of popes and emperors whom heretics have actually surprised. For you say that Apollinaris surprised Pope Damasus in the same way as Celestius surprised Zozimus. You say, moreover, a person of the name of Athanasius deceived the Emperor Heraclius, and led him to persecute the orthodox; and that, in fine, Sergius, by what you call " playing the humble servant to the pope," obtained from Honorius the decree which was burned at the sixth Council.

It is clear, then, from yourself, father, that those who act thus towards kings and popes, sometimes artfully engage them to persecute those who defend the faith, while thinking to put down heresies. And hence it is that the popes, who abhor nothing so much as these surprises, have converted a letter of Alexander III. into an ecclesiastical enactment, inserted in the canon law, and allowing the execution of their bulls and decrees to be suspended when it is thought that they have been deceived. This pope, writing to the Archbishop of Ravenna, says, " If we occasionally send your fraternity decrees which run counter to your feelings, give yourself no uneasiness. For either you will execute them with respect, or you will state to us your reason for not doing it; because we will approve of your not executing a decree which may have been drawn from us by surprise or artifice." Thus act the popes who only seek to remove the differences among Christians, and not to gratify the passion of those who would produce disturbances among them. They do not employ domination, as St. Peter and St. Paul express it after Jesus Christ; but the spirit apparent in all their conduct is that of peace and truth. Hence they usually put into their letters this clause, which is always to be understood; "*Si ita est; si preces veritate nitantur;* If the thing is as we have been given to understand; if the facts are true." Hence it is plain, that since the popes enforce their bulls only in so far as they rest on true facts, mere bulls do not prove the truth of the facts, but, on the contrary, the truth of the facts makes the bulls receivable.

How, then, shall we learn the truth of facts? By the eyes, father, which are the legitimate judges of them, just as reason is of natural and intelligible things, and faith of things supernatural and revealed. For since you oblige me, father, I will tell you, that according to the two greatest doctors of the Church, St. Augustine and St. Thomas, these three sources of our knowledge, the senses, reason, and faith, have each their separate objects, and their certainty within this sphere. And as God has been pleased to make use of the medium of the senses to give an entrance to faith, *fides ex auditu*, so far is faith from destroying the certainty of the senses, that, on the contrary, to throw doubt on the report of the senses, would be to destroy faith. And this is the reason why St. Thomas says expressly, that God has been pleased that the sensible accidents should subsist in the Eucharist, in order that the senses which only judge of these accidents might not be deceived: *Ut sensus a deceptione reddantur immunes.*

Hence let us conclude, that when any proposition is presented to us for examination, the first thing necessary is to ascertain its nature, to see to which of the three principles we ought to refer it. If it relates to something supernatural, we will not judge of it either by the senses or by reason, but by Scripture and the decisions of the Church. If it relates to a proposition not revealed, and proportioned to natural reason, reason will be the proper judge; and if, in fine, it relates to a point of fact, we will believe the senses, to which the knowledge of facts naturally belongs.

This rule is so general, that, according to St. Augustine and St. Thomas, when Scripture even presents to us some passage, the primary literal sense of which is opposed to what the senses or reason recognise with certainty, we must not resolve to disavow them on this occasion, in order to subject them to this apparent sense of Scripture, but we must interpret Scripture, and search for another meaning in accordance with this sensible truth; because, the Word of God being infallible even in facts, and the report of the senses and of reason acting within their sphere being also certain, these two must agree: and as Scripture may be interpreted in different manners, while the report of the senses is single, we must in these matters hold that to be the true interpretation of Scripture which agrees with the faithful report of the senses. "It is necessary," says St. Thomas, 1 p. q. 68, a. 1, "to observe two things, according to St. Augustine: the one, That Scripture has always a true sense; the other, That as it may receive several senses, when we find one which reason proves to be certainly false, we must not persist in saying that it is the natural sense, but seek another which agrees with it."

This he illustrates by the passage in Genesis, in which is said that God created "two great lights, the sun and the moon, and the stars also." Here Scripture seems to say that the moon is greater than all the stars; but because it is clear, from indubitable demonstration, that this is false, we should not, says this saint, obstinately defend this literal sense, but seek another conformable to this true fact, as in saying, "That the word *great light* means only the greatness of the moon as it appears to us, and not its magnitude considered in itself."

Were we disposed to act otherwise, we should not thereby render Scripture venerable, but, on the contrary, expose it to the contempt of infidels; "because," as St. Augustine says, "when they come to learn that we believe, on the authority of Scripture, things which they certainly know to be false, they will laugh at our credulity in other things of a more recondite nature, as the resurrection of the dead, and eternal life." "And thus," adds St. Thomas, "we should make our religion contemptible to them, and even close the entrance against them."

We should also close the entrance against heretics, and make the authority of the pope contemptible to them, were we to deny the orthodoxy of those who refuse to believe that certain words are in a book, in which they cannot be found, because a pope had asserted it through surprise. Only by examining a book can we ascertain what words are in it. Matters of fact are proved only by the senses. If what you maintain is true, show it; if not, do not urge any one to believe it; it would be to no purpose. All the powers in the world cannot by authority prove a point of fact, any more than change it. For nothing can make that which is, not to be.

In vain for example did monks of Ratisbon obtain from Leo. IX. a formal decree declaring that the body of St. Dionysius, the first bishop of Paris, who is commonly held to be the Areopagite, had been carried out of France, and deposited in the church of their monastery. That does not prevent the body of this saint from having always been, and from still being, in the celebrated abbey which bears his name, in which you would find it difficult to make this bull be received, although the pope therein declares that he had examined the matter "with all possible care, *diligentissimè*, and with the advice of several bishops and prelates, so that he strictly enjoins all the French to acknowledge and confess that they no longer have these holy relics." And yet the French, who knew the falsehood of the fact by their own eyes, and who, having opened the crypt, found all those relics entire, as the historians of that period testify, believed then, and have ever since believed, the contrary of what the pope enjoined them to believe, knowing well that even saints and prophets are liable to be surprised.

In vain also did you obtain from Rome a decree against Galileo, condemning his opinion concerning the motion of the earth. That will not prove it to be at rest; and if we had uniform observations proving that it turns, all men could not prevent it from revolving, nor themselves from revolving with it. No more imagine, that the letters of Pope Zachariah, excommunicating St. Virgilius because he held there were antipodes, have annihilated this New World; and that, although he had declared this opinion to be a very dangerous error, the king of Spain has not found his advantage in having believed Christopher Columbus, who came from it, rather than this pope who had not been there, and that the Church has not received a great advantage from it, inasmuch as it has brought a knowledge of the Gospel to many nations that must have perished in their unbelief.

Thus, father, you see the nature of matters of fact, and the principles by which they are to be judged; and hence, with reference to our subject, it is easy to conclude, that if the five propositions are not in Jansenius, it is impossible that they can have been extracted from it, and that the only means of judging of them, and satisfying people in regard to them, is to examine the book at a regular conference, as you have long been asked to do. Till then, you have no right to call your opponents obstinate; for they will be without blame on the point of fact, as they are without error on the point of faith; orthodox as regards the doctrine, reasonable as regards the fact, and innocent in both.

Who then, father, would not be astonished at seeing on the one side a justification so complete, and, on the other, accusations so violent? Who would think that there is no question between you but a fact of no importance, which you insist as being believed without showing it? And who could venture to imagine that so much noise should be made throughout the Church for nothing, *pro nihilo*, father, as St. Bernard says. But herein lies the most artful part of your conduct. By making it believed that every thing is at stake, in an affair of nothing, and by giving persons in power, who listen to you, to understand that your disputes involve the most pernicious errors of Calvin, and the most important principles of faith, you enlist all their zeal and all their authority against those whom you combat, as if the safety of the Catholic religion depended upon it; whereas if they came to know that the only question is this minute point of fact, they would take no interest in it, but, on the contrary, deeply regret that they had done so much to gratify your private passions, in an affair which is of no consequence to the Church.

In fine, to take things at the worst, were it even true that Jansenius held these propositions, what misfortune could arise because some individuals doubt this, provided they detest them as they publicly declare they do? Is it not enough that they are condemned by all the world without exception, in the very sense in which you have explained that you wish them condemned? Would they be more censured from its being said that Jansenius held them? Of what use, then, to demand this acknowledgment, except to decry a doctor and a bishop who died in the communion of the Church? I do not see any so great good in this, as to justify the purchase of it by so many troubles. What interest in it have the State, the Pope, the bishops, the doctors, the whole Church? It does not affect them in any way, father. It is only your Society that would truly receive any pleasure from the defamation of an author who has done you some harm. Still all is in commotion, because you give out that all is threatened. This is the secret cause which gives the impulse to all these great movements, which would cease the moment the true state of the dispute was known. It is because the repose of the Church depends on this explanation, that it becomes of the utmost importance to give it, in order that, all your disguises being discovered, it may be apparent to the whole world that your accusations are without foundation, your opponents without error, and the Church without heresy.

Such, father, is the good which it has been my aim to accomplish, and which seems to me of such importance to religion, that I have difficulty in comprehending how those to whom you give so much cause to speak can remain silent. Though they should be unscathed by the insults which you offer them, those which the Church suffers ought, methinks, to lead them to complain: besides, I doubt if ecclesiastics can abandon their reputation to calumny, especially in a matter of faith. Still they allow you to say whatever you please, so that, but for the occasion which you have accidentally given me, perhaps no opposition would have been made to the scandalous impressions which you disseminate on all sides. Their patience astonishes me; and the more that it cannot be suspected either of timidity or powerlessness, knowing well that they want neither arguments for their justification, nor zeal for the truth. I see them, nevertheless, so religiously silent, that I fear there is excess in it. For my part, father, I do not believe I can do so. Leave the Church in peace, and I will leave you with all my heart. But so long as you shall labour to keep her in trouble, doubt not that there are children of peace, who will think themselves obliged to employ all their efforts to preserve her tranquillity.

THE END.

www.ingramcontent.com/pod-product-compliance
Lightning Source LLC
Chambersburg PA
CBHW032101220426
43664CB00008B/1095